i-Ready® Classroom
Mathematics

Grade 8 • Volume 2

NOT FOR RESALE

978-1-7280-1303-9
©2021–Curriculum Associates, LLC
North Billerica, MA 01862
12 13 14 15   24 23 22

BTS21

Curriculum Associates

803997

Contents

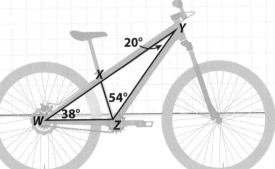

UNIT 2

Geometric Figures

Transformations, Similarity, and Angle Relationships

iii

Contents (continued)

UNIT 4

Functions

Linear and Nonlinear Relationships

Contents (continued)

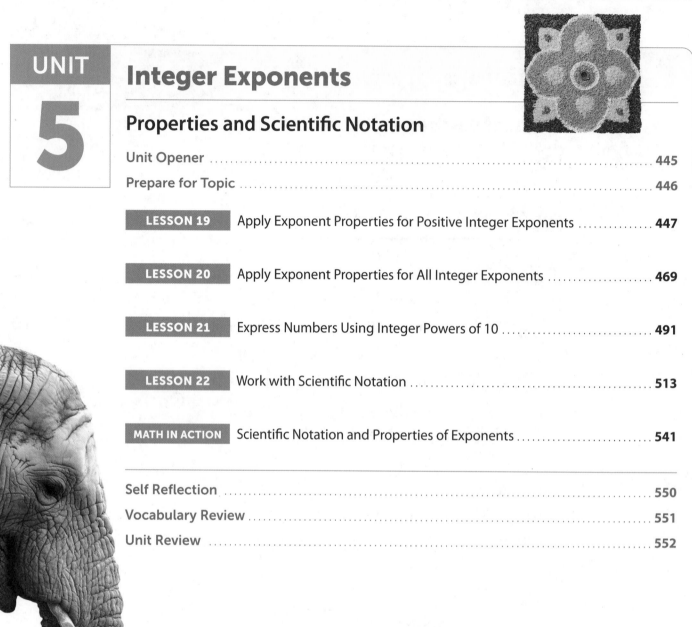

UNIT 5

Integer Exponents

Properties and Scientific Notation

UNIT 6

Real Numbers

Rational Numbers, Irrational Numbers, and the Pythagorean Theorem

$A = 9$ in.^{2}

Contents (continued)

Unit 5

Integer Exponents

Properties and Scientific Notation

✓ **Self Check**	Before starting this unit, check off the skills you know below. As you complete each lesson, see how many more skills you can check off!

I can . . .	Before	After
Simplify expressions with two or more powers using exponent properties.	☐	☐
Apply exponent properties to rewrite or simplify expressions with zero and negative integer exponents.	☐	☐
Express, estimate, and compare quantities using integer powers of 10.	☐	☐
Perform operations with numbers in scientific notation.	☐	☐
Work with scientific notation to solve problems.	☐	☐
Listen carefully during discussion in order to understand and explain another person's ideas.	☐	☐

Prepare for Exponent Properties and Scientific Notation

➤ **You have learned to use reasoning about powers, exponents, and factors. Write what you know about the term *cube* in the boxes. Share your ideas with a partner and add new information to the boxes as needed.**

Numerical Expressions

How to Say the Expression

cube

Related Words

Dear Family,

This week your student is learning how to simplify expressions with two or more powers. Students learned previously that a power is an expression with a **base** and an **exponent** that represents repeated multiplication.

$$3^4 = 3 \cdot 3 \cdot 3 \cdot 3$$

Students will now encounter expressions with more than one power, like $(3^4)^2$ or $\dfrac{5^{11}}{5^8}$. Such expressions can be simplified by using repeated multiplication or by using properties of exponents. Here are some properties for rewriting expressions with more than one power:

Power of a Power	Powers with the Same Base	Powers with the Same Exponent
$(a^m)^n = a^{m \cdot n}$	$a^m \cdot a^n = a^{m+n}$ $\dfrac{a^m}{a^n} = a^{m-n}, a \neq 0$	$(a \cdot b)^m = a^m \cdot b^m$ $\left(\dfrac{a}{b}\right)^m = \dfrac{a^m}{b^m}, b \neq 0$

Students will solve problems like the one below.

How can you write $\dfrac{(7^2)^3}{7^4}$ as a single power of 7?

➤ **ONE WAY** to write as a single power is to use repeated multiplication.

$$\frac{(7^2)^3}{7^4} = \frac{(7^2) \cdot (7^2) \cdot (7^2)}{7 \cdot 7 \cdot 7 \cdot 7}$$

$$= \frac{(7 \cdot 7) \cdot (7 \cdot 7) \cdot (7 \cdot 7)}{(7 \cdot 7) \cdot (7 \cdot 7)}$$

$$= 7 \cdot 7$$

$$= 7^2$$

➤ **ANOTHER WAY** is to use properties of exponents.

$$\frac{(7^2)^3}{7^4} = \frac{(7^{2 \cdot 3})}{7^4}$$

$$= \frac{7^6}{7^4}$$

$$= 7^{6-4}$$

$$= 7^2$$

Using either method, $\dfrac{(7^2)^3}{7^4} = 7^2$.

▶ Use the next page to start a conversation about exponent properties.

Activity Thinking About Exponent Properties

➤ **Do this activity together to investigate exponent properties in the real world.**

You can compare quantities more easily using properties of exponents! For example, you can use exponent properties to compare the weights of a 3,125-lb mother hippopotamus and her 125-lb baby. If you know that $3{,}125 = 5^5$ and $125 = 5^3$, you can use the expression $\dfrac{5^5}{5^3}$ to find that the mother hippo is 5^2, or 25, times the weight of her baby.

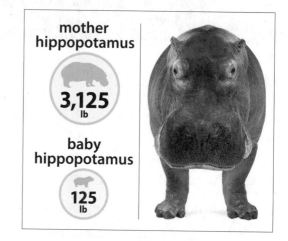

mother hippopotamus

3,125 lb

baby hippopotamus

125 lb

? When else might you want to use exponent properties?

Explore Exponent Properties for Positive Integer Exponents

10^3

10^2

10^1

Previously, you learned how to evaluate powers. In this lesson, you will learn ways to simplify expressions involving two or more powers.

➤ **Use what you know to try to solve the problem below.**

How can you write $(10^3)^2$ as a single power of 10? A single power has one base and one exponent.

TRY IT

DISCUSS IT

Ask: How did you find the exponent in your answer?

Share: I found the exponent by . . .

◎ **Learning Target** SMP 1, SMP 2, SMP 3, SMP 4, SMP 5, SMP 6, SMP 7, SMP 8
Know and apply the properties of integer exponents to generate equivalent numerical expressions.

3 **a.** How can you write $(10^2)^4$ as a single power of 10? Show your work.

SOLUTION _____

b. Check your answer to problem 3a. Show your work.

Develop Applying Properties for Powers with the Same Base

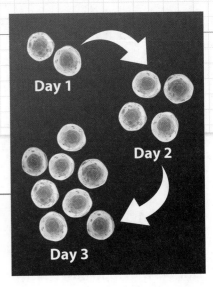

Day 1

Day 2

Day 3

➤ **Read and try to solve the problem below.**

One population of single-celled bacteria doubles each day. On Day x, the population of the colony is 2^x. How many times as large is the population of the colony on Day 7 than on Day 4?

TRY IT

DISCUSS IT

Ask: How did you use powers and exponents to solve the problem?

Share: I used powers and exponents when I . . .

➤ **Explore different ways to divide powers with the same base.**

One population of single-celled bacteria doubles each day. On Day x, the population of the colony is 2^x. How many times as large is the population of the colony on Day 7 than on Day 4?

Model It

You can start with the population on Day 4.

Double the population each day after that until Day 7.

Day	Population
4	2^4
5	$2 \cdot 2^4$
6	$2 \cdot 2 \cdot 2^4$
7	$2 \cdot 2 \cdot 2 \cdot 2^4$

The relationship between the population on Day 7 and the population on Day 4 is $\dfrac{(2 \cdot 2 \cdot 2) \cdot 2^4}{2^4}$.

Model It

You can write each power as repeated multiplication of the same factor.

$$\frac{\text{population on Day 7}}{\text{population on Day 4}} = \frac{2^7}{2^4}$$

$$= \frac{2 \cdot 2 \cdot 2 \cdot 2 \cdot 2 \cdot 2 \cdot 2}{2 \cdot 2 \cdot 2 \cdot 2}$$

$$= \frac{2}{2} \cdot \frac{2}{2} \cdot \frac{2}{2} \cdot \frac{2}{2} \cdot 2 \cdot 2 \cdot 2$$

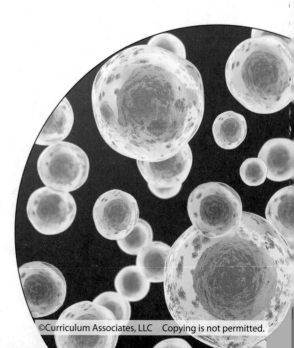

▶ **Use the problem from the previous page to help you understand how to multiply and divide powers with the same base.**

1 **a.** What single power of 2 represents the relationship between the population of the colony on Day 7 and the population on Day 4? Use your answer to complete the equation. How many times as large is the population of the colony on Day 7 than on Day 4?

$$\frac{2^7}{2^4} = \underline{\hspace{3cm}}$$

b. Look at the equation you completed in problem 1a. How are the exponents on the left side of the equation related to the exponent on the right side?

2 **a.** Look at the first **Model It**. The table shows the population of the colony on Day 7 as $(2 \cdot 2 \cdot 2) \cdot 2^4$. How can you write this expression as a product of two powers?

b. What power represents the population of the colony on Day 7? Write an equation by writing your answer to problem 2a equal to this power.

c. How are the exponents in your equation related?

3 Explain why you can write the product $(-6)^{23} \cdot (-6)^{15}$ as the single power $(-6)^{38}$.

4 **Reflect** Think about all the models and strategies you have discussed today. Describe how one of them helped you better understand how to multiply and divide powers with the same base.

Apply It

➤ **Use what you learned to solve these problems.**

5 Which expressions are equal to $\dfrac{(7^4 \cdot 7^8)}{7^2}$? Select all that apply.

A 7^{10}

B $7^4 \cdot 7^4 \cdot 7^2$

C 7^{16}

D $(7^2)^5$

E $\dfrac{7^{15}}{7^5}$

F 7^{14}

6 Write each side of the equation as a single power. Then write and solve an equation to find the value of n. Show your work.

$$23^8 \cdot 23^n = (23^5)^3$$

SOLUTION _____

7 Evaluate the expression $\left(\dfrac{(-2)^3}{-2}\right)^3$. Show your work.

SOLUTION _____

Practice Applying Properties for Powers with the Same Base

➤ Study the Example showing how to simplify an expression involving powers that have the same base. Then solve problems 1–5.

Example

Rewrite the expression $\dfrac{(6^9 \cdot 6^4)}{6^{11}}$ as a single power.

$$\frac{(6^9 \cdot 6^4)}{6^{11}} = \frac{6^{9+4}}{6^{11}}$$

$$= \frac{6^{13}}{6^{11}}$$

$$= 6^{13-11}$$

$$= 6^2$$

1. Rewrite each expression as a single power.

   a. $(-4)^6(-4)^5$

   b. $13^7 \cdot 13^2$

   c. $\dfrac{9^{14}}{9^7}$

   d. $\dfrac{(-24)^5}{-24}$

2. A certain type of bacteria reproduces so that after x hours there are 15^x cells. What single power represents the size relationship between the cell population after 24 hours and the cell population after 8 hours? Show your work.

SOLUTION _____

3. Cody tried to rewrite the expression $2^9 \cdot 3^4$ as a single power. His work is shown below. What was Cody's mistake?

   $$2^9 \cdot 3^4 = 6^{9+4}$$

   $$= 6^{13}$$

Vocabulary

power
an expression with a base and an exponent.

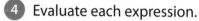

④ Evaluate each expression.

a. $2(2^5)$

b. $(-10)^4(-10)^3$

c. $\dfrac{(-11)^3(-11)^6}{(-11)^7}$

d. $\dfrac{(3^2)^7}{3^{10}}$

e. $(10^2 \cdot 10^3)^2$

f. $\left(\dfrac{4^7}{4^5}\right)^2$

⑤ What value of n makes the equation true? Show your work.

a. $\dfrac{(-5)^{11}}{(-5)^n} = (-5)^2 \cdot (-5)^1$

SOLUTION _____

b. $8^9 \cdot 8^4 = \dfrac{(8^n)^3}{8^2}$

SOLUTION _____

c. $(7^5 \cdot 7^n)^4 = \left(\dfrac{7^{16}}{7^n}\right)^3$

SOLUTION _____

Develop Applying Properties for Powers with the Same Exponent

➤ **Read and try to solve the problem below.**

Rani makes a special design called a rangoli for Diwali. Her design is square with a side length of 15 in. Rani then makes a larger rangoli by tripling this side length. How many times as large is the area of the new rangoli than the area of the original rangoli?

 TRY IT

Math Toolkit grid paper, straightedges

DISCUSS IT

Ask: What was your first step in solving the problem?

Share: The first thing I did was . . .

➤ **Explore different ways to find the power of a product.**

Rani makes a special design called a rangoli for Diwali. Her design is square with a side length of 15 in. Rani then makes a larger rangoli by tripling this side length. How many times as large is the area of the new rangoli than the area of the original rangoli?

Model It

You can use a fraction to compare the areas.

original rangoli side length (in.): 15

new rangoli side length (in.): 3 • 15

$$\frac{\text{area of new rangoli (in.}^2)}{\text{area of original rangoli (in.}^2)} = \frac{(3 \cdot 15)(3 \cdot 15)}{15 \cdot 15}$$

$$= \frac{(3 \cdot 3)(15 \cdot 15)}{15 \cdot 15}$$

$$= \frac{3 \cdot 3}{1} \cdot \frac{15 \cdot 15}{15 \cdot 15}$$

Model It

You can use a power expression for the area of the new rangoli.

The area of the original rangoli is 15 • 15. Find the area of the new rangoli in terms of the area of the original rangoli.

area of new rangoli (in.²): $(3 \cdot 15)^2$

$$(3 \cdot 15)^2 = (3 \cdot 15) \cdot (3 \cdot 15)$$

$$= (3 \cdot 3) \cdot (15 \cdot 15)$$

CONNECT IT

➤ **Use the problem from the previous page to help you understand powers of products and powers of quotients.**

1 How many times as large is the area of the new rangoli than the area of the original rangoli?

2 a. The second **Model It** shows that $(3 \cdot 15)^2 = (3 \cdot 3) \cdot (15 \cdot 15)$. Rewrite the right side of the equation as a product of two powers.

b. How can you write an expression equivalent to $(a \cdot b)^n$ as a product of two powers? Explain why the expressions are equivalent.

c. The expression $(3 \cdot 15)^2$ is a power of a product. How can you write the expression $18^3 \cdot 35^3$ as the power of a product?

3 a. The side length of the original rangoli in feet is 1.25, or $\frac{5}{4}$. The area of this rangoli in square feet can be written as a power of a quotient.

$$\left(\frac{5}{4}\right)^2 = \frac{5}{4} \cdot \frac{5}{4} = \frac{5 \cdot 5}{4 \cdot 4}$$

Rewrite $\frac{5 \cdot 5}{4 \cdot 4}$ as a quotient of two powers.

b. Write the expression $\left(\frac{5}{4}\right)^6$ as a quotient of two powers. Show that the expressions are equivalent by writing the powers as repeated multiplication.

4 Reflect Think about all the models and strategies you have discussed today. Describe how one of them helped you better understand powers of products and powers of quotients.

Apply It

➤ **Use what you learned to solve these problems.**

5 How can you write $8^4 \cdot 7^4$ as a single power? Show your work.

SOLUTION _____

6 Which expressions are equal to $\dfrac{(12 \cdot 17^4)^5}{17^{10}}$? Select all that apply.

A $12^5 \cdot 17^2$

B $\left(\dfrac{12 \cdot 17^4}{17^2}\right)^5$

C $12^5 \cdot 17^{10}$

D $(12 \cdot 17^2)^5$

E $\dfrac{12^5 \cdot 17^9}{17^{10}}$

F $\dfrac{12 \cdot 17^{20}}{17^{10}}$

7 When a rubber ball is dropped on a particular surface, it bounces back to $\dfrac{8}{10}$ of its drop height. The ball's height after bounce x is $\left(\dfrac{8}{10}\right)^x$ times its drop height. What fraction of its drop height will the ball bounce up to after its fourth bounce? Show your work.

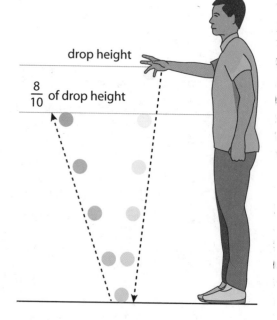

drop height

$\dfrac{8}{10}$ of drop height

SOLUTION _____

Practice Applying Properties for Powers with the Same Exponent

➤ **Study the Example showing how to evaluate an expression that involves powers with the same exponent. Then solve problems 1–6.**

Example

Evaluate the expression $\left(\frac{(-3)}{2^4}\right)^2$.

$$\left(\frac{(-3)}{2^4}\right)^2 = \frac{(-3)^2}{(2^4)^2}$$

$$= \frac{9}{2^8}$$

$$= \frac{9}{256}$$

1 Evaluate the expression.

a. $((-10)^3 \cdot 6)^3$

b. $\left(\frac{3^2}{5}\right)^3$

2 Rewrite each expression as a product of two powers or a quotient of two powers.

a. $(6 \cdot 13)^8$

b. $\left(\frac{9}{14}\right)^7$

c. $3^{10}(32^5 \cdot 3)^2$

d. $\left(\frac{4^5}{9^7 \cdot 4}\right)^5$

e. $\left(\frac{7^4 \cdot 24^3}{24}\right)^5$

f. $\left(\frac{15^9}{8^3}\right)^6$

3 What is the value of the expression $\left(\frac{5^4 \cdot 2^4}{10}\right)^3$? Show your work.

Vocabulary

power
an expression with a base and an exponent.

SOLUTION _____

4. When a ball is dropped, the height it reaches after it bounces is a fraction of its original drop height. The expression shown for each ball gives the fraction of the drop height that the ball reaches after x bounces. What fraction of its original height does each ball bounce up to after the third bounce?

   a. basketball: $\left(\frac{3}{4}\right)^x$

   b. tennis ball: $\left(\frac{2}{3}\right)^x$

   c. softball: $\left(\frac{3}{10}\right)^x$

5. Moses is creating a large cube sculpture for a city park. He first makes a smaller cube to use as a rough model of his sculpture. The edge lengths of the model are each 25 in. The edge lengths of the sculpture will be 3 times the model's edge lengths. How many times as large is the volume of the sculpture than the volume of the model? Show your work.

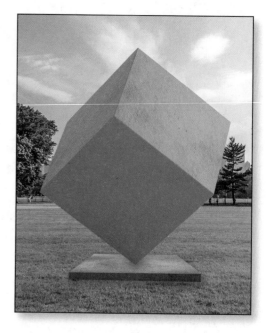

SOLUTION _____

6. What value of n makes the equation true? Show your work.

$$\left(\frac{19^8}{7^n}\right)^4 = \left(\frac{19^4}{7^3}\right)^8$$

SOLUTION _____

Refine Applying Exponent Properties for Positive Integer Exponents

➤ **Complete the Example below. Then solve problems 1–10.**

Example

Write the expression $\dfrac{6^2 \cdot 24^9}{4^9}$ as a single power.

Look at how you could combine powers with the same exponent.

$$\frac{6^2 \cdot 24^9}{4^9} = 6^2 \cdot \left(\frac{24}{4}\right)^9$$
$$= 6^2 \cdot 6^9$$
$$= 6^{2+9}$$

SOLUTION _____

CONSIDER THIS...
How are the bases of the powers in the numerator related to the base of the power in the denominator?

PAIR/SHARE
What is the value of the expression?

Apply It

1 What is the value of n? Show your work.

$$22^n \cdot 22^6 = (22^8)^3$$

CONSIDER THIS...
How can you rewrite each side of the equation as a single power?

PAIR/SHARE
Suppose the left side of the equation was $(22^n \cdot 22)^6$. How would the solution change?

SOLUTION _____

2 Rewrite $\left(\dfrac{5^7(-3)^4}{5^6}\right)^2$ as a product of two powers. Show your work.

CONSIDER THIS...
How can you combine powers that have the same base?

SOLUTION _____

PAIR/SHARE
What is the value of the expression inside the large parentheses?

3 Which expression is equivalent to $\dfrac{(15^4 \cdot 7^6)^3}{15^2}$?

A $15^2 \cdot 7^9$

B $15^2 \cdot 7^{18}$

C $15^5 \cdot 7^9$

D $15^{10} \cdot 7^{18}$

Caitlin chose C as the correct answer. How might she have gotten that answer?

CONSIDER THIS...
Which exponents do you need to work with first?

PAIR/SHARE
Think of another expression involving powers that is equivalent to the expression in the problem.

4 Which expressions are equivalent to $8^3 10^6$? Select all that apply.

A $(8 \cdot 10^3)^3$

B $\dfrac{8^5 \cdot 10^{15}}{10^9 \cdot 8^2}$

C $\dfrac{(8 \cdot 10)^6}{8^2}$

D $8 \cdot 10^4 \cdot (8 \cdot 10)^2$

E $\left(\dfrac{8 \cdot 10^5}{10^3}\right)^3$

5 Tell whether $n = 4$ makes the equation true.

	Yes	No
a. $(7^n)^2 = 7^8$	○	○
b. $(-5)^3 \cdot (-5)^n = (-5)^{12}$	○	○
c. $\dfrac{19^4}{19} = 19^n$	○	○
d. $(3n)^2 = 144$	○	○
e. $\left(-\dfrac{2}{5}\right)^2 = \dfrac{n}{25}$	○	○

6 Explain why the number $(-99)^n(-99)^n$ is positive.

7 What is the value of the expression $\dfrac{5^{18} \cdot 5^6}{(5^{10})^2}$? Show your work.

SOLUTION _____

8 Paulo used clay to make the cube shown. He wants to make a larger cube with an edge length that is twice as long. How many ounces of clay does he need to make this larger cube? Show your work.

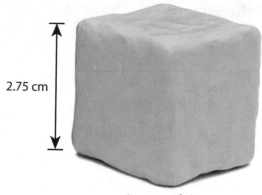

2.75 cm

1 ounce of clay

SOLUTION _____

9 The expression $(9^3 \cdot 9)^5$ written as repeated multiplication has _____ factors of 9.

10 **Math Journal** Rewrite each expression as a single power. Use repeated factors to explain your answers.

a. $(38^5)^2$

b. $\dfrac{20^6}{20^3}$

 End of Lesson Checklist

☐ **INTERACTIVE GLOSSARY** Write a new entry for *related*. Explain why you might want to know how bases are *related* when rewriting an expression involving powers.

☐ **SELF CHECK** Go back to the Unit 5 Opener and see what you can check off.

Dear Family,

Previously, your student learned about properties of exponents. They used these properties to simplify powers with positive integer exponents. This week, students will be learning how to apply these properties and others to powers with zero and negative integer exponents.

Students will learn how to simplify and evaluate expressions containing powers such as 5^{-3} and 25^0 by using these new properties:

Negative Exponents	Zero as an Exponent
$a^{-n} = \dfrac{1}{a^n}, a \neq 0$	$a^0 = 1, a \neq 0$

Applying these properties, $5^{-3} = \dfrac{1}{5^3}$ or $\dfrac{1}{125}$, and $25^0 = 1$.

Students will solve problems like the one below.

Evaluate the expression $\dfrac{3^{-4}}{3^0}$.

➤ **ONE WAY** to evaluate is to simplify the fraction.

$$\frac{3^{-4}}{3^0} = \frac{1}{3^4} \cdot 3^0$$

$$= \frac{1}{3^4} \cdot \frac{1}{3^0}$$

$$= \frac{1}{81} \cdot \frac{1}{1}$$

$$= \frac{1}{81}$$

➤ **ANOTHER WAY** is to use properties of exponents.

$$\frac{3^{-4}}{3^0} = \frac{1}{3^4 \cdot 3^0}$$

$$= \frac{1}{3^{4+0}}$$

$$= \frac{1}{3^4}$$

$$= \frac{1}{81}$$

Using either method, $\dfrac{3^{-4}}{3^0} = \dfrac{1}{81}$.

 Use the next page to start a conversation about integer exponents and their properties.

Apply Exponent Properties for All Integer Exponents

Activity Thinking About Exponent Properties for All Integer Exponents

➤ **Do this activity together to investigate integer exponent properties.**

You can use any integer—positive, zero, or negative—as an exponent. Expressions with negative exponents are often used to describe very small quantities, such as the diameter of a blood cell. Sizes of microscopic cells are often measured in micrometers, where 1 micrometer is one millionth of a meter, or 10^{-6} m. Look at these equations that relate expressions with integer exponents. What patterns do you notice in each set?

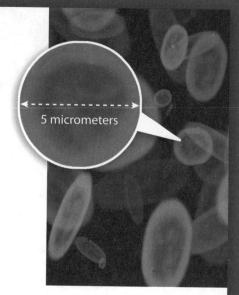

5 micrometers

EQUATION SET 1

$$4^2 \cdot 4^5 = 4^7$$
$$4^2 \cdot 4^0 = 4^2$$
$$4^{-2} \cdot 4^5 = 4^3$$

EQUATION SET 2

$$5^2 \cdot 5^2 = 5^4$$
$$5^0 \cdot 5^4 = 5^4$$
$$5^{-1} \cdot 5^{-2} = 5^{-3}$$

EQUATION SET 3

$$(-2)^3 \cdot (-2)^4 = (-2)^7$$
$$(-2)^{-2} \cdot (-2)^1 = (-2)^{-1}$$
$$(-2)^0 \cdot (-2)^3 = (-2)^3$$

? Did you notice any patterns in each set? How could seeing a pattern help you evaluate expressions involving integer exponents?

Explore Exponent Properties for Zero Exponents

Previously, you learned how to work with positive exponents and their properties. In this lesson, you will learn about exponents that are not positive.

➤ **Use what you know to try to solve the problem below.**

A colony of microalgae is being studied. The mass of the colony doubles every day. On Day x of the study, the colony has a mass of 2^x mg. What is the mass of the colony on Days 3, 2, and 1? What is the mass of the colony on Day 0, when the study begins?

Day 4 mass: 16 mg

TRY IT

DISCUSS IT

Ask: How did you find the mass for each day?

Share: I found the mass by . . .

◎ **Learning Target**   SMP 1, SMP 2, SMP 3, SMP 4, SMP 5, SMP 6, SMP 7, SMP 8
Know and apply the properties of integer exponents to generate equivalent numerical expressions.

CONNECT IT

1 **Look Back** Complete the table to show the mass of the colony on Days 3, 2, 1, and 0. How did you get your answers?

x	2^x	Mass (mg)
3		
2		
1		
0		

2 **Look Ahead** Consider the expressions shown.

$$\frac{2^5}{2^5} \qquad\qquad \frac{10^8}{10^8} \qquad\qquad \frac{25^{13}}{25^{13}}$$

a. What is the value of each expression? How do you know?

b. Write each expression as a single power.

c. The value of any power with a nonzero base and an exponent of 0 is 1. How do your answers to problems 2a and 2b show that this is true?

3 **Reflect** Write an equation showing the expression $6^3 \cdot 6^0$ as a single power. How does your answer show that $6^0 = 1$?

Prepare for Applying Exponent Properties for All Integer Exponents

1 Think about what you know about powers and exponents. Fill in each box. Use words, numbers, and pictures. Show as many ideas as you can.

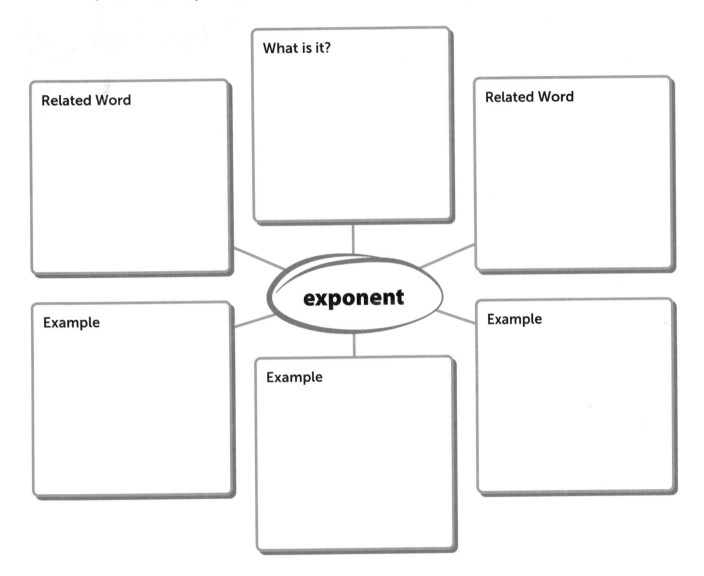

What is it?

Related Word

Related Word

Example

exponent

Example

Example

2 Evaluate the power. What is the exponent in the expression?

   a. 10^7 **b.** 18^1 **c.** $(-5)^4$

➤ **Explore different ways to write powers.**

A Chinese restaurant calculates that there are 2^{14} ways to order dim sum by choosing from the dishes they offer. They also calculate that there are 2^{10} ways to order dim sum from another restaurant in town. They want to advertise that the other restaurant offers only a small fraction of the possibilities that they do. Evaluate the expression $\frac{2^{10}}{2^{14}}$ to find that fraction.

Model It

You can simplify the fraction.

$$\frac{2^{10}}{2^{14}} = \frac{2^{10}}{2^{10} \cdot 2^4}$$

$$= \frac{2^{10}}{2^{10}} \cdot \frac{1}{2^4}$$

$$= 1 \cdot \frac{1}{2^4}$$

$$= \frac{1}{2^4}$$

Model It

You can use what you know about exponents to write the expression as a single power.

$$\frac{2^{10}}{2^{14}} = 2^{10 - 14}$$

$$= 2^{-4}$$

➤ **Use the problem from the previous page to help you understand how to work with negative exponents.**

1 Look at the last line of the first **Model It**. What fraction will the restaurant use in their advertisement?

2 The equation shown is written by setting the last expressions of the two **Model Its** equal to one another.

$$\frac{1}{2^4} = 2^{-4}$$

You can show that this equation is true. Begin with $\frac{1}{2^4}$ and rewrite the numerator as a power of 2. Then use what you know about exponents to rewrite the expression as a single power.

$$\frac{1}{2^4} = \frac{2^?}{2^4}$$

3 Use $2^{-4} = \frac{1}{2^4}$ to show that $\frac{1}{2^{-4}} = 2^4$.

4 Rewrite each expression using only positive exponents.

$10^{-8} =$ $\qquad$ $(-5)^{-3} =$ $\qquad$ $\frac{1}{17^{-1}} =$

5 **Reflect** Think about all the models and strategies you have discussed today. Describe how one of them helped you better understand how to work with negative exponents.

Apply It

➤ **Use what you learned to solve these problems.**

6 Which expressions are equivalent to $\dfrac{17^{-5}}{29^3}$? Select all that apply.

A $\dfrac{1}{17^5 \cdot 29^3}$

B $\dfrac{29^3}{17^5}$

C $17^{-5} \cdot 29^{-3}$

D $\left(\dfrac{17^5}{29^{-3}}\right)^{-1}$

E $17^5 \cdot 29^{-3}$

F $\dfrac{29^{-3}}{17^{-5}}$

7 Fill in the missing exponents to complete the pattern. Use the pattern to explain how to evaluate 0 and negative exponents.

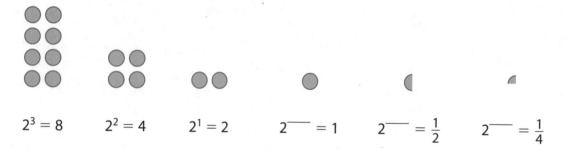

$2^3 = 8$ $\qquad$ $2^2 = 4$ $\qquad$ $2^1 = 2$ $\qquad$ $2^{\rule{1em}{0.4pt}} = 1$ $\qquad$ $2^{\rule{1em}{0.4pt}} = \dfrac{1}{2}$ $\qquad$ $2^{\rule{1em}{0.4pt}} = \dfrac{1}{4}$

8 Rewrite the expression $\dfrac{9^{-8} \cdot 3^0}{2^{-1}}$ using only positive exponents. Show your work.

SOLUTION _____

Practice Applying Properties of Negative Exponents

 Study the Example showing how to rewrite expressions involving negative exponents. Then solve problems 1–4.

Example

Rewrite the expression using only positive exponents.

$$\frac{14^0 \cdot 15^{-9}}{2^{-5} \cdot 99^3} = \frac{1 \cdot 15^{-9}}{2^{-5} \cdot 99^3} \quad \longleftarrow \quad 14^0 = 1$$

$$= \frac{2^5}{15^9 \cdot 99^3} \quad \longleftarrow \quad 15^{-9} = \frac{1}{15^9}; \; \frac{1}{2^{-5}} = 2^5$$

1 Rewrite each expression using only positive exponents.

a. $6^{-10} \cdot 41^{-4} \cdot 11^{-13}$

b. $\dfrac{(-2)^7 \cdot 19^{-3}}{31^{-1}}$

c. $15^0 \cdot 8^{-6} \cdot 23^5$

d. $\dfrac{3^{25} \cdot 16^0}{5^{-9} \cdot 52^{-3}}$

2 Which expressions have a value between 0 and 1? Select all that apply.

A $\left(\dfrac{4}{5}\right)^{-3}$

B $5^{-7} \cdot 4^2$

C $\dfrac{5^{-3}}{4^6}$

D $\dfrac{4^{-2}}{5^{-3}}$

E $4^{-3} \cdot 5^{-9}$

➤ **Explore different ways to work with integer exponents.**

Adriana and Katrina are evaluating the expression shown. Adriana thinks the value is between 0 and 1, while Katrina thinks the value is greater than 1.

Evaluate the expression. Who is correct?

I think the value is between 0 and 1.

I think the value is greater than 1.

$$\left(\frac{81^{-2}}{27^{-3}}\right)^5$$

Model It

You can begin by eliminating the parentheses.

$$\left(\frac{81^{-2}}{27^{-3}}\right)^5 = \frac{81^{-10}}{27^{-15}}$$

$$= \frac{27^{15}}{81^{10}}$$

$$= \frac{27^{15}}{(3 \cdot 27)^{10}}$$

$$= \frac{27^{15}}{3^{10} \cdot 27^{10}}$$

$$= \frac{27^{5}}{3^{10}}$$

$$= \frac{(3^3)^5}{3^{10}}$$

$$= \frac{3^{15}}{3^{10}}$$

Model It

You can rewrite the powers so that they have the same base.

$$\left(\frac{81^{-2}}{27^{-3}}\right)^5 = \left(\frac{(3^4)^{-2}}{(3^3)^{-3}}\right)^5$$

$$= \left(\frac{3^{-8}}{3^{-9}}\right)^5$$

$$= (3^{-8-(-9)})^5$$

$$= (3^{-8+9})^5$$

$$= (3^1)^5$$

➤ **Use the problem from the previous page to help you understand how to work with integer exponents.**

1 Look at the last expression of each **Model It**. Rewrite each expression as a single power. Do they both simplify to the same power? Explain.

2 What is the value of the expression? Who is correct?

3 Do you need to find the exact value of the expression in order to tell whether it is less than or greater than 1? Explain.

4 **a.** What is the simplest form of the expression you could write without changing the bases of any of the powers? How would you evaluate this expression?

b. Can you tell whether the expression in problem 4a is less than or greater than 1? Why or why not?

5 Did you or your classmates evaluate the expression in a different way than shown in the **Model Its**? Which ways seem simpler or more efficient? Explain.

6 **Reflect** Think about all the models and strategies you have discussed today. Describe how one of them helped you better understand how to solve the **Try It** problem.

Apply It

➤ **Use what you learned to solve these problems.**

7 Which expressions have a value between 0 and 1? Select all that apply.

A $\left(\dfrac{54}{29^{-2}}\right)^{-3}$

B $(54^2 \cdot 29^{-2})^{-1}$

C $\left(\dfrac{54^{-7}}{29^0}\right)^{-3}$

D $54^{-2}(29^3 \cdot 54^{-1})^0$

E $\dfrac{54^{-2} \cdot 29^5}{29^{-7} \cdot 54^2}$

8 Evaluate the expression $24^{-3} \cdot 6^4$. Show your work.

SOLUTION _____

9 Rewrite the expression $\dfrac{(75^{-6} \cdot 31^0)^{-3}}{75^{10} \cdot 31^{-9}}$ with no parentheses and using only positive exponents. Show your work.

SOLUTION _____

Practice Applying Properties of Integer Exponents

➤ **Study the Example showing how to evaluate expressions involving integer exponents. Then solve problems 1–4.**

Example

Evaluate the expression $\dfrac{(4^{-3} \cdot 9^0)^2}{4^{-5}}$.

$$\dfrac{(4^{-3} \cdot 9^0)^2}{4^{-5}} = \dfrac{4^{-6} \cdot 9^0}{4^{-5}} \quad \longleftarrow \quad (4^{-3})^2 = 4^{-6}; (9^0)^2 = 9^0$$

$$= \dfrac{4^{-6}(1)}{4^{-5}} \quad \longleftarrow \quad 9^0 = 1$$

$$= \dfrac{4^5}{4^6} \quad \longleftarrow \quad 4^{-6} = \dfrac{1}{4^6}; \dfrac{1}{4^{-5}} = 4^5$$

$$= \dfrac{1}{4} \quad \longleftarrow \quad (4^{5-6}) = 4^{-1}$$

1 Evaluate each expression.

a. $(12^0)^4$

b. $7^{-4} \cdot 7^4$

c. $(3^0 \cdot 8^2)^{-2}$

d. $\left(\dfrac{5^{-4} \cdot 5^7}{10^2}\right)^{-1}$

2 Rewrite each expression using only positive exponents.

a. $39^{-5}(39^{-6} \cdot 39)^{-2}$

b. $\dfrac{11^{-3} \cdot 40^{-2}}{40^6 \cdot 11^{-8}}$

c. $16^{-10} \cdot 16^4(16^{-5})^2$

d. $\left(\dfrac{21^2}{21^{-9} \cdot 21^5}\right)^{-7}$

3 Glen rewrote an expression as shown. $\left(\frac{2}{5}\right)^4 \left(\frac{2}{5}\right) \left(\frac{2}{5}\right)^{-3} = \left(\frac{8}{125}\right)^2$

   a. What was Glen's mistake?

   b. Rewrite the expression correctly as a single power. Show your work.

 SOLUTION _____

4 What value of n makes the equation true? Show your work.

   a. $(8^{-n})^5 = \dfrac{8}{8^{-14}}$

 SOLUTION _____

   b. $\left(\dfrac{3^4}{3^n}\right)^2 = 3^6$

   SOLUTION _____

Refine Applying Exponent Properties for All Integer Exponents

➤ **Complete the Example below. Then solve problems 1–9.**

Example

Esteban has some money in a savings account that earns interest each year. The amount of money in his account x years from now will be $250(1.05)^x$. How much money is in the account right now? How much was in the account 1 year ago?

Look at how you could use 0 and negative exponents.

Right now is 0 years from now, so $x = 0$. The amount of money now is $250(1.05)^0 = 250(1)$.

1 year ago is −1 year from now, so $x = -1$. The amount of money 1 year ago is $250(1.05)^{-1} = \dfrac{250}{1.05}$.

SOLUTION _____

CONSIDER THIS...
Do positive or negative
x-values represent
the past?

PAIR/SHARE
How do you know
which amount of
money should
be greater?

Apply It

1. What value of n makes the equation true? Show your work.

   $$\frac{85^n}{85^6} = 85^{-6}$$

CONSIDER THIS...
Write an equation that
you can solve for n.

PAIR/SHARE
How would the problem
change if the powers
had different bases?

SOLUTION _____

2 Evaluate the expression $\dfrac{3^2 \cdot 5^{-7}}{15^{-3}}$. Show your work.

CONSIDER THIS...
How can you rewrite 15^{-3} as a product of two powers?

PAIR/SHARE
Could you tell whether the expression was less than or greater than 1 before evaluating the powers?

SOLUTION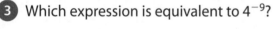

3 Which expression is equivalent to 4^{-9}?

A $4^9 \cdot 4^{-1}$

B $(4^{-9})^0$

C $\dfrac{1}{4^9}$

D $\dfrac{4^9}{4^0}$

Benjamin chose A as the correct answer. How might he have gotten that answer?

CONSIDER THIS...
How can you combine powers that have the same base?

PAIR/SHARE
How can you change each of the other expressions so that they are all equivalent to 4^{-9}?

4 Which expressions are equivalent to 28^{-3}? Select all that apply.

A $\dfrac{28^{-5}}{28^{-2}}$ B $28^0 \cdot 28^3$ C $\left(\dfrac{1}{28^{-3}}\right)^{-1}$

D $(7^{-3} \cdot 4^{-3})^{-1}$ E $28^{-2} \cdot 28^5$ F $\dfrac{7^{-3}}{4^3}$

5 Angel says that raising a fraction to the power of -1 is the same as finding the reciprocal of the fraction. Do you agree? Explain.

6 What value of n makes the equation true? Show your work.

$$\dfrac{42^n}{42} = \dfrac{1}{42^{-8}}$$

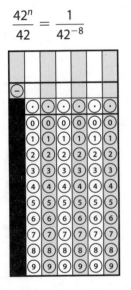

7 Tell whether each expression is equivalent to 7^4, 7^{-4}, or *Neither*.

	7^4	7^{-4}	Neither
a. $\dfrac{1}{7^{-4}}$	○	○	○
b. $7^2 \cdot 7^{-2}$	○	○	○
c. $(7^2)^{-2}$	○	○	○
d. $\left(\dfrac{1}{7^4}\right)^{-1}$	○	○	○

8 The value of Serafina's car is decreasing by 10% each year.

Its value in dollars x years from now will be $12{,}000\left(\dfrac{9}{10}\right)^{x}$.

a. How much is the car worth right now? Show your work.

Value decreases by 10% each year.

SOLUTION _____

b. How much was the car worth one year ago? Show your work.

SOLUTION _____

9 **Math Journal** Explain how to find if the value of the expression $\left(\dfrac{26^{3}}{15^{-8}}\right)^{-1}$ is between 0 and 1. Do you have to find the exact value of the expression?

✔ **End of Lesson Checklist**

☐ **INTERACTIVE GLOSSARY** Find the entry for *simplify*. Write a new entry for *simplify*. Tell what you do when you *simplify* an expression.

☐ **SELF CHECK** Go back to the Unit 5 Opener and see what you can check off.

Dear Family,

This week your student is learning to express numbers using integer powers of 10. Students will be able to use single-digit factors and integer powers of 10 to express very large and very small numbers without writing a lot of zeros, as shown in the table.

Single Digit × Power of 10	2×10^{-6}	2×10^{-4}	2×10^{4}	2×10^{6}
Standard Form	0.000002	0.0002	20,000	2,000,000

Students will use integer powers of 10 to estimate and compare quantities, like in the problem below.

> The population of a small city is 626,299. Write an estimate for the population as a single digit times an integer power of 10.

➤ **ONE WAY** to solve is to round the number and then factor out a power of 10.

626,300 is about 600,000.

$600,000 = 6 \times 100,000$

$600,000 = 6 \times 10^5$ ◁ Write the standard form of the power of 10 as a single power.

➤ **ANOTHER WAY** is to round and then use decimal point patterns.

626,300 is about 600,000.

$600,000. \div 10^1 = 60,000.0$ ⟶ $60,000.0 \times 10^1 = 600,000.$

$600,000. \div 10^2 = 6,000.00$ ⟶ $6,000.00 \times 10^2 = 600,000.$

. . .

$600,000. \div 10^5 = 6.00000$ ⟶ $6.00000 \times 10^5 = 600,000.$

You can use arrows to show the decimal point movement more simply.

$6,0,0,0,0,0 = 6 \times 10^5$ ◁ The number of places the decimal point moves helps you write the exponent.

Using either method, the city's population is about 6×10^5.

 Use the next page to start a conversation about integer powers of 10.

Activity Thinking About Expressing Numbers Using Integer Powers of 10

➤ **Do this activity together to investigate integer powers of 10 in the real world.**

Integer powers of 10 are useful when working with very large or very small numbers! For example, 5 nanobytes of memory is equivalent to 5×10^{-9} of a byte. Five gigabytes of memory is equivalent to 5×10^9 bytes. Writing these numbers as a single digit times an integer power of 10 is much easier than writing 0.000000005 or 5,000,000,000. There is also less chance of making an error.

? Can you think of other real-world situations where integer powers of 10 would be useful?

Explore Using Integer Powers of 10

Previously, you learned about properties of integer exponents.
In this lesson, you will learn how to express and estimate quantities using integer powers of 10.

➤ **Use what you know to try to solve the problem below.**

According to the U.S. Mint, the number of quarters minted in 2018 was about 2×10^9. The mass of a quarter is about 6×10^{-3} kg. Write the number of quarters and the mass of a quarter in standard form.

TRY
IT

DISCUSS IT

Ask: How did you use the exponents in the powers of 10 to help you solve the problem?

Share: I used the exponents to . . .

Learning Target   SMP 1, SMP 2, SMP 3, SMP 4, SMP 5, SMP 6, SMP 7, SMP 8
Use numbers expressed in the form of a single digit times an integer power of 10 to estimate very large or very small quantities, and to express how many times as much one is than the other.

3 One ounce of gold can be made into a wire that is 8×10^4 m long and 5×10^{-6} m thick.

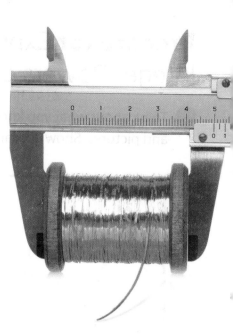

a. Write the length and thickness of the wire in standard form. Show your work.

SOLUTION _____

b. Check your answer to problem 3a. Show your work.

Develop Estimating Quantities Using Integer Powers of 10

➤ **Read and try to solve the problem below.**

Claudia's family has a soybean farm. They plant 175,000 soybeans on each acre of the farm. Each soybean weighs about 0.0057 oz. Write an estimate for both the number of soybeans per acre and the weight of a soybean as a single digit times an integer power of 10.

weight of a soybean: 0.0057 oz

TRY IT

➤ **Explore different ways to write estimates for quantities using integer powers of 10.**

Claudia's family has a soybean farm. They plant 175,000 soybeans on each acre of the farm. Each soybean weighs about 0.0057 oz. Write an estimate for both the number of soybeans per acre and the weight of a soybean as a single digit times an integer power of 10.

Model It

You can round and then factor out a power of 10.

Round to the greatest place value with a nonzero digit:

175,000 is about 200,000   0.0057 is about 0.006

Rewrite the rounded number as the product of a **single nonzero digit** and a **power of 10**.

200,000 = 2 × 100,000   0.006 = 6 × 0.001

Write the standard form of the power of 10 as a single power.

Model It

You can use what you know about decimal point patterns after you round.

Recall that every time you multiply or divide a number by 10, the decimal point moves one place. For example:

$200,000. \div 10^1 = 20,000.0$ ⟶ $20,000.0 \times 10^1 = 200,000.$

$200,000. \div 10^2 = 2,000.00$ ⟶ $2,000.00 \times 10^2 = 200,000.$

Similarly:

$0.006 \times 10^1 = 00.06$

$0.006 \times 10^2 = 000.6$

Continue until there is a single nonzero digit to the left of the decimal point. This is the single-digit factor.

The absolute value of the exponent in the power of 10 is equal to the number of places the decimal point moves to get the single-digit factor. The sign of the exponent is determined by whether the original number is greater or less than 1.

$2\,0\,0\,0\,0\,0 = 2 \times$ _____ $0.0\,0\,6 = 6 \times$ _____

➤ **Use the problem from the previous page to help you understand how to write estimates for quantities using integer powers of 10.**

 Look at the first **Model It**. Why do you round each number to the greatest place value with a nonzero digit?

 Look at the second **Model It**. Why does moving the decimal point help you find the correct exponent for the power of 10?

 a. Fill in the powers of 10 in the second **Model It**. How do you know whether the exponent in the power of 10 is positive or negative?

b. Write an estimate for both the number of soybeans per acre and the weight of a soybean as a single digit times an integer power of 10.

 How can you write an estimate for a number as a single digit times an integer power of 10?

 Reflect Think about all the models and strategies you have discussed today. Describe how one of them helped you better understand how to solve the **Try It** problem.

Apply It

> **Use what you learned to solve these problems.**

6 Astronomers use light years to measure large distances. A light year is the distance light travels in one year. Write an estimate for the number of miles in a light year as a single digit times an integer power of 10. Show your work.

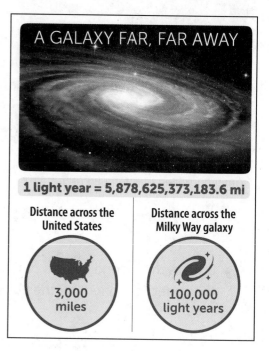

A GALAXY FAR, FAR AWAY

1 light year = 5,878,625,373,183.6 mi

Distance across the United States	Distance across the Milky Way galaxy
3,000 miles	100,000 light years

SOLUTION _____

7 The population of a city is 809,762. Which is the best estimate for the population?

A 8×10^5

B 9×10^5

C 8×10^6

D 9×10^6

8 Silt is like sand but with smaller grains. The smallest diameter of a grain of silt is 0.0000039 m. Write an estimate for the smallest diameter of a grain of silt as a single digit times an integer power of 10. Show your work.

SOLUTION _____

Practice Estimating Quantities Using Integer Powers of 10

➤ **Study the Example showing how to write an estimate for a quantity as a single digit times an integer power of 10. Then solve problems 1–5.**

Example

The average mass of one grain of rice is 0.000029 kg. Write an estimate for the average mass of one grain of rice as a single digit times an integer power of 10.

Round 0.000029 to the greatest place value with a nonzero digit.

   0.000029 is about 0.00003

Rewrite 0.00003 as a single nonzero digit times a power of 10.

   $0.00003 = 3 \times 0.00001$

Write the standard form of the power of 10 as a single power.

   $0.00001 = 10^{-5}$

The average mass of one grain of rice is about 3×10^{-5} kg.

---

1 The average thickness of a chicken eggshell is 0.000356 m. Write an estimate for the average thickness of a chicken eggshell as a single digit times an integer power of 10. Show your work.

SOLUTION _____

2 A news podcast has 77,000 subscribers. Write an estimate for the number of subscribers as a single digit times an integer power of 10. Show your work.

SOLUTION _____

3 A standard baseball has a mass of 0.148835 kg. A student was asked to write an estimate for the mass as a single digit times an integer power of 10. The student's work is shown at the right.

0.148835 is about 0.05.

$0.05 = 5 \times 0.01$

$= 5 \times 10^{-2}$

The mass is about 5×10^{-2} kg.

a. Explain the student's error.

b. Show how to solve the problem correctly.

4 According to a recent survey, the number of pet dogs and cats in the United States is about 183,900,000. Write an estimate for the number of pet dogs and cats as a single digit times an integer power of 10. Show your work.

SOLUTION _____

5 a. Which is a better estimate for 682,000: 6×10^5 or 7×10^6? Explain.

b. Is there a better way to write an estimate for 682,000 as a single digit times an integer power of 10? Explain.

Develop Comparing Quantities Involving Integer Powers of 10

➤ **Read and try to solve the problem below.**

The people planning Fourth of July fireworks in City A expect 3×10^5 people to attend. The people planning Fourth of July fireworks in City B expect 6×10^4 people to attend. Which city is expecting more people to attend the fireworks? How many times as many people are expected in that city?

TRY IT

Apply It

➤ **Use what you learned to solve these problems.**

7 A movie star's social media account has 8×10^5 subscribers. An athlete's social media account has 4×10^3 subscribers. How many times as many subscribers are there to the movie star's account than to the athlete's account? Show your work.

SOLUTION _____

8 The population of Elmwood is about 4×10^6. This is about 20 times the population of Midville. Which of the following could be the population of Midville?

A 2×10^5

B 2×10^6

C 8×10^6

D 8×10^7

9 A deer's hair has a diameter of about 4×10^{-4} m. A dog's hair has a diameter of about 8×10^{-5} m. Which animal's hair has a greater diameter? How many times as great? Show your work.

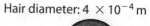
Hair diameter: 4×10^{-4} m

Hair diameter: 8×10^{-5} m

SOLUTION _____

_____

Practice Comparing Quantities Involving Integer Powers of 10

➤ **Study the Example showing how to compare quantities involving integer powers of 10. Then solve problems 1–5.**

Example

Linda is comparing densities of materials. The density of red oak is about 2×10^{-2} pound per cubic inches. The density of stainless steel is about 3×10^{-1} pound per cubic inches. Which material has a greater density? How many times as great?

Both numbers are written as a single digit times a power of 10, so compare the powers of 10. 10^{-1} is greater than 10^{-2}, so the density of stainless steel is greater than the density of red oak.

Compare the single digits and the integer powers of 10.

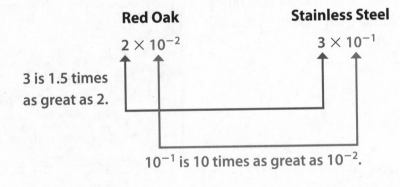

Red Oak

2×10^{-2}

Stainless Steel

3×10^{-1}

3 is 1.5 times as great as 2.

10^{-1} is 10 times as great as 10^{-2}.

$1.5 \times 10 = 15$

The density of stainless steel is 15 times as great as that of red oak.

1   Use information from the Example. The density of brick is about 7×10^{-2} lb per in.^{3}. Which material has a greater density, brick or red oak? How do you know?

2   Which number is greater: 3×10^{-12} or 9×10^{-11}? How many times as great? Show your work.

SOLUTION _____

3 The Boston Public Library has about 2×10^7 books. The Dallas Public Library has about 5×10^6 books.

   a. Which library has a greater number of books? How do you know?

   b. How many times as many books? Show your work.

SOLUTION _____

4 The 2019 population of California was 39,776,830. The 2019 population of New Mexico was about 2×10^6. How many times as large was the population of California than the population of New Mexico in 2019? Show your work.

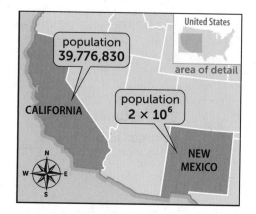

SOLUTION _____

5 A geologist is studying a sample of chalk and a sample of marble. The chalk sample has a mass of 8×10^{-2} kg. The marble sample has a mass of 2×10^2 kg. Which sample has a greater mass? How many times as great? Show your work.

SOLUTION _____

Refine Expressing Numbers Using Integer Powers of 10

➤ **Complete the Example below. Then solve problems 1–9.**

CONSIDER THIS...
The phrase *About how many times...* means you can solve the problem by estimating.

Example

Last year, Company A earned about 3×10^5 dollars. Company B earned about 7×10^8 dollars. About how many times as much did Company B earn than Company A?

Look at how you could solve the problem by comparing the single digits and the powers of 10.

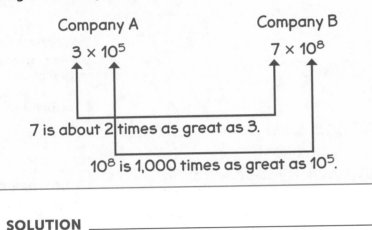

Company A

3×10^5

Company B

7×10^8

7 is about 2 times as great as 3.

10^8 is 1,000 times as great as 10^5.

SOLUTION _____

_____

PAIR/SHARE
How would your answer be different if the income for Company A was 3×10^6 dollars?

Apply It

1 The height of the statue of Abraham Lincoln at the Lincoln Memorial in Washington, DC, is 5.7912 m. Write an estimate for the height of the statue as a single digit times an integer power of 10. Show your work.

CONSIDER THIS...
The integer exponent in the power of 10 can be positive, negative, or zero.

PAIR/SHARE
How can you check that your estimate for the height is correct?

SOLUTION _____

2 The table shows the approximate lengths of some rivers in the United States. Which of the rivers is the longest? Show your work.

River	Length (m)
Copper	500,000
Missouri	4×10^6
Ohio	2,000,000
Porcupine	9×10^5
Rio Grande	3×10^6

CONSIDER THIS...
How can you use powers of 10 to help order the numbers?

PAIR/SHARE
What can you say about the single digit and the power of 10 for any river longer than those in the table?

SOLUTION _____

3 The volume of a small spoon is 0.00438 L. Which is the best estimate for the volume?

A 5×10^{-2} L

B 4×10^{-2} L

C 5×10^{-3} L

D 4×10^{-3} L

Tiana chose C as the correct answer. How might she have gotten that answer?

CONSIDER THIS...
You can think of this problem as comparing 0.00438 to the numbers written as a single digit times a power of 10.

PAIR/SHARE
How would your answer change if the volume were 0.00431 L?

4 The table shows the number of grams of vitamin A in a 100-gram serving of several foods. List the foods from the greatest amount of vitamin A to the least. Show your work.

Food	Vitamin A (g)
Beef liver	6×10^{-3}
Egg	7×10^{-5}
Red grapefruit	1×10^{-4}
Salmon	2×10^{-4}
Sweet potato	2×10^{-3}

SOLUTION _____

5 Which of the following values are between 6×10^{-5} and 3×10^{-4}? Select all that apply.

A 8×10^{-5} **B** 5×10^{-5}

C 1×10^{-4} **D** 7×10^{-5}

E 5×10^{-4} **F** 7×10^{-4}

6 Tell whether each statement is *Always, Sometimes,* or *Never* true.

	Always	Sometimes	Never
a. If n is an integer, then 3×10^n is negative.	○	○	○
b. If p is a positive single-digit number, then $p \times 10^{-2}$ is positive.	○	○	○
c. If m is an integer, then 5×10^m equals 50^m.	○	○	○
d. If q is a positive single-digit number, then $q \times 10^{-1}$ is greater than 1.	○	○	○

7 Kwame compares the number of people that can be seated in two stadiums. Stadium A can seat 82,933 people. Stadium B can seat 29,005 people.

a. Write an estimate for the seating capacity of each stadium as a single digit times a power of 10.

b. About how many times as great is the seating capacity of Stadium A than the seating capacity of Stadium B? Show your work.

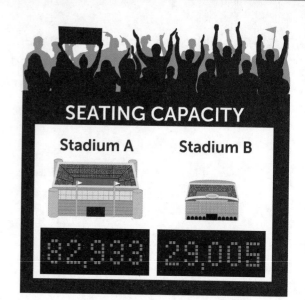

SEATING CAPACITY

Stadium A   Stadium B

82,933   29,005

SOLUTION _____

8 Eldora was asked to determine which is greater, 5×10^8 or 3×10^9, and how many times as great it is. Her work is shown here. Is she correct? Explain her strategy if she is correct. Explain her error if she is not correct.

$$5 \times 10^8 \qquad 3 \times 10^9$$
$$\downarrow \qquad\qquad \downarrow$$
$$5 \times 10^8 \qquad 30 \times 10^8$$

$30 > 5$, so 3×10^9 is greater.

$30 \div 5 = 6$, so 3×10^9 is 6 times as great.

9 **Math Journal** Choose a 6-digit whole number. Each digit in the number should be different. Explain how to write an estimate for the number as a single digit times an integer power of 10.

✓ End of Lesson Checklist

☐ **INTERACTIVE GLOSSARY** Write a new entry for *express*. Tell what you do when you *express* a quantity as a single digit times an integer power of 10.

☐ **SELF CHECK** Go back to the Unit 5 Opener and see what you can check off.

Dear Family,

This week your student is learning to perform operations with numbers in **scientific notation**. A number in scientific notation is written as the product of two factors: a number greater than or equal to 1 and less than 10, and an integer power of 10. The number factor is written as a single digit or a decimal, never as a fraction.

For example, a large number like 124,000,000 would be written as 1.24×10^8 in scientific notation. A small number like 0.000000371 would be written as 3.71×10^{-7}. The first factor in each product, 1.24 and 3.71, are each greater than or equal to 1 and less than 10.

Students will learn to solve problems like the one below.

> A scientific scale measures the mass of a monarch butterfly to be 0.00041 kilograms. What is the mass of the butterfly written using scientific notation?

➤ **ONE WAY** to write 0.00041 in scientific notation is to use the definition of scientific notation.

4.1 is greater than or equal to 1 and less than 10. Multiply by the correct power of 10.

$0.00041 = 4.1 \times 0.0001$
$= 4.1 \times 10^{-4}$

Write the **standard form** of the power of 10 as a **single power**.

➤ **ANOTHER WAY** is to move the decimal point.

Move the decimal point until there is a single nonzero digit to the left of the decimal point. The absolute value of the exponent is equal to the number of places the decimal point moved. The original number is less than 1, so the exponent is negative.

$0.00041 = 4.1 \times 10^{-4}$

Using either method, the mass of the butterfly is 4.1×10^{-4} kg.

 Use the next page to start a conversation about scientific notation.

Work with Scientific Notation

LESSON 22

©Curriculum Associates, LLC   Copying is not permitted.

LESSON 22 Work with Scientific Notation   **513**

Activity Thinking About Scientific Notation

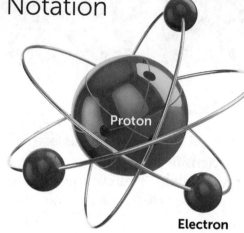

➤ **Do this activity together to investigate working with scientific notation in the real world.**

Scientific notation can be used to compare very large or very small quantities. For example, the mass of a proton is about 1.7×10^{-24} grams, and the mass of an electron is about 9.1×10^{-28} grams. You can compare the masses to see that a proton is about 1.868×10^3, or over 1,800, times the size of an electron!

Proton

Electron

 Can you think of other quantities that would be easier to compare using scientific notation?

Explore Scientific Notation

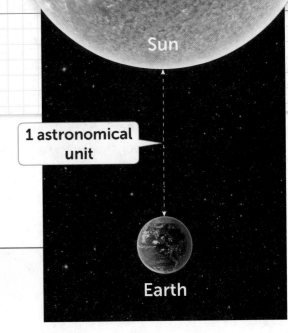

Sun

1 astronomical unit

Earth

Previously, you learned how to use powers of 10 to write estimates of very large and small numbers. In this lesson, you will learn about scientific notation.

➤ **Use what you know to try to solve the problem below.**

The average distance between Earth and the sun is about 9.296×10^7 mi. This distance is called an *astronomical unit*. How can you write 9.296×10^7 in standard form?

TRY IT

DISCUSS IT

Ask: What did you do first to write 9.296×10^7 in standard form?

Share: I knew . . . so I . . .

◎ **Learning Target** SMP 1, SMP 2, SMP 3, SMP 4, SMP 5, SMP 6, SMP 7
Perform operations with numbers expressed in scientific notation, including problems where both decimal and scientific notation are used. Use scientific notation and choose units of appropriate size for measurements of very large or very small quantities. Interpret scientific notation that has been generated by technology.

CONNECT IT

1 **Look Back** What is 9.296×10^7 written in standard form? Explain how you found your answer.

2 **Look Ahead** The number 9.296×10^7 is written in a form called **scientific notation**. Scientific notation is often used to write equivalent forms of very large or very small numbers. Numbers written in scientific notation are written as a product of two factors:

a decimal number ≥ 1 and < 10 ⟶ 9.296×10^7 ⟵ an integer power of 10

In scientific notation, the number factor is never written as a fraction.

a. Are 3.01×10^{-8} and 7.25×10^1 both written in scientific notation? Explain.

b. Are 42.655×10^{-5}, 0.6×10^6, and 2.539×3^5 written in scientific notation? Explain.

c. Desiderio says that 4.13×10^0 is not written in scientific notation. Explain why Desiderio is incorrect.

3 **Reflect** How are numbers written in scientific notation and numbers written as a single digit times an integer power of 10 similar? How are they different?

Prepare for Working with Scientific Notation

1 Think about what you know about powers. Fill in each box. Use words, numbers, and pictures. Show as many ideas as you can.

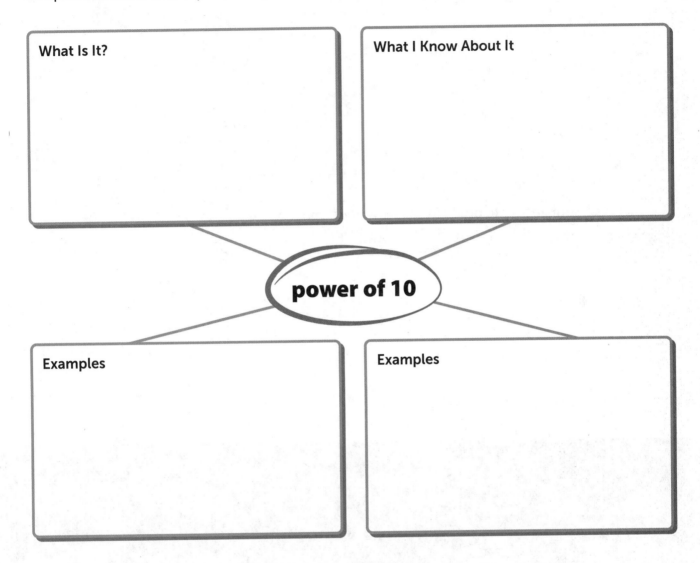

What Is It?

What I Know About It

power of 10

Examples

Examples

2 How can you write 5,000,000 as a product of a single digit and a power of 10?

3 On average, Neptune is about 2.795×10^9 mi from the sun.

 a. How can you write 2.795×10^9 in standard form? Show your work.

 SOLUTION _____

 b. Check your answer to problem 3a. Show your work.

$2.795 \times 10^9 \text{ mi}$

Sun

Neptune

Develop Writing Numbers in Scientific Notation

seas

+

oceans

+

bays

≈

➤ **Read and try to solve the problem below.**

Almost 97% of all water on Earth is in oceans, seas, and bays. Together, they hold about 1,338,000,000 cubic kilometers of water. What is 1,338,000,000 written in scientific notation?

97% of all water on Earth

TRY IT

DISCUSS IT

Ask: How do you know your answer is reasonable?

Share: I know the number . . .

➤ **Explore different ways to write a large number in scientific notation.**

Almost 97% of all water on Earth is in oceans, seas, and bays. Together, they hold about 1,338,000,000 cubic kilometers of water. What is 1,338,000,000 written in scientific notation?

Model It

You can use the definition of scientific notation.

Scientific notation is written as a product of two factors:

a decimal number ≥ 1 and $< 10 \times$ an integer power of 10

1.338 is greater than or equal to 1 and less than 10. Multiply by the correct power of 10.

$$1,338,000,000 = 1.338 \times 1,000,000,000$$

Write the standard form of the power of 10 as a single power.

Model It

You can use what you know about decimal point patterns to move the decimal point.

Repeatedly move the decimal point one place until there is a single nonzero digit to the left of the decimal point.

The absolute value of the exponent in the power of 10 is equal to the number of places the decimal point moves.

The sign of the exponent depends on whether the original number is greater than or less than 1.

$$1\,3\,3\,8\,0\,0\,0\,0\,0\,0 = 1.338 \times \underline{\hspace{2cm}}$$

Glaciers, ice caps, and permanent snow hold 1.74% of Earth's total water.

CONNECT IT

> Use the problem from the previous page to help you understand how to write very large and very small numbers in scientific notation.

1 Look at both **Model Its**. Fill in the power of 10 in the second **Model It**. What is 1,338,000,000 written in scientific notation?

2 **a.** Use patterns to complete the table.

Standard Form	Scientific Notation
13.003	1.3003×10^1
1.3003	1.3003×10^0
0.13003	1.3003×10^{-1}
0.013003	
0.0013003	

b. To write 0.000013003 in scientific notation, how many places will you move the decimal point to get the number factor? Explain.

c. To write 0.000013003 in scientific notation, will the exponent of the power of 10 be positive or negative? Explain.

d. Write 0.000013003 in scientific notation.

3 Suppose you are writing the number a in scientific notation. Write *positive, zero,* or *negative* to complete each sentence.

If $a \geq 10$, the power of 10 has a _____ exponent.

If $a < 1$, the power of 10 has a _____ exponent.

If $1 \leq a < 10$, the power of 10 has a _____ exponent.

4 **Reflect** Think about all the models and strategies you have discussed today. Describe how one of them helped you better understand how to solve the **Try It** problem.

4. Write $3,901\frac{1}{4}$ in scientific notation.

5. Anders made a mistake while writing 4,050,000 in scientific notation. His work is shown. What error did Anders make? What is the correct answer?

   $$4,050,000 = 4.5 \times 1,000,000$$
   $$= 4.5 \times 10^6$$

6. The length of a cell is 0.000909 mm. Which of the following is the best estimate of the length written using scientific notation?

   A 909×10^{-4} mm

   B 91×10^{-4} mm

   C 9.1×10^{-4} mm

   D 9.1×10^{-5} mm

7. Write the number 6 in scientific notation.

8. The circumference of Earth at the equator is about 131,300,000 ft.

   a. What is 131,300,000 written in scientific notation?

   b. Explain how you know your answer to problem 8a is written in scientific notation.

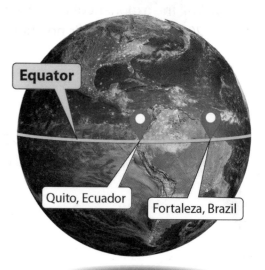

Equator

Quito, Ecuador

Fortaleza, Brazil

Develop Adding and Subtracting with Scientific Notation

➤ **Read and try to solve the problem below.**

The 48 contiguous states have an area of about 3.12×10^6 mi^2. The area of Alaska is about 6.63×10^5 mi^2. How many fewer square miles in area is Alaska? Write your answer using scientific notation.

DISCUSS IT

Ask: How did you know which operation to use?

Share: The problem is asking . . .

➤ **Explore different ways to add and subtract with numbers written in scientific notation.**

The 48 contiguous states have an area of about 3.12×10^6 mi². The area of Alaska is about 6.63×10^5 mi². How many fewer square miles in area is Alaska? Write your answer using scientific notation.

Model It

You can rewrite both areas with the power 10^5 and subtract.

Use the distributive property to rewrite the difference as a product of two factors.

$$(3.12 \times 10^6) - (6.63 \times 10^5) = (31.2 \times 10^5) - (6.63 \times 10^5)$$
$$= (31.2 - 6.63) \times 10^5$$

Factor out the common factor, 10^5.

Model It

You can rewrite both areas with the power 10^6 and subtract.

Use the distributive property to rewrite the difference as a product of two factors.

$$(3.12 \times 10^6) - (6.63 \times 10^5) = (3.12 \times 10^6) - (0.663 \times 10^6)$$
$$= (3.12 - 0.663) \times 10^6$$

Factor out the common factor, 10^6.

Denali National Park, Alaska

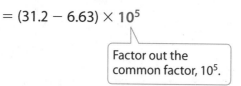

©Curriculum Associates, LLC Copying is not permitted.

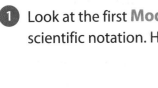

> **Use the problem from the previous page to help you understand how to add and subtract numbers written in scientific notation.**

1 Look at the first **Model It**. Complete the solution and write your answer using scientific notation. How many fewer square miles in area is Alaska?

2 Look at the second **Model It**. Complete the solution and write your answer using scientific notation. How many fewer square miles in area is Alaska?

3 Why does the second **Model It** require one less step when you complete the solution?

4 Suppose you want to know the sum of the areas. Add the areas using the methods from both **Model Its**. Write your answers using scientific notation. Do the methods also work for addition? Explain.

5 What must be true about numbers written in scientific notation before you can add or subtract? Explain.

6 **Reflect** Think about all the models and strategies you have discussed today. Describe how one of them helped you better understand how to add or subtract numbers written in scientific notation.

3 The population of Kansas City, Missouri, is about 4.9×10^5. The population of Kansas City, Kansas, is about 153,000.

  a. What is the combined population of the two cities? Write your answer using scientific notation. Show your work.

  SOLUTION _____

  b. The state of Missouri has a population of a little more than 6 million people. About how many people live in Missouri, but not in Kansas City, Missouri? Write your answer using scientific notation. Show your work.

  SOLUTION _____

4 Two numbers are written in scientific notation. What must be true of their powers of 10 before you can add or subtract the numbers using scientific notation?

5 Evaluate $(7.5 \times 10^{12}) + (2.2 \times 10^{14}) - (3 \times 10^{10})$. Write your answer in scientific notation. Show your work.

SOLUTION _____

Develop Multiplying and Dividing with Scientific Notation

➤ **Read and try to solve the problem below.**

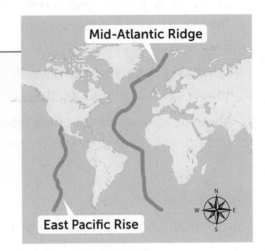

Mid-Atlantic Ridge

East Pacific Rise

Over time, the ocean floor moves apart along underwater mountains and trenches. The Mid-Atlantic Ridge moves an average of 3.5×10^{-2} m per year. The East Pacific Rise has moved about 6.6×10^6 m in 60 million years.

How many meters has the Mid-Atlantic Ridge moved in 60 million years? Write your answer using scientific notation.

About how many times as many meters has the East Pacific Rise moved than the Mid-Atlantic Ridge in 60 million years?

TRY IT

DISCUSS IT

Ask: How can you state what the problems is asking in your own words?

Share: The problem asks . . .

➤ **Explore different ways to multiply and divide numbers written in scientific notation.**

Over time, the ocean floor moves apart along underwater mountains and trenches. The Mid-Atlantic Ridge moves an average of 3.5×10^{-2} m per year. The East Pacific Rise has moved about 6.6×10^6 m in 60 million years.

How many meters has the Mid-Atlantic Ridge moved in 60 million years? Write your answer using scientific notation.

About how many times as many meters has the East Pacific Rise moved than the Mid-Atlantic Ridge in 60 million years?

Model It

You can multiply using properties of integer exponents to answer the first question.

60 million $= 6 \times 10^7$

$$(3.5 \times 10^{-2}) \times (6 \times 10^7) = (3.5 \times 6) \times (10^{-2} \times 10^7)$$
$$= 21 \times 10^{-2+7}$$
$$= 21 \times 10^5$$
$$= 2.1 \times 10^6$$

Model It

You can divide using properties of integer exponents to answer the second question.

$$(6.6 \times 10^6) \div (2.1 \times 10^6) = \frac{6.6 \times 10^6}{2.1 \times 10^6}$$
$$= \frac{6.6}{2.1} \times \frac{10^6}{10^6}$$
$$\approx 3 \times 10^{6-6}$$

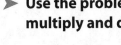

CONNECT IT

➤ **Use the problem from the previous page to help you understand how to multiply and divide numbers written in scientific notation.**

1 Look at the first **Model It**. How many meters has the Mid-Atlantic Ridge moved in 60 million years?

2 Look at the second **Model It**. Complete the solution. About how many times as many meters has the East Pacific Rise moved than the Mid-Atlantic Ridge during this time?

3 What properties of integer exponents are used in the **Model Its**? How are the properties used?

4 What must be true about the powers of 10 when adding or subtracting numbers written in scientific notation? Is this also true when multiplying or dividing numbers written in scientific notation? Explain.

5 **Reflect** Think about all the models and strategies you have discussed today. Describe how one of them helped you better understand how to solve the **Try It** problem.

Apply It

➤ **Use what you learned to solve these problems.**

6 An entomologist estimates there are 1.5 billion ants in the territory he studies. He divides the territory into 23 equal-sized sections. On average, how many ants are in each section? Show your work. Write your answer using scientific notation.

Ant hills can grow to be several feet high.

SOLUTION _____

7 The driving distance from Casablanca, Morocco, to Gaborone, Botswana, is about 1.1×10^4 km. A GPS map of Africa has a scale factor of 2×10^{-8}.

a. Multiply the actual distance by the scale factor to find how long a web designer should make this distance on the map. Write your answer using scientific notation. Show your work.

SOLUTION _____

b. Rewrite your answer to problem 7a using a more appropriate unit for the web designer to use on the map.

8 Find the product of (5×10^{-16}) and (1.7×10^9). Write your answer in scientific notation. Show your work.

SOLUTION _____

Name:

Practice Multiplying and Dividing with Scientific Notation

➤ **Study the Example showing how to multiply numbers written in scientific notation. Then solve problems 1–5.**

Example

Colorado's shape is almost a rectangle. It measures about 2×10^6 ft long by 1.478×10^6 ft wide. What is the estimated area of the state? Write your answer using scientific notation.

$$(2 \times 10^6) \times (1.478 \times 10^6) = (2 \times 1.478) \times (10^6 \times 10^6)$$
$$= 2.956 \times 10^{6+6}$$
$$= 2.956 \times 10^{12}$$

The area of Colorado is approximately 2.956×10^{12} ft^2.

1 Look at the Example. The area of Rhode Island is about 43.07 billion square feet. About how many times as great is the area of Colorado than the area of Rhode Island? Show your work.

SOLUTION _____

2 The water in Earth's oceans has a volume of about 3.2×10^8 cubic miles. There are about 1.1×10^{12} gallons in 1 cubic mile. How many gallon jugs would it take to hold all the ocean water on Earth? Show your work. Write your answer using scientific notation.

Vocabulary

scientific notation
a way of expressing a number as a product in the form $n \times 10^a$, where a is an integer and n is a decimal number such that $1 \le n < 10$.

SOLUTION _____

3 A hydrogen atom has a mass of about 1.67×10^{-24} g. An oxygen atom has a mass of about 2.66×10^{-23} g. About how many times as great is the mass of an oxygen atom than the mass of a hydrogen atom? Show your work.

SOLUTION _____

4 Write *add* or *subtract* to complete each sentence.

When multiplying two numbers written in scientific notation, you can _____ the exponents of the powers of 10.

When dividing two numbers written in scientific notation, you can _____ the exponents of the powers of 10.

5 Look at the blueprint for a new mall.

a. What is the area of Section A, written using scientific notation?

b. Section B has area 2.88×10^6 in.^{2}. What is the unknown length of Section B, written using scientific notation?

c. The builder's assistant solved problem 5b and got 2.4×10^9 in. What mistake do you think the assistant made?

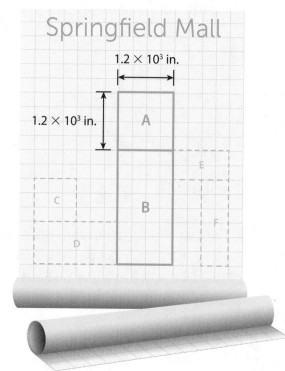

Springfield Mall

1.2×10^3 in.

1.2×10^3 in.   A

E

C

B

F

D

Refine Working with Scientific Notation

➤ **Complete the Example below. Then solve problems 1–11.**

Example

Jia's classmates send an average of 85 text messages per day. At this rate, how many texts would all of the eighth graders in the U.S. send in a year? There are about 3,500,000 eighth graders in the U.S. Jia uses her calculator to multiply $85 \times 365 \times 3{,}500{,}000$ and gets the result 1.086E+11. What does this answer mean?

Look at how you can use scientific notation to analyze the answer.

$$85 \times 365 \times (3.5 \times 10^6) = (3.1025 \times 10^4) \times (3.5 \times 10^6)$$
$$= 1.086 \times 10^{11}$$

E+11 means the exponent on the power of 10 is positive 11.

SOLUTION _____

CONSIDER THIS...
Many calculators use a special notation to display answers that are longer than 10 digits.

PAIR/SHARE
What do you think 1.086E−11 means?

Apply It

1. Complete the table. Then use scientific notation to find the difference in the masses of a giraffe and a giant squid. Show your work.

Insect or Animal	Average Mass (g) Standard Form	Average Mass (g) Scientific Notation
Ant	0.004	
Hummingbird		3.6×10^0
House cat		4.5×10^3
Giant squid	200,000	
Giraffe	1,190,000	

CONSIDER THIS...
How could you use patterns in powers of 10 to help complete the table?

PAIR/SHARE
How many times as great is the mass of a giraffe than the mass of a giant squid?

SOLUTION _____

2 What is the perimeter of the triangle written using scientific notation? Show your work.

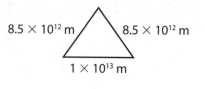

8.5×10^{12} m 8.5×10^{12} m

1×10^{13} m

SOLUTION _____

3 Scientists estimate there are about 7.5×10^{18} grains of sand on Earth. They estimate there could be as many as 4×10^{11} stars in the Milky Way galaxy. How many times as many grains of sand are there on Earth than stars in the galaxy?

A   1.875

B 1.875×10^7

C 7.5×10^{18}

D 1.875×10^{29}

Amelia chose D as the correct answer. How might she have gotten that answer?

4 Scientists estimate there are about 7.5×10^{18} grains of sand on Earth. The mass of one grain of sand is about 1.1×10^{-13} kg. What is the mass of all the sand on Earth? Write your answer using scientific notation.

micrograph of
1 grain of sand

5 A student determines he lives 2.5×10^5 cm from school. What might be a better way to communicate this distance to a friend? Choose an appropriate unit and write the answer using standard form.

6 To add 8.5×10^{12} and 2.7×10^{13}, Muna and Kevin write different first steps. Who is correct? Explain.

Muna's First Step

$(8.5 \times 10^{12}) + (27 \times 10^{12})$

Kevin's First Step

$(0.85 \times 10^{13}) + (2.7 \times 10^{13})$

7 Which statements are true about the spreadsheet? Select all that apply.

A Cell A1 shows the number 6.7×10^{-9}.

B Cell A2 shows the number 3.9×10^{11}.

C Cell A3 shows the difference of cell A1 minus cell A2.

D To find the product of cells A1 and A2, you would add the exponents $-9 + (-11)$.

E To find the sum of cells A1 and A2, you would add the exponents $-9 + (-11)$.

	A	B
1	6.7E-09	
2	3.9E-11	
3	6.661E-09	
4		

8 North Dakota is roughly shaped liked a rectangle. The state is about 5.45×10^5 m long and 3.4×10^5 m wide. South Dakota has an area of about 1.997×10^{11} m^2. What is the estimated combined area of the two states? Write your answer using scientific notation. Show your work.

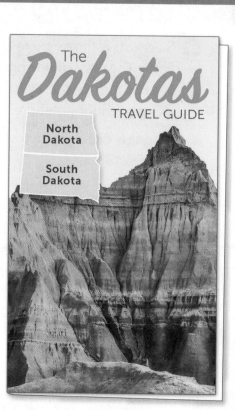

SOLUTION _____

9 Write a number that is greater than 1 and less than 10 in scientific notation.

10 4.6×10^{71} is the product of 2.3×10^{71} and what number?

11 **Math Journal** Use the table to write an addition, subtraction, or division word problem. Then solve your problem. Write your answer using scientific notation.

Lake	Volume (m^3)
Superior	1.21×10^{13}
Erie	4.84×10^{11}

✓ **End of Lesson Checklist**

☐ **INTERACTIVE GLOSSARY** Find the entry for _scientific notation_. Write a definition and give examples of numbers written in scientific notation.

☐ **SELF CHECK** Go back to the Unit 5 Opener and see what you can check off.

Study an Example Problem and Solution

SMP 1 Make sense of problems and persevere in solving them.

➤ **Read this problem involving scientific notation. Then look at one student's solution to this problem on the following pages.**

Planetary Orbits

Jamal attends an event about careers in the space industry. He meets with an astronomer who talks about a planet's orbital period, which is the amount of time it takes the planet to orbit the sun once.

Read the information about the orbits of the planets in our solar system. Choose a planet and use its data to determine about how far it would travel along its orbit in 7 Earth days. Use an appropriately sized unit.

Planetary Orbits in Our Solar System

A planet's orbit around the sun is not an exact circle, so its distance from the sun changes as it orbits.

A planet's distance from the sun affects its orbital speed. The closer a planet is to the sun, the faster it moves.

Although a planet's orbital speed is constantly changing, you can use the average speed to estimate how far it travels over a given period of time.

Jupiter

Uranus

Mercury   Earth

Venus   Mars   Saturn   Neptune

	Mercury	Venus	Earth	Mars	Jupiter	Saturn	Uranus	Neptune
Length of Orbit (meters)	3.6×10^{11}	6.8×10^{11}	9.4×10^{11}	1.4×10^{12}	4.9×10^{12}	9.0×10^{12}	1.8×10^{13}	3.7×10^{13}
Orbital Period (seconds)	7.6×10^{6}	1.9×10^{7}	3.2×10^{7}	5.9×10^{7}	3.7×10^{8}	9.3×10^{8}	2.6×10^{9}	5.2×10^{9}

Try Another Approach

➤ **There are many ways to solve problems. Think about how you might solve the Planetary Orbits problem in a different way.**

Planetary Orbits

Jamal attends an event about careers in the space industry. He meets with an astronomer who talks about a planet's orbital period, which is the amount of time it takes the planet to orbit the sun once.

Read the information about the orbits of the planets in our solar system. Choose a planet and use its data to determine about how far it would travel along its orbit in 7 Earth days. Use an appropriately sized unit.

Planetary Orbits in Our Solar System

A planet's orbit around the sun is not an exact circle, so its distance from the sun changes as it orbits.

A planet's distance from the sun affects its orbital speed. The closer a planet is to the sun, the faster it moves.

Although a planet's orbital speed is constantly changing, you can use the average speed to estimate how far it travels over a given period of time.

	Mercury	Venus	Earth	Mars	Jupiter	Saturn	Uranus	Neptune
Length of Orbit (meters)	3.6×10^{11}	6.8×10^{11}	9.4×10^{11}	1.4×10^{12}	4.9×10^{12}	9.0×10^{12}	1.8×10^{13}	3.7×10^{13}
Orbital Period (seconds)	7.6×10^{6}	1.9×10^{7}	3.2×10^{7}	5.9×10^{7}	3.7×10^{8}	9.3×10^{8}	2.6×10^{9}	5.2×10^{9}

Plan It

➤ **Answer these questions to help you start thinking about a plan.**

a. How could you solve this problem without determining how far the planet travels in 1 second?

b. How will the properties of exponents help you solve this problem?

Solve It

➤ **Find a different solution for the Planetary Orbits problem. Show all your work on a separate sheet of paper. You may want to use the Problem-Solving Tips to get started.**

PROBLEM-SOLVING TIPS

Key Terms

scientific notation	standard form	exponent
product	quotient	base
power		

Models You may want to use . . .

• properties of exponents to multiply and divide numbers written in scientific notation.

• scientific notation to write very large or very small numbers.

Questions

• Do the units of your final answer make sense? Would another unit be more appropriate?

• How far does the planet you chose travel on an average day?

Reflect

Use Mathematical Practices As you work through the problem, discuss these questions with a partner.

• **Use Models** How can using scientific notation and the properties of exponents help you solve this problem?

• **Reason Mathematically** Does it make sense for the planet to travel farther in 1 second or 1 day?

Discuss Models and Strategies

➤ **Read the problem. Write a solution on a separate sheet of paper. Remember, there can be lots of ways to solve a problem.**

Insulating Blankets

An aerospace engineer explains that insulating blankets protect spacecraft from damaging heat and radiation from the sun. He tells Jamal that the blankets are constructed using several layers of special materials. Read the information about the design of these blankets.

Jamal notices that the blankets seem very thin and wonders how thick one might be. Use the specifications below to describe a blanket for a spacecraft. Then find the thickness of the blanket.

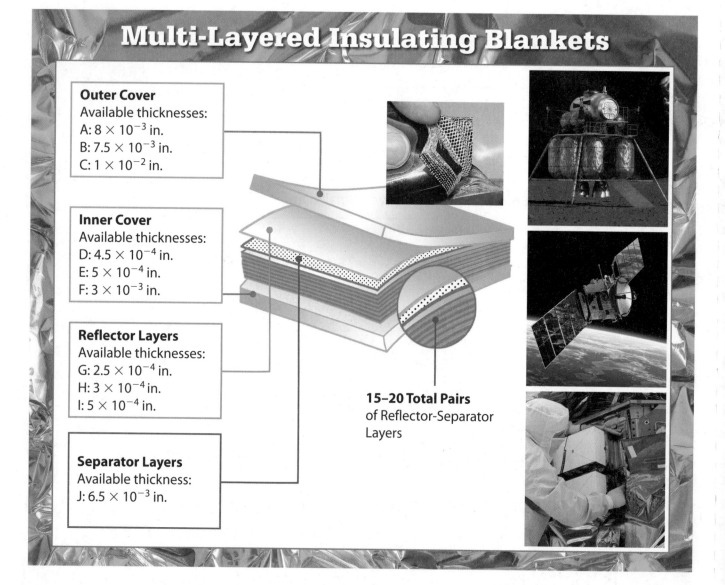

Multi-Layered Insulating Blankets

Outer Cover
Available thicknesses:
A: 8×10^{-3} in.
B: 7.5×10^{-3} in.
C: 1×10^{-2} in.

Inner Cover
Available thicknesses:
D: 4.5×10^{-4} in.
E: 5×10^{-4} in.
F: 3×10^{-3} in.

Reflector Layers
Available thicknesses:
G: 2.5×10^{-4} in.
H: 3×10^{-4} in.
I: 5×10^{-4} in.

Separator Layers
Available thickness:
J: 6.5×10^{-3} in.

15–20 Total Pairs of Reflector-Separator Layers

Plan It and Solve It

➤ **Find a solution to the Insulating Blankets problem.**

Write a detailed plan and support your answer. Be sure to include:

- the thicknesses of the inner and outer covers you will use.
- the thicknesses of the reflector and separator layers you will use.
- the number of pairs of reflector and separator layers in your blanket.
- the total thickness of the blanket.

PROBLEM-SOLVING TIPS

Key Terms

scientific notation	standard form	power
product	quotient	sum
properties of exponents	factor	

Models You may want to use . . .

- properties of exponents to simplify an expression.
- decimal point patterns to rewrite numbers so that all numbers in an expression have the same power of 10.

Questions

- What is the total thickness of 1 reflector layer and 1 separator layer? What is the total thickness of all the reflector and separator layers in the blanket?
- Will you use scientific notation or standard form to do your calculations?

Reflect

Use Mathematical Practices As you work through the problem, discuss these questions with a partner.

- **Make Sense of Problems** What operations will you use to determine the total thickness of the insulating blanket?

- **Make an Argument** Does it make sense to write your final answer in scientific notation or standard form? Why?

Insulating "space blankets" are often given to runners at the end of a long-distance race to help regulate body temperature.

Persevere On Your Own

➤ **Read the problem. Write a solution on a separate sheet of paper.**

Satellites

Jamal meets a satellite technologist. She explains to Jamal that satellites travel faster the closer they are to Earth, just as planets move faster the closer they are to the sun. Jamal wonders how long it takes for a satellite to complete one orbit around Earth.

The satellite technologist shows Jamal this diagram, which gives information about the orbits of three types of satellites. Choose one type of satellite and calculate the time it takes to complete one orbit of Earth.

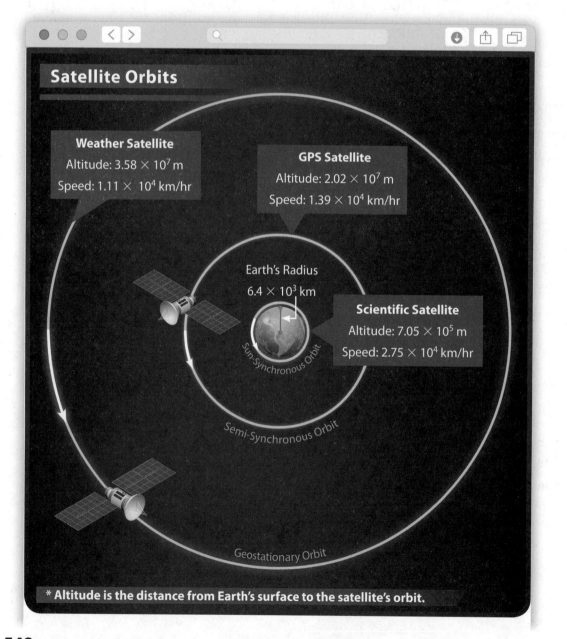

Satellite Orbits

Weather Satellite
Altitude: 3.58×10^7 m
Speed: 1.11×10^4 km/hr

GPS Satellite
Altitude: 2.02×10^7 m
Speed: 1.39×10^4 km/hr

Earth's Radius
6.4×10^3 km

Scientific Satellite
Altitude: 7.05×10^5 m
Speed: 2.75×10^4 km/hr

Sun-Synchronous Orbit

Semi-Synchronous Orbit

Geostationary Orbit

* **Altitude is the distance from Earth's surface to the satellite's orbit.**

Solve It

➤ **Find a solution to the Satellites problem.**

- Calculate the distance one type of satellite will travel to complete one orbit. (The formula for the circumference of a circle with radius r is $C = 2\pi r$.)

- Determine how long it will take the satellite to complete one orbit.

Reflect

Use Mathematical Practices After you complete the problem, choose one of these questions to discuss with a partner.

- **Be Precise** What units did you use when doing your calculations? What units did you use to give your final answer?

- **Persevere** What models or strategies did you use to determine your answer?

A satellite dish is a bowl-shaped antenna that transmits and receives information from a communication satellite.

In this unit you learned to . . .

Skill	Lesson
Simplify expressions with two or more powers using exponent properties.	**19, 20, 21, 22**
Apply exponent properties to rewrite or simplify expressions with zero and negative integer exponents.	**20, 21, 22**
Express, estimate, and compare quantities using integer powers of 10.	**21**
Perform operations with numbers in scientific notation.	**22**
Work with scientific notation to solve problems.	**22**
Listen carefully during discussion in order to understand and explain another person's ideas.	**19–22**

Think about what you have learned.

➤ **Use words, numbers, and drawings.**

1 One topic I could use in my everyday life is _____ because . . .

2 Something I know well is . . .

3 One thing I still need to work on is . . .

Vocabulary Review

➤ **Review the unit vocabulary. Put a check mark by items you can use in speaking and writing. Look up the meaning of any terms you do not know.**

Math Vocabulary		Academic Vocabulary
☐ absolute value	☐ power of 10	☐ express
☐ base (of a power)	☐ standard form	☐ mass
☐ evaluate	☐ scientific notation	☐ molecule
☐ exponent		☐ simplify

➤ **Use the unit vocabulary to complete the problems.**

1 Tell whether you would most likely use standard form or scientific notation to represent each quantity.

   a. The diameter of a basketball in inches

   b. The distance from Earth to Mars in miles

   c. The world population

2 Select a positive number greater than 10,000,000 and a positive number less than 0.000001. Express both numbers in standard form and in scientific notation. Use *scientific notation* and *standard form* to label your numbers.

3 Explain what you do when you simplify an expression. How is it the same or different from what you do when you evaluate an expression?

4 Label this expression with at least three math or academic vocabulary terms.

$$1.685 \times 10^4$$

➤ **Use what you have learned to complete these problems.**

1 Which expressions are equivalent to $7^4 \cdot 9^8$? Choose all the correct answers.

A $7 \cdot 9^5 \cdot (7 \cdot 9)^3$

B $\left(\dfrac{7 \cdot 9^6}{9^4}\right)^4$

C $(7 \cdot 9^4)^4$

D $\dfrac{7^5 \cdot 9^{12}}{9^4 \cdot 7}$

E $\dfrac{(7 \cdot 9)^8}{7^2}$

2 Which expression is equivalent to 3^{-5}?

A $\dfrac{3^5}{3^0}$

B $(3^5)^0$

C $3^5 \cdot 3^{-1}$

D $\dfrac{1}{3^5}$

3 A geology class is studying a sample of rock and a sample of dry sponge. The rock sample has a mass of 1×10^1 kg. The dry sponge sample has a mass of 2×10^{-3} kg. Which sample has a greater mass? How many times greater? Show your work.

SOLUTION _____

_____

4 Find the perimeter of the triangle using scientific notation. Write your answers in the blanks.

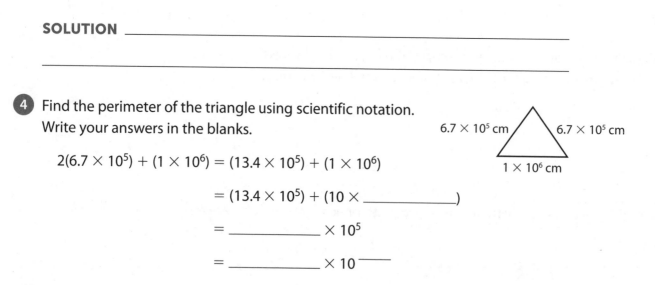

6.7 × 10⁵ cm   6.7 × 10⁵ cm

1 × 10⁶ cm

$2(6.7 \times 10^5) + (1 \times 10^6) = (13.4 \times 10^5) + (1 \times 10^6)$

$= (13.4 \times 10^5) + (10 \times \underline{\hspace{1.5cm}})$

$= \underline{\hspace{1.5cm}} \times 10^5$

$= \underline{\hspace{1.5cm}} \times 10^{\underline{\hspace{0.5cm}}}$

5 Evaluate the expression $\dfrac{2^3 \cdot 7^{-8}}{14^{-5}}$. Show your work.

SOLUTION _____

6 Which of the following values are between 7×10^{-6} and 6×10^{-5}?
Choose all the correct answers.

A 6×10^{-6}

B 8×10^{-5}

C 9×10^{-6}

D 4×10^{-5}

E 8×10^{-6}

F 7×10^{-5}

7 The mass of one grain of sand is about 6.7×10^{-7} kg. An hourglass is estimated to contain 2.1×10^4 grains of sand. What is the mass of the sand in the hourglass? Write your answer using scientific notation. Show your work.

SOLUTION _____

Performance Task

➤ **Answer the questions and show all your work on separate paper.**

A company that harvests and produces sugar has three refineries. The table shows how much sugar each refinery can produce in one hour.

Refinery	Hourly Production (cm^3)
A	1.6×10^5
B	2.1×10^5
C	2.4×10^5

Each refinery can produce sugar for a maximum of 10 h each day. Also, a cubic centimeter of sugar has a mass of 8.5×10^{-4} kg.

The company receives large orders from national grocery stores. It must produce between 3,000,000 cm^3 and 5,000,000 cm^3 of sugar each day to fill the orders.

Create a plan for the refineries to produce the amount of sugar needed to fill the grocery store orders. Describe the following in your plan:

• how much sugar, in cubic centimeters, will be produced in one day;

• how many hours each refinery will produce sugar;

• total mass of sugar produced using your one-day plan.

Use scientific notation for your calculations.

Reflect

Use Mathematical Practices After you complete the task, choose one of the following questions to answer.

• **Use Reasoning** How can you use what you know about scientific notation to make sure your plan uses powers of 10 correctly?

• **Be Precise** How could you test your solution to make sure it answers the task?

Unit 6

Real Numbers

Rational Numbers, Irrational Numbers, and the Pythagorean Theorem

---

 **Self Check** | Before starting this unit, check off the skills you know below. As you complete each lesson, see how many more skills you can check off!

I can . . .	Before	After
Recognize numbers as perfect squares and perfect cubes.	☐	☐
Take the square root or cube root of a number to solve problems.	☐	☐
Know every rational number can be written as a repeating or a terminating decimal.	☐	☐
Write repeating decimals as fractions.	☐	☐
Find rational approximations of irrational numbers and locate them on the number line.	☐	☐
Explain the Pythagorean Theorem and its converse.	☐	☐
Apply the Pythagorean Theorem to find an unknown length in a figure or distance between two points in the coordinate plane.	☐	☐
Know the volume formulas for cones, cylinders, and spheres and use them to solve problems.	☐	☐
Actively participate in discussions by asking questions and rephrasing or building on my classmates' ideas.	☐	☐

Prepare for Rational and Irrational Numbers

➤ **Continue the pattern below by drawing the figures for Steps 4 and 5. Express the total number of unit squares as an addition expression, a sum, and a power.**

	Squares	Addition Expression	Sum	Power
Step 1	■	1	1	1
Step 2		$1 + 3$	4	2^2
Step 3		$1 + 3 + 5$	9	
Step 4				
Step 5				

Meet with a partner and compare your answers. Discuss the answers on which you disagree. You may revise or add to your work. With your partner, answer the following two questions.

1 What relationship do you see between the step number and the power?

2 What relationship do you see between the step number and the sum?

Dear Family,

This week your student is learning how to recognize numbers that are **perfect squares** and **perfect cubes**. A perfect square is the product of an integer and itself. For example, $3 \times 3 = 3^2 = 9$, so 9 is a perfect square. A perfect cube is the product when an integer is used as a factor three times. For example, $2 \times 2 \times 2 = 2^3 = 8$, so 8 is a perfect cube.

A **square root of x** is a number that when multiplied by itself is equal to x. The square roots of 9 are 3 and -3 because $3^2 = 9$ and $(-3)^2 = 9$. Similarly, the **cube root of x** is the number that when cubed is equal to x. The cube root of 8 is 2 because $2^3 = 8$. Your student will evaluate square roots and cube roots to solve problems, such as the one below.

> An artist paints on a square canvas with an area of 49 ft². What is the side length of the canvas?

➤ **ONE WAY** to find the length is to write and solve an equation.

The area, A, of a square with side length, s, is $A = s^2$.

$$A = s^2$$
$$49 = s^2 \quad \longleftarrow \text{Substitute 49 for } A.$$
$$\pm\sqrt{49} = s \quad \longleftarrow \text{Take the square root of both sides of the equation.}$$

The side length cannot be negative, so $s = \sqrt{49}$.

$7 \times 7 = 49$, so $s = 7$.

➤ **ANOTHER WAY** is to check a list of perfect squares.

s	1	2	3	4	5	6	7
s²	1	4	9	16	25	36	49

The square root is 7.

Look for 49 in the perfect squares.

Using either method, the side length of the canvas is 7 ft.

 Use the next page to start a conversation about square roots and cube roots.

Activity Thinking About Square Roots and Cube Roots

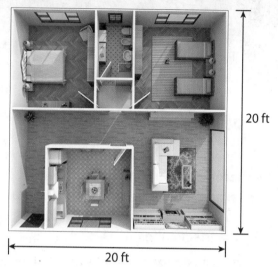

20 ft

20 ft

➤ **Do this activity together to investigate square roots and cube roots in the real world.**

Square roots and cube roots are often used to solve problems involving area and volume. For example, an apartment with a square floor plan has an area of 400 ft². To figure out the length and width of the apartment, you can find the square root of 400, or $\sqrt{400}$. The apartment measures 20 ft by 20 ft because $20^2 = 400$.

? What other problems might you solve by finding a square root or cube root?

Explore Square Roots

Previously, you learned about powers of numbers. In this lesson, you will learn about square roots and cube roots of numbers.

➤ **Use what you know to try to solve the problem below.**

Miguel has a box of small square tiles. Each tile has an area of 1 in.^{2}. He wants to put some of the tiles together to make larger squares. Which areas listed below are possible areas of the larger squares Miguel can make? What side length will each of those larger squares have?

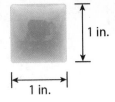

1 in.

1 in.

Area 4 in.^{2} Area 8 in.^{2} Area 9 in.^{2} Area 12 in.^{2}

TRY IT

Math Toolkit grid paper, paper squares, unit tiles

DISCUSS IT

Ask: What strategy did you use to decide which areas are possible?

Share: My strategy was . . .

◎ **Learning Target**   SMP 1, SMP 2, SMP 3, SMP 4, SMP 5, SMP 6, SMP 7
Use square root and cube root symbols to represent solutions to equations of the form $x^2 = p$ and $x^3 = p$, where p is a positive rational number. Evaluate square roots of small perfect squares and cube roots of small perfect cubes. Know that $\sqrt{2}$ is irrational.

CONNECT IT

1 **Look Back** Which areas in the list are possible areas of the larger squares Miguel can make? What side lengths do these larger squares have? How do you know?

2 **Look Ahead** A **perfect square** is the product of an integer and itself.

a. Complete the table at the right. Which numbers in the table are perfect squares? Why?

x	x^2
1	
2	
3	
4	
5	
6	
7	
8	
9	
10	
11	
12	

b. The inverse operation of squaring is finding a square root. A **square root of x** is a number that when multiplied by itself is equal to x. So, a square root of 9 is 3 because $3 \cdot 3 = 9$. Another square root of 9 is -3. Why?

c. A square root can be positive or negative. The symbol $\sqrt{}$ means the *positive* square root. So, $\sqrt{9} = 3$, but not -3. Complete the following.

$\sqrt{81} =$ _____ $\sqrt{144} =$ _____

To solve an equation like $x^2 = 17$, note that the variable is squared. To find the value of the variable, perform the inverse of squaring. Take the square root of both sides of the equation.

$x^2 = 17$

$x = \pm\sqrt{17}$

When you take a square root, both the positive and the negative square root are possible answers. Since 17 is not a perfect square, you cannot write $\sqrt{17}$ or $-\sqrt{17}$ as integers. Write the solution as $\pm\sqrt{17}$.

3 **Reflect** Explain how to find all the square roots of 16.

Prepare for Finding Square Roots and Cube Roots to Solve Problems

1 Think about what you know about operations with rational numbers. Fill in each box. Use words, numbers, and pictures. Show as many ideas as you can.

In My Own Words	My Illustrations

product

Examples	Non-Examples

2 Which of the expressions at the right are examples of a product? Explain.

$2(10 + y)$

x^4

$-7a$

$(3 + 4)(3 - 4)$

3 Garrett is cutting square patches from old sports jerseys. Each patch has an area of 1 ft². He wants to put some of the patches together to make square quilts.

a. Which areas listed below are possible areas of the square quilts Garrett can make? What side length will each of those square quilts have? Show your work.

Area 5 ft²   Area 16 ft²   Area 18 ft²   Area 25 ft²

SOLUTION _____

_____

b. Check your answer to problem 3a. Show your work.

Develop Finding a Square Root to Solve Problems

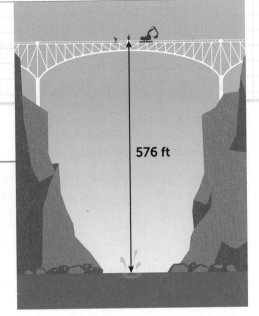

576 ft

➤ **Read and try to solve the problem below.**

A worker on the Rio Grande Gorge Bridge in New Mexico drops a bolt that lands in the water 576 feet below. The equation $\frac{d}{16} = t^2$ represents the distance in feet, d, that an object falls in t seconds. How long does it take the bolt to hit the water?

TRY IT

Math Toolkit grid paper, paper squares, unit tiles

DISCUSS IT

Ask: How can you check your answer?

Share: I can check my answer by . . .

➤ **Explore different ways to find a square root to solve a problem.**

A worker on the Rio Grande Gorge Bridge in New Mexico drops a bolt that lands in the water 576 feet below. The equation $\frac{d}{16} = t^2$ represents the distance in feet, d, that an object falls in t seconds. How long does it take the bolt to hit the water?

Model It

You can solve the given equation for t.

The distance the bolt falls is 576 feet.

Substitute 576 for d in the equation.

$$\frac{d}{16} = t^2$$

$$\frac{576}{16} = t^2$$

$$36 = t^2$$

Take the square root of both sides of the equation.

$$\pm\sqrt{36} = t$$

Model It

You can check a list of perfect squares to try to find the value of t.

The value of t cannot be negative, so $t = \sqrt{36}$.

Look for 36 in a table of perfect squares.

t	1	2	3	4	5	6	7	8	9
t^2	1	4	9	16	25	36	49	64	81

➤ **Use the problem from the previous page to help you understand how to find a square root to solve a problem.**

1 Look at the steps taken to solve the equation in the first **Model It**. Why do you write $\pm\sqrt{36}$ after you take the square root of both sides of the equation?

2 Look at the second **Model It**. How do you know that the value of t cannot be negative?

3 How long does it take the bolt to hit the water?

4 Suppose the first **Model It** ended with $t = \pm\sqrt{47}$. What would the solution to the problem be in this case? Why?

5 When you solve a real-world problem, you may get an equation of the form $x^2 = a$. How do you use this equation to solve the problem?

6 **Reflect** Think about all the models and strategies you have discussed today. Describe how one of them helped you better understand how to solve the **Try It** problem.

Apply It

➤ **Use what you learned to solve these problems.**

7 Brianna is solving the equation $t^2 = \frac{36}{121}$. Her work is shown at the right. Is Brianna correct? Explain.

Brianna's work:

$$t^2 = \frac{36}{121}$$

$$t = \pm\sqrt{\frac{36}{121}}$$

$$t = \pm\frac{6}{11}$$

8 Yesterday, there were b mg of bacteria in a lab experiment. Today, there are b^2 mg of bacteria. There are 400 mg of bacteria today. How many milligrams of bacteria were there yesterday?

A 20 mg

B 200 mg

C 1,600 mg

D 160,000 mg

9 The equation $P^2 = 16A$ represents the perimeter, P, of a square with area, A. A square stained-glass window has an area of 4 ft². What is the perimeter of the window? Show your work.

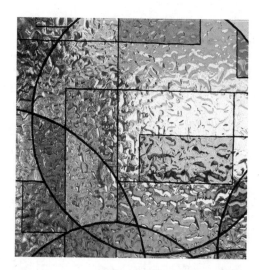

$A = 4$ ft²

SOLUTION _____

Name:

Practice Finding a Square Root to Solve Problems

➤ **Study the Example showing how to find a square root to solve a problem. Then solve problems 1–5.**

Example

The equation $e^2 = \dfrac{S}{6}$ represents the edge length, e, of a cube with surface area, S. What is the edge length of a cube with surface area 90 cm²?

Substitute 90 for S in the equation.

$$e^2 = \frac{90}{6}$$

$$e^2 = 15$$

Take the square root of both sides of the equation.

$$e = \pm\sqrt{15}$$

The edge length cannot be negative, so $e = \sqrt{15}$. 15 is not a perfect square. The edge length is $\sqrt{15}$ cm.

---

1 Suppose the cube in the Example has surface area 486 cm². What is the edge length in this case? Show your work.

SOLUTION _____

2 What is the solution of the equation $w^2 = \dfrac{4}{9}$? Show your work.

Vocabulary

square root of x
the number that when multiplied by itself is equal to x.

perfect square
the product of an integer and itself.

SOLUTION _____

3 The equation $s^2 = 2A$ represents the area, A, of an isosceles right triangle with two short sides of length, s. A model sailboat has a sail that is an isosceles right triangle. The sail's area is 9 in.^{2}. What is the length of a short side of the sail? Show your work.

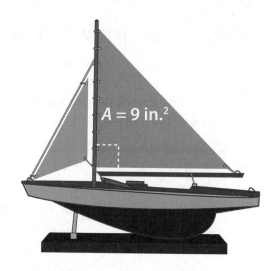

$A = 9$ in.^{2}

SOLUTION _____

4 What is the solution of the equation $x^2 - 7 = 42$? Show your work.

SOLUTION _____

5 A square playground has an area of 10,000 ft^2. What is the side length of the playground? Show your work.

SOLUTION _____

Develop Finding a Cube Root to Solve Problems

➤ **Read and try to solve the problem below.**

Carolina works at a museum. She is looking online for a storage case for some large fossils. She wants the case to have a volume of 27 ft³. Carolina would like the case to be a cube. What edge length should the case have?

TRY IT

Math Toolkit unit cubes

DISCUSS IT

Ask: How did you get started solving the problem?

Share: The first thing I did was . . .

➤ **Explore different ways to find a cube root to solve a problem.**

Carolina works at a museum. She is looking online for a storage case for some large fossils. She wants the case to have a volume of 27 ft³. Carolina would like the case to be a cube. What edge length should the case have?

Model It

You can write and solve an equation.

The volume, V, of a cube with edge length, s, is given by $V = s^3$.

Substitute 27 for V in the equation.

$$27 = s^3$$

Take the cube root of both sides of the equation. The **cube root of x** is the number that when cubed, or raised to the third power, is equal to x. The symbol for cube root is $\sqrt[3]{}$.

$$\sqrt[3]{27} = s$$

Model It

You can check a list of perfect cubes to try to find the value of s.

A **perfect cube** is the product when an integer is used as a factor three times.

Look for 27 in a table of perfect cubes.

s	1	2	3	4	5	6	7	8	9
s^3	1	8	27	64	125	216	343	512	729

➤ **Use the problem from the previous page to help you understand how to find a cube root to solve a problem.**

1 Look at the steps taken to solve the equation in the first **Model It**. Why do you take the cube root of both sides of the equation?

2 Look at the table in the second **Model It**. What edge length should the case have?

3 In the first **Model It**, the $\pm$ symbol was not used when taking the cube root of both sides of the equation. How do you know that s must be positive even before you realize that a negative edge length does not make sense?

4 Suppose Carolina wants a box with a volume of 50 ft³. How would you write the edge length of the box? Why?

5 How do you solve an equation of the form $x^3 = a$?

6 **Reflect** Think about all the models and strategies you have discussed today. Describe how one of them helped you better understand how to find a cube root to solve a problem.

Apply It

➤ **Use what you learned to solve these problems.**

7) What is the solution of the equation $m^3 = \dfrac{8}{27}$? Show your work.

SOLUTION _____

8) For which value of x is $5 < \sqrt[3]{x} < 10$?

A 2

B 8

C 27

D 216

9) The equation $P^3 = 64V$ represents the perimeter, P, of one face of a cube with volume, V. A sculpture in the shape of a cube has a volume of 3 m³. What is the perimeter of one face of the cube? Show your work.

$V = 3$ m³

SOLUTION _____

Name: _____

Practice Finding a Cube Root to Solve Problems

➤ **Study the Example showing how to find a cube root to solve a problem. Then solve problems 1–5.**

Example

What is the solution of the equation $x^3 = 343$?

Take the cube root of both sides of the equation.

$$x^3 = 343$$
$$x = \sqrt[3]{343}$$

Look for 343 in a table of perfect cubes.

x	1	2	3	4	5	6	7	8	9
x^3	1	8	27	64	125	216	343	512	729

The cube root of 343 is 7.

The solution of the equation is $x = 7$.

---

1 Suppose the equation in the Example was $x^3 = 344$. How would the solution be different? Explain.

2 Tyler knows that $\frac{6}{5} \cdot \frac{6}{5} \cdot \frac{6}{5} = \frac{216}{125}$. Explain how he can use this to find the solution of the equation $c^3 = \frac{216}{125}$.

Vocabulary

cube root of x
the number that when cubed is equal to x.

perfect cube
the product when an integer is used as a factor three times.

3 In 2018, there were z zebra mussels in a section of a river. In 2019, there were z^3 zebra mussels in that same section. There were 729 zebra mussels in 2019. How many zebra mussels were there in 2018? Show your work.

zebra mussel

SOLUTION _____

4 What is the solution of the equation $y^3 + 15 = 140$? Show your work.

SOLUTION _____

5 Complete the following.

$\sqrt{0} = $ _____ $\sqrt{1} = $ _____

$\sqrt[3]{0} = $ _____ $\sqrt[3]{1} = $ _____

Refine Finding Square Roots and Cube Roots to Solve Problems

➤ **Complete the Example below. Then solve problems 1–9.**

Example

The expression $4\sqrt{2}$ means $4 \cdot \sqrt{2}$. Use this information to write $(4\sqrt{2})^2$ without using a square root symbol.

Look at how you could use what you know about squares and square roots to rewrite the expression.

An expression squared means that the expression is multiplied by itself.

$$(4\sqrt{2})^2 = (4 \cdot \sqrt{2})(4 \cdot \sqrt{2})$$
$$= 4 \cdot 4 \cdot \sqrt{2} \cdot \sqrt{2}$$
$$= 16 \cdot 2$$

SOLUTION _____

CONSIDER THIS . . .
The commutative and associative properties say that you can change the order and the grouping of the factors in a product.

PAIR/SHARE
How do you know that your answer makes sense?

Apply It

1 A square window has an area of $\frac{16}{25}$ m². What is the perimeter of the window? Show your work.

CONSIDER THIS . . .
The perimeter of a square is 4 times the length of a side.

PAIR/SHARE
What is a different way that you could solve the problem?

SOLUTION _____

7 The area of a square rug is the same as the area of a rectangular rug that is 9 ft long and 4 ft wide. Write and solve an equation to find the side length of the square rug. Show your work.

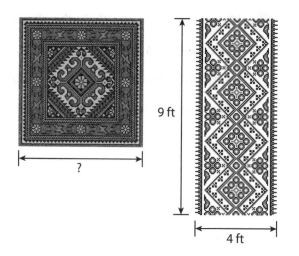

9 ft

?

4 ft

SOLUTION _____

8 Lucía says that 25 is a perfect square, but not a perfect cube. She says this means the equation $x^2 = 25$ has two solutions, but the equation $x^3 = 25$ has no solutions. Do you agree? Explain.

9 **Math Journal** Choose a two-digit number, p. Write the equations $x^2 = p$ and $x^3 = p$. Explain how to solve the two equations you wrote.

✔ **End of Lesson Checklist**

☐ **INTERACTIVE GLOSSARY** Find the entry for *square root of x*. Write a definition for a younger student. Show an example.

☐ **SELF CHECK** Go back to the Unit 6 Opener and see what you can check off.

Dear Family,

This week your student is learning how to express rational numbers as fractions and decimals. Previously, students learned how to write fractions as decimals and how to write terminating decimals as fractions. Now they will work more with repeating decimals.

Repeating decimals repeat the same digit or digits without end. An overbar is often used to identify which digits repeat. For example, $0.\overline{57} = 0.575757\ldots$. Students will learn how to write repeating decimals as fractions to solve problems like the one below.

> Galeno knows that $0.\overline{1} = \frac{1}{9}$. How can he write $0.\overline{2}$ as a fraction?

➤ **ONE WAY** to write the fraction is to use what you know about $0.\overline{1}$.

$$0.\overline{1} = \frac{1}{9}$$
$$0.\overline{1} + 0.\overline{1} = 0.\overline{2}, \text{ so } \frac{1}{9} + \frac{1}{9} = \frac{2}{9}.$$

➤ **ANOTHER WAY** is to write and solve an equation.

$$x = 0.\overline{2}$$
$$10x = 2.\overline{2}$$
$$10x - x = 2.\overline{2} - 0.\overline{2} \quad \boxed{x = 0.\overline{2}; \text{ Subtract } x \text{ from one side and } 0.\overline{2} \text{ from the other.}}$$
$$9x = 2$$
$$x = \frac{2}{9}$$

Using either method, $0.\overline{2} = \frac{2}{9}$.

 Use the next page to start a conversation about rational numbers.

LESSON 24 Express Rational Numbers as Fractions and Decimals

Express Rational Numbers as Fractions and Decimals

Activity Thinking About Rational Numbers

➤ **Do this activity together to investigate different ways to express rational numbers.**

Students will learn to express rational numbers as fractions and decimals in order to solve problems. Below are three decimals and three fractions. Decide which fraction equals each decimal. Draw lines to show your answers.

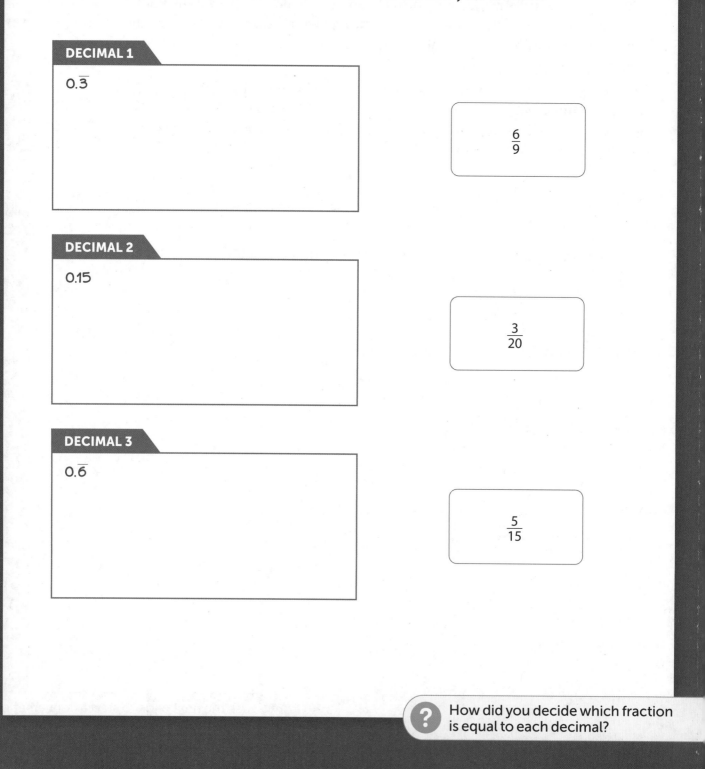

DECIMAL 1

$0.\overline{3}$

$\dfrac{6}{9}$

DECIMAL 2

0.15

$\dfrac{3}{20}$

DECIMAL 3

$0.\overline{6}$

$\dfrac{5}{15}$

? How did you decide which fraction is equal to each decimal?

Explore Writing Fractions as Decimals

Previously, you learned about rational numbers. In this lesson, you will learn about expressing rational numbers as fractions and decimals.

➤ **Use what you know to try to solve the problem below.**

Chantel is designing a poster for a hip-hop concert. She uses art software to create a poster from her sketch. The software program requires her to use decimal measurements. Are both fractions in the poster repeating decimals? How do you know?

Math Toolkit grid paper

DISCUSS IT

Ask: How does your model or strategy show whether a decimal is a repeating decimal?

Share: I can tell a decimal is a repeating decimal by . . .

◎ **Learning Target** SMP 1, SMP 2, SMP 3, SMP 4, SMP 5, SMP 6, SMP 7, SMP 8

Know that numbers that are not rational are called irrational. Understand informally that every number has a decimal expansion; for rational numbers show that the decimal expansion repeats eventually, and convert a decimal expansion which repeats eventually into a rational number.

CONNECT IT

1 Look Back How did you decide if the decimals are repeating?

2 Look Ahead You have already worked with rational numbers. A *rational number* is a number that can be expressed as the fraction $\frac{a}{b}$ where a and b are integers and $b \neq 0$.

a. Recall that repeating decimals repeat the same digit or digits without end. When you use long division to write a fraction as a decimal, how are the remainders related to the repeating digits in the quotient?

b. The fraction $\frac{1}{2}$ can be written as the terminating decimal 0.5. What digit will repeat in the quotient when you use division to write $\frac{1}{2}$ as a decimal? Explain why terminating decimals are also considered repeating decimals.

c. An overbar is often used to identify which digits repeat in a repeating decimal. For example, $0.\overline{3}$ means 0.333 . . . and $0.\overline{45}$ means 0.454545 . . ..

Write the repeating decimals using an overbar.

0.777 . . . = _____   0.358358358 . . . = _____

How could you write the terminating decimal using an overbar?

0.58 = _____

3 Reflect Explain why you can think of every rational number as a number whose decimal expansion repeats eventually.

Prepare for Expressing Rational Numbers as Fractions and Decimals

1 Think about what you know about different types of numbers. Fill in each box. Use words, numbers, and pictures. Show as many ideas as you can.

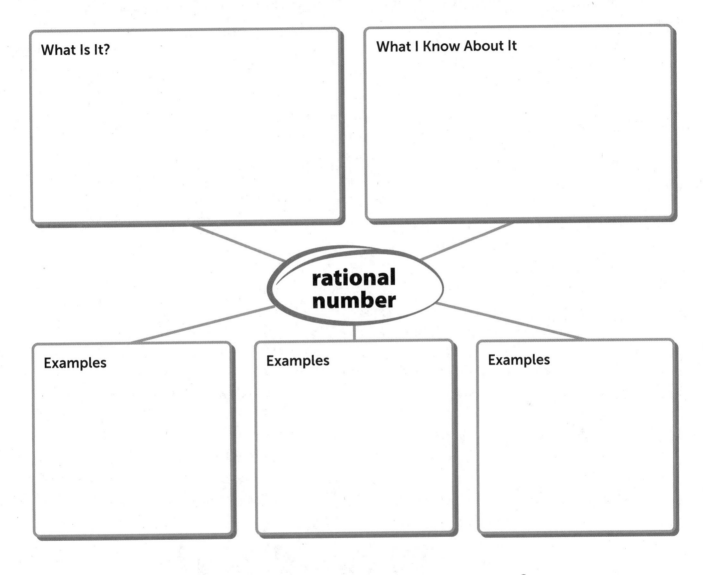

What Is It?

What I Know About It

rational number

Examples

Examples

Examples

2 Ana says $5\frac{1}{3}$ is not a rational number because it is not a fraction of the form $\frac{a}{b}$, where a and b are integers and $b \neq 0$. Do you agree? Explain.

3 Deyvi is comparing the weights of two groups of rabbits on different diets. In Group A, $\frac{7}{11}$ of the rabbits gained weight. In Group B, $\frac{7}{8}$ of the rabbits gained weight. He needs to record this information in a spreadsheet, which requires him to use decimals.

Rabbits	Weight Gain
Group A	$\frac{7}{11}$
Group B	$\frac{7}{8}$

a. Are both fractions in the table repeating decimals? Show your work.

SOLUTION _____

b. Check your answer to problem 3a. Show your work.

Develop Writing a Repeating Decimal as a Fraction

➤ **Read and try to solve the problem below.**

A grocery store has large wheels of cheese. The owner keeps track of the portion of each wheel that has been sold.

Write $\frac{1}{9}$ as a decimal. Then use your answer to write $0.\overline{4}$ as a fraction.

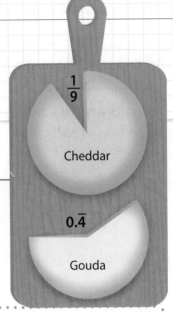

$\frac{1}{9}$

Cheddar

$0.\overline{4}$

Gouda

TRY IT

Math Toolkit grid paper

➤ **Explore different ways to write a repeating decimal as a fraction.**

A grocery store has large wheels of cheese. The owner keeps track of the portion of each wheel that has been sold.

Write $\frac{1}{9}$ as a decimal. Then use your answer to write $0.\overline{4}$ as a fraction.

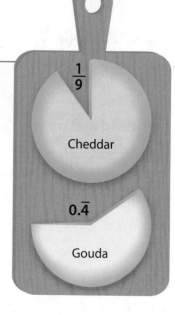

Model It

You can use long division to write a fraction as a decimal.

$$
\begin{array}{r}
0.111\ldots \\
9\overline{)1.000} \\
\underline{-9} \\
10 \\
\underline{-9} \\
10 \\
\underline{-9} \\
1
\end{array}
$$

You can use this result to write $0.\overline{4}$ as a fraction.

Model It

You can also use an equation to write a repeating decimal as a fraction.

$x = 0.\overline{4}$

Multiply both sides of the equation by a power of 10 to get a new equation. The number on the right side of the new equation should have the same repeating part as the number in the original equation. For $0.\overline{4}$, the repeating part of the decimal ends at the tenths place. So multiply both sides of the equation by 10. The number $4.\overline{4}$ has the same repeating part as $0.\overline{4}$.

$10 \cdot x = 10 \cdot 0.\overline{4}$

$10x = 4.\overline{4}$

Now subtract x from the left side and $0.\overline{4}$ from the right side of the equation.

$10x - x = 4.\overline{4} - 0.\overline{4}$

$9x = 4$

➤ **Use the problem from the previous page to help you understand how to write a repeating decimal as a fraction.**

1 Look at the first **Model It**. What is the decimal form of $\frac{1}{9}$? How can you use this answer to help you write $0.\overline{4}$ as a fraction?

2 Look at the second **Model It**. Why can you subtract x from the left side and $0.\overline{4}$ from the right side of the equation $10x = 4.\overline{4}$? What does this step eliminate from the equation?

3 What is $0.\overline{4}$ written as a fraction?

4 **a.** To use an equation to write $0.\overline{36}$ as a fraction, multiply both sides of the equation by 100. Show how to write $0.\overline{36}$ as a fraction.

  b. What power of 10 would you use to find a fraction for $0.\overline{123}$? Why?

5 How can you use an equation to write a repeating decimal as a fraction?

6 **Reflect** Think about all the models and strategies you have discussed today. Describe how one of them helped you better understand how to solve the **Try It** problem.

Apply It

➤ **Use what you learned to solve these problems.**

7 Show that $0.\overline{47}$ is a rational number.

8 Which fraction is equivalent to $1.\overline{1}$?

A $\frac{1}{9}$

B $\frac{10}{11}$

C $\frac{100}{99}$

D $\frac{10}{9}$

9 Tiffany weighs a bunch of avocados. She divides their total weight by the number of avocados to find the average weight of one avocado. The result is $0.\overline{23}$ lb. Write $0.\overline{23}$ as a fraction. Show your work.

SOLUTION _____

Practice Writing a Repeating Decimal as a Fraction

➤ **Study the Example showing how to write a repeating decimal as a fraction. Then solve problems 1–5.**

Example

Write $0.\overline{348}$ as a fraction.

$$x = 0.\overline{348}$$

The repeating part of the decimal ends at the thousandths place, so multiply both sides of the equation by 1,000.

$$1,000x = 348.\overline{348}$$

$$1,000x - x = 348.\overline{348} - 0.\overline{348}$$

$$999x = 348$$

$$x = \frac{348}{999} \text{ or } \frac{116}{333}$$

---

1. Write $0.\overline{721}$ as a fraction. Show your work.

SOLUTION _____

2. Jacob wrote $0.\overline{8}$ as a fraction by first writing $x = 0.\overline{8}$. Then he multiplied both sides of the equation by 100. Will this method work? If it will work, complete the calculation. If it will not work, explain why not.

Vocabulary

repeating decimals
decimals that repeat the same digit or sequence of digits forever.

---

3 The mass of a crystal is $0.\overline{49}$ kg.

a. Write $0.\overline{49}$ as a fraction. Show your work.

mass $= 0.\overline{49}$ kg

SOLUTION _____

b. Use your answer from problem 3a to write $9.\overline{49}$ as a fraction.

4 Use the fact that $0.\overline{1} = \frac{1}{9}$ and $0.\overline{4} = \frac{4}{9}$ to write $0.\overline{5}$ as a fraction. Show your work.

SOLUTION _____

5 Inés finds the population density of a county. She divides the population by the area in square miles. The result is $0.\overline{3648}$ people per square mile. Write $0.\overline{3648}$ as a fraction. Show your work.

SOLUTION _____

Refine Expressing Rational Numbers as Fractions and Decimals

➤ **Complete the Example below. Then solve problems 1–9.**

Example

Write $0.2\overline{5}$ as a fraction.

Look at how you could multiply by two different powers of 10 to get numbers that will help you eliminate the repeating part of the decimal.

$$x = 0.2\overline{5}$$
$$10x = 2.\overline{5}$$
$$100x = 25.\overline{5}$$
$$100x - 10x = 25.\overline{5} - 2.\overline{5}$$
$$90x = 23$$

SOLUTION _____

CONSIDER THIS ...
You can multiply by two different powers of 10 to get two different numbers with repeating 5s to the right of the decimal point.

PAIR/SHARE
How can you check that the fraction you wrote is correct?

Apply It

1 Write $0.\overline{9}$ as a fraction. Show your work. (*Hint*: The result may surprise you.)

CONSIDER THIS ...
$0.\overline{9}$ is greater than 0.9, greater than 0.99, greater than 0.999, and so on.

PAIR/SHARE
What do you think is another way to write $5.\overline{9}$?

SOLUTION _____

2 Write $0.33\overline{4}$ as a fraction. Show your work.

CONSIDER THIS...
Multiplying by what powers of 10 will give answers where only the repeating part of the number is to the right of the decimal point?

SOLUTION _____

PAIR/SHARE
How can you use your work to predict the fraction form of $0.33\overline{5}$?

3 Which of the following shows that the decimal expansion of $\frac{16}{33}$ eventually repeats?

A 0.48

B $0.\overline{48}$

C $0.4\overline{8}$

D $0.48\overline{0}$

Rolando chose C as the correct answer. How might he have gotten that answer?

CONSIDER THIS...
How might long division help you find the decimal expansion for $\frac{16}{33}$?

PAIR/SHARE
What is an example of another fraction that has the same decimal expansion as $\frac{16}{33}$?

4 Stalagmites are rock and mineral formations that build up on a cave floor. A geologist finds that the average rate of growth of a stalagmite in a cave is $0.00\overline{35}$ inch per year. Write $0.00\overline{35}$ as a fraction. Show your work.

stalagmite average growth:
$0.00\overline{35}$ in. per year

SOLUTION _____

5 Write $0.\overline{1}$, $0.\overline{01}$, and $0.\overline{001}$ as fractions. Then explain how you can use the results to predict how to write $0.\overline{0001}$ as a fraction.

6 Tell whether each statement is *True* or *False*.

	True	False
a. The numbers 0.4 and $0.\overline{4}$ are equal to the same fraction.	○	○
b. The number $0.101100111000\ldots$ is a repeating decimal.	○	○
c. The fraction $\frac{1}{7}$ is equal to a repeating decimal.	○	○
d. The fraction $\frac{5}{8}$ is equal to $0.\overline{625}$.	○	○

7 Quinn picks lemons from a tree. He finds the average weight of a lemon is 0.275 lb. He reads this as *275 thousandths* and writes the fraction as $\frac{275}{1,000}$. Hasina uses the strategies from this lesson to write a fraction as shown below. Who is correct? Explain.

$$x = 0.275$$

$$1,000x = 275.0$$

$$10,000x = 2,750.0$$

$$10,000x - 1,000x = 2,750.0 - 275.0$$

$$9,000x = 2,475$$

$$x = \frac{2,475}{9,000}$$

8 Do the strategies you learned for writing a repeating decimal as a fraction work for the decimal 0.12112111211112…? Why or why not?

9 **Math Journal** Write a repeating decimal that includes the digits 7 and 8. Then show how to write the decimal as a fraction.

☑ **End of Lesson Checklist**

☐ **INTERACTIVE GLOSSARY** Write a new entry for *eventually*. Write at least one synonym for *eventually*.

☐ **SELF CHECK** Go back to the Unit 6 Opener and see what you can check off.

Dear Family,

This week your student is learning about **irrational numbers**. Irrational numbers are numbers that cannot be expressed as a quotient of two integers, a terminating decimal, or a repeating decimal. Some examples are the square root of a nonperfect square, such as $\sqrt{3}$, or nonterminating and nonrepeating decimals, such as $\pi = 3.14159\ldots$.

Together, rational and irrational numbers are called the set of **real numbers**, which are all the numbers on the number line. Students will find rational approximations of irrational numbers to solve problems like the one below.

> Find an approximate value for $\sqrt{8}$.

➤ **ONE WAY** to find an approximate value for $\sqrt{8}$ is to find which perfect squares $(\sqrt{8})^2$ lies between.

x	1	2	3	4
x^2	1	4	9	16

$(\sqrt{8})^2 = 8$, and 8 is between the perfect squares 4 and 9.

$4 < 8 < 9$, so $\sqrt{4} < \sqrt{8} < \sqrt{9}$. Since 8 is closer to 9, $\sqrt{8}$ is closer to $\sqrt{9}$.

$\sqrt{8}$ is close to 3.

➤ **ANOTHER WAY** is to find a better approximation to more decimal places.

Since $\sqrt{8}$ is close to 3, start by squaring decimal values close to 3.

x	2.7	2.8	2.9	3
x^2	7.29	7.84	8.41	9

$7.84 < 8 < 8.41$, so $2.8 < \sqrt{8} < 2.9$. $\sqrt{8}$ is closer to 2.8 than 2.9.

$\sqrt{8}$ is close to 2.8.

Using either method, $\sqrt{8}$ is between 2 and 3, but closer to 3.

 Use the next page to start a conversation about irrational numbers.

Activity Thinking About Irrational Numbers

➤ **Do this activity together to investigate irrational numbers.**

Whole numbers, integers, rational numbers, and irrational numbers are all part of the set of real numbers. Below is a set of irrational numbers and a set of rational numbers.

? What patterns do you notice in the set of irrational numbers?
What patterns do you notice in the set of rational numbers?

Irrational numbers

3.14159 . . .

$\sqrt{2}$

2.71828 . . .

1.61803 . . .

$\sqrt{7}$

Rational numbers

6

1.25

$0.\overline{3}$

0.1

$\frac{2}{5}$

Explore Numbers That Are Not Rational

Previously, you learned about rational numbers. In this lesson, you will learn about numbers that are not rational.

➤ **Use what you know to try to solve the problem below.**

Which of the following numbers do you think are rational? Which do you think are not rational? Justify your answers.

0.23764   0.$\overline{5467}$ $\pi = 3.14159\ldots$

$\sqrt{64}$ $\dfrac{2}{3}$ 1.010010001 . . .

"The Passage," part of *Metronome*, a public art installation in Union Square, New York City

TRY IT   **Math Toolkit** grid paper

DISCUSS IT

Ask: What strategy did you use to decide if a number is rational?

Share: The strategy I used was . . .

🎯 **Learning Targets**   SMP 1, SMP 2, SMP 3, SMP 4, SMP 5, SMP 6, SMP 7, SMP 8
- Know that numbers that are not rational are called irrational.
- Use rational approximations of irrational numbers to compare the size of irrational numbers, locate them approximately on a number line diagram, and estimate the value of expressions.
- Know that $\sqrt{2}$ is irrational.

CONNECT IT

1 **Look Back** Which of the numbers do you think are rational? Which do you think are not rational? Justify your answers.

2 **Look Ahead** An **irrational number** is a number that cannot be expressed as a quotient of two integers, a terminating decimal, or a repeating decimal.

a. The square root of any whole number that is not a perfect square is irrational. Write *rational* or *irrational* for each of the following.

$\sqrt{2}$ _____ $\sqrt{8}$ _____

$\sqrt{4}$ _____ $\sqrt{9}$ _____

$\sqrt{5}$ _____ $\sqrt{12}$ _____

b. An irrational number can be expressed with a nonterminating, nonrepeating decimal. For example, 1.010010001 . . . is an irrational number.

Note that an overbar (for example, $0.\overline{1}$) indicates a repeating decimal. An ellipsis (. . .) indicates a nonterminating, nonrepeating decimal.

Together, the rational numbers and irrational numbers are called the **real numbers**. The real numbers are all the numbers on a number line. Write an example of each number in each region of the Venn diagram.

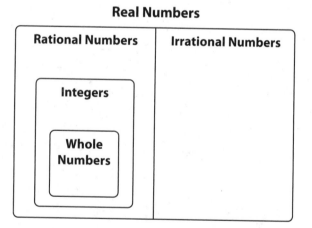

Real Numbers

Rational Numbers	Irrational Numbers
Integers	
Whole Numbers	

3 **Reflect** What is one way you can determine whether a number is rational or irrational?

Prepare for Finding Rational Approximations of Irrational Numbers

1 Think about what you know about rational numbers. Fill in each box. Use words, numbers, and pictures. Show as many ideas as you can.

Word	In My Own Words	Example
rational number		
repeating decimals		
terminating decimals		

2 Look at the long division shown at the right.

a. What rational number of the form $\frac{a}{b}$ is shown by the long division?

b. Explain how you can use the long division to see that the rational number is equivalent to a repeating decimal.

c. What is the repeating decimal?

$$
\begin{array}{r}
0.444 \\
9)\overline{4.000} \\
-3.6 \\
\hline
40 \\
-36 \\
\hline
40 \\
-36 \\
\hline
4
\end{array}
$$

3 Consider the numbers shown below.

$\sqrt{7} = 2.64575\ldots$ 0.366 $1.0\overline{2}$

$0.151551555\ldots$ $\dfrac{2}{9}$ $\sqrt{100}$

a. Which of the numbers do you think are rational? Which do you think are not rational? Justify your answers.

b. Check your answer to problem 3a. Show your work.

Develop Finding Rational Approximations and Locating Them on the Number Line

➤ **Read and try to solve the problem below.**

Mei is building a raised bed in her garden to grow lettuce. She wants the base of the bed to be a square with an area of 2 square meters. Find an approximate side length of the base of the bed. Plot the value on the number line.

0   1   2

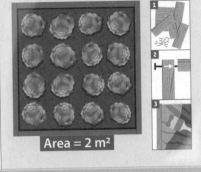

DO IT YOURSELF
Square Garden Bed

Area = 2 m²

TRY IT   **Math Toolkit** grid paper

DISCUSS IT

Ask: What did you do first to solve the problem?

Share: The first thing I did was . . .

➤ **Explore different ways to find a rational approximation for an irrational number.**

Mei is building a raised bed in her garden to grow lettuce. She wants the base of the bed to be a square with an area of 2 square meters. Find an approximate side length of the base of the bed. Plot the value on the number line.

Model It

You can solve an area equation. You can find a rational approximation if the side length is irrational.

A square with side length, s, has area, s^2.

$s^2 = 2$ square meters, so $s = \sqrt{2}$ meters.

$\sqrt{2}$ is irrational, so you must find a rational approximation.

Look for the given area value in a table of perfect squares.

The given area value, 2, is between the perfect squares 1 and 4.

x	1	2	3
x^2	1	4	9

$1 < 2 < 4$

So, $\sqrt{1} < \sqrt{2} < \sqrt{4}$. This means $1 < \sqrt{2} < 2$.

The side length is between 1 and 2 meters.

Analyze It

You can improve your rational approximation by estimating to more decimal places.

You know the value of $\sqrt{2}$ is between 1 and 2. Now improve your approximation to the tenths place by squaring 1.1, 1.2, and so on.

x	1.1	1.2	1.3	1.4	1.5
x^2	1.21	1.44	1.69	1.96	2.25

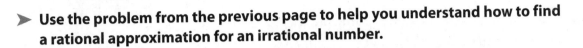

➤ **Use the problem from the previous page to help you understand how to find a rational approximation for an irrational number.**

1 Look at **Analyze It**. How do you use the table to find the approximate value of $\sqrt{2}$ to the nearest tenth?

2 What is the side length of the base of the garden bed to the nearest tenth? Plot the value on the number line.

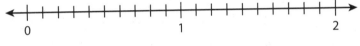

3 Suppose you want to find the approximate value of $\sqrt{2}$ to the nearest hundredth. What would you do next?

4 Suppose you continue to approximate the value of $\sqrt{2}$ to the nearest hundredth, then nearest thousandth, and so on. Could you continue this process forever or would it eventually end? Why?

5 All real numbers can be plotted on a number line. Why does it make sense that any rational or irrational number can be plotted on a number line?

6 **Reflect** Think about all the models and strategies you have discussed today. Describe how one of them helped you better understand how to solve the **Try It** problem.

Apply It

➤ **Use what you learned to solve these problems.**

7 A park has three square-shaped fountains. The side lengths of the fountains, in feet, are $\sqrt{81}$, $\sqrt{144}$, and $\sqrt{151}$. Identify the side length that is an irrational number. Then approximate that value to the nearest tenth. Show your work.

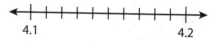

SOLUTION _____

8 Which of the following has the greatest value?

A 8

B $\sqrt{8}$

C $\sqrt{65}$

D $\sqrt{62}$

9 Elijah knows that $\sqrt{17}$ is between 4.1 and 4.2. He wants to find the approximate value of $\sqrt{17}$ to the nearest hundredth. Show how Elijah can find this value. Then plot the value on the number line.

Practice Finding Rational Approximations and Locating Them on the Number Line

➤ **Study the Example showing how to find a rational approximation of an irrational number. Then solve problems 1–5.**

Example

Find the approximate value for $\sqrt{7}$ to the nearest hundredth.

7 is between the perfect squares 4 and 9, and closer to 9. So, $\sqrt{4} < \sqrt{7} < \sqrt{9}$.
$\sqrt{7}$ is between 2 and 3, and closer to 3.

x	2.5	2.6	2.7
x^2	6.25	6.76	7.29

$\sqrt{7}$ is between 2.6 and 2.7, and slightly closer to 2.6.

x	2.63	2.64	2.65
x^2	6.9169	6.9696	7.0225

$\sqrt{7}$ is between 2.64 and 2.65, and closer to 2.65.

So, $\sqrt{7}$ is approximately 2.65.

1 Plot the approximate value of $\sqrt{7}$ from the Example on the number line.

2 Explain how you could continue the work in the Example to approximate $\sqrt{7}$ to the nearest thousandth.

3 An outdoor square chessboard has an area of 10 m².

    a. Find the approximate length of a side of the chessboard to the nearest tenth. Show your work.

SOLUTION _____

b. Use your answer to problem 3a to plot the approximate value of $\sqrt{10}$ on the number line.

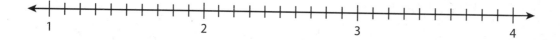

4 Ian wants to plot $\sqrt{33}$ on a number line that is only marked with whole numbers. Between which consecutive whole numbers should he plot the value? Which of those whole numbers should the value be closer to? Explain.

5 Order the following numbers from least to greatest: $\sqrt{16}$, $\sqrt{15}$, 3.8. Show your work.

SOLUTION _____

Develop Estimating the Value of Irrational Expressions

➤ **Read and try to solve the problem below.**

Jiro is a member of a taiko drumming group. He plays an odaiko drum that has a circular playing surface with a diameter of 6 feet. Jiro wants to paint the playing surface with a mitsudomoe symbol.

What is the exact area of the drum's playing surface? What is an approximation of the area? Round your approximation to the nearest hundredth of a square foot. $(A = \pi r^2; \pi \approx 3.14, \pi \approx \frac{22}{7})$

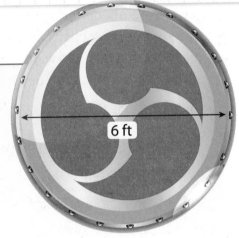

odaiko drum with mitsudomoe symbol

TRY IT

Math Toolkit compasses, grid paper, rulers

DISCUSS IT

Ask: How can you restate the problem in your own words?

Share: The problem is asking . . .

➤ **Explore different ways to estimate the value of an irrational expression.**

Jiro is a member of a taiko drumming group. He plays an odaiko drum that has a circular playing surface with a diameter of 6 feet. Jiro wants to paint the playing surface with a mitsudomoe symbol.

What is the exact area of the drum's playing surface?

What is an approximation of the area? Round your approximation to the nearest hundredth of a square foot. ($A = \pi r^2$; $\pi \approx 3.14$, $\pi \approx \frac{22}{7}$)

Picture It

You can make a sketch and find the exact area using the formula for the area of a circle.

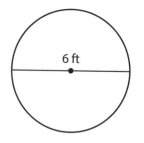

6 ft

Since the diameter, d, is 6 ft, the radius, r, is $\frac{d}{2}$, or 3 ft.

$A = \pi r^2$

$ = \pi(3)^2$

Model It

You can use an approximate value for π to find an approximate area.

Use $\pi \approx 3.14$.

$A = \pi(3)^2$

$ \approx 3.14(3)^2$

CONNECT IT

➤ **Use the problem from the previous page to help you understand how to estimate the value of an irrational expression.**

1 Look at **Picture It**. Why do you use π rather than 3.14 or $\frac{22}{7}$ in the calculation to find the exact area of the drum's surface?

2 Look at **Model It**. Why might you need a numerical value for the answer? Why use an approximation for π in this case?

3 What is the exact area of the drum's playing surface? Based on **Model It**, what is an approximation of the area to the nearest hundredth of a square foot?

4 You can use a calculator to approximate some irrational numbers. For example, many calculators use 3.141592654 as an approximation for π. Would using this value for π give a more accurate final answer than using 3.14? Explain.

5 How do you write an exact value for an irrational expression? How do you write an approximate value?

6 **Reflect** Think about all the models and strategies you have discussed today. Describe how one of them helped you better understand how to estimate the value of an irrational expression.

Apply It

➤ **Use what you learned to solve these problems.**

7 Consider the values $\sqrt{26}$, 2π, $-(\pi \times \frac{1}{3})$, and $-\sqrt{10}$. Plot and label the approximate location of each value on the number line. ($\pi \approx 3.14$)

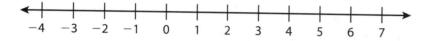

8 Which of the following has the greatest value? ($\pi \approx 3.14$)

A 4π

B 12

C $\sqrt{13}$

D $\sqrt{16} + \pi$

9 A yield sign on a highway has the shape of an equilateral triangle with sides that are 4 feet long. The height of this triangle is $2\sqrt{3}$ feet. What is the exact area of the triangle? What is an approximation of the area to the nearest tenth? Show your work. (*Hint:* $\sqrt{3} \approx 1.73$)

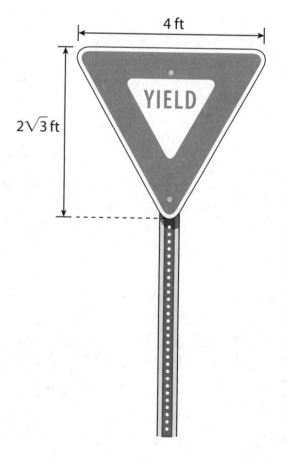

SOLUTION _____

Name:

Practice Estimating the Value of Irrational Expressions

➤ **Study the Example showing how to estimate the value of an irrational expression. Then solve problems 1–5.**

Example

Write an approximate value for the expression π^2 that is accurate to the nearest tenth.

π is irrational, but an approximate value is 3.14159 . . ..

Use $\pi \approx 3.14$ to get an answer accurate to the nearest tenth.

$\pi^2 \approx 3.14^2$

$\quad = 9.8596$

Round to the nearest tenth.

$\pi^2 \approx 9.9$

---

1 Write an approximate value for π^3 that is accurate to the nearest tenth. Show your work. ($\pi \approx 3.14$)

SOLUTION

2 Consider the values $\pi - 3$, $-\sqrt{17}$, $\frac{\pi}{3}$, and $2\sqrt{2}$. Plot and label the approximate location of each value on the number line. ($\pi \approx 3.14$)

Vocabulary

irrational number
a number that cannot be expressed as a quotient of two integers.

③ Soledad wants to make a frame for a square painting. The area of the painting is 2 ft². Soledad wants to know the perimeter of the painting.

a. What is the exact perimeter? Show your work.

SOLUTION _____

b. What is an approximation of the perimeter to the nearest tenth of a foot? Show your work. (*Hint*: $\sqrt{2} \approx 1.414$)

SOLUTION _____

④ Destiny says that 7π is a rational number because $7\left(\frac{22}{7}\right) = 22$, and 22 is a rational number. Do you agree or disagree with Destiny's reasoning? Explain.

⑤ Which is greater, -9 or -3π? How do you know? ($\pi \approx 3.14$)

Refine Finding Rational Approximations of Irrational Numbers

➤ **Complete the Example below. Then solve problems 1–9.**

Example

Is $\sqrt{2}$ greater than, less than, or equal to $1\frac{206}{500}$?

Look at how you could use a rational approximation for $\sqrt{2}$ to compare.

You can use a calculator to find that $\sqrt{2} \approx 1.414$.

Write a fraction for 1.414.

$$1.414 = 1 + 0.414$$

$$= 1 + \frac{414}{1,000}$$

$$= 1 + \frac{207}{500}$$

$$= 1\frac{207}{500}$$

SOLUTION _____

Apply It

1 Find an approximate value for $\sqrt{9} + \sqrt{10}$ to the nearest tenth. Show your work.

SOLUTION _____

2 Is π greater than, less than, or equal to $3\frac{6}{50}$? Show your work. (π ≈ 3.14)

> **CONSIDER THIS . . .**
> You can write an approximate decimal value for π to the nearest hundredth. Then write the decimal as a fraction.

SOLUTION _____

> **PAIR/SHARE**
> How does π compare to $3\frac{7}{50}$?

3 Which of the following has the least value? (π ≈ 3.14)

A $-\sqrt{25}$

B $\sqrt{37}$

C $\pi - 8$

D $-(\pi + 2)$

Adoncia chose C as the correct answer. How might she have gotten that answer?

> **CONSIDER THIS . . .**
> You can find the approximate value of the irrational numbers to the nearest tenth for this problem.

> **PAIR/SHARE**
> Can you eliminate any of the choices before doing any calculations or finding any approximate values?

4 A playground has square rubber tiles under a play structure. The tiles are arranged in 6 rows of 6 tiles each to make a large square play surface. The area of each tile is 5 ft².

What is the exact perimeter of the play surface? What is an approximation of the perimeter to the nearest tenth of a foot? Show your work.
(*Hint*: Use a calculator to get an approximation.)

$A = 5$ ft²

SOLUTION _____

5 The decimal expansion for π begins 3.14159 . . .. A common rational approximation for π is $\frac{22}{7}$. Is $\frac{22}{7}$ greater than or less than π? Explain.

6 Tell whether each value is *Rational* or *Irrational*.

	Rational	Irrational
a. $\sqrt{2} \cdot \sqrt{2}$	○	○
b. 0.20220222022220 . . .	○	○
c. $-\sqrt{11}$	○	○
d. $\pi - \pi$	○	○

7 Wind turbines convert wind into energy. A wind turbine has blades that are each 116 feet long. To the nearest tenth of a foot, how many feet does the tip of one blade move in one full rotation? ($C = 2\pi r$; $\pi \approx 3.14$)

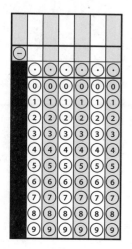

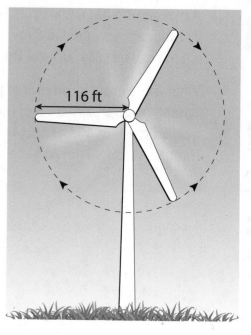

wind turbine

8 Hugo says that $\frac{2\pi}{3}$ is a rational number because it is expressed as a fraction.

Do you agree or disagree? Explain.

9 **Math Journal** Choose a two-digit number that is not a perfect square. Show how to find the approximate value of the square root of that number to the nearest tenth.

✓ End of Lesson Checklist

☐ **INTERACTIVE GLOSSARY** Find the entry for *irrational number*. Tell how irrational numbers and rational numbers are different.

☐ **SELF CHECK** Go back to the Unit 6 Opener and see what you can check off.

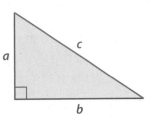

Dear Family,

This week your student is exploring the **Pythagorean Theorem**. This theorem describes a relationship between the side lengths of a right triangle. The side of a right triangle opposite the right angle is called the **hypotenuse**. The two sides that meet to form the right angle are called the **legs**.

Consider a right triangle with legs of lengths a and b and a hypotenuse of length c. The relationship $a^2 + b^2 = c^2$ is true based on the Pythagorean Theorem. The **converse of the Pythagorean Theorem** uses this relationship in reverse. Consider a triangle with side lengths p, q, and r, where $p^2 + q^2 = r^2$. According to the converse of the Pythagorean Theorem, this triangle is a right triangle.

➤ **ONE WAY** to use the Pythagorean Theorem is to find an unknown side length.

The legs of a right triangle are 4 units and 3 units long. You can use the Pythagorean Theorem to find the length of the hypotenuse.

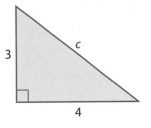

$$4^2 + 3^2 = c^2$$
$$16 + 9 = c^2$$
$$25 = c^2$$
$$5 = c$$

The hypotenuse is 5 units long.

➤ **ANOTHER WAY** is to use the converse of the Pythagorean Theorem to check if a triangle is a right triangle.

Consider a triangle with side lengths **6** units, **8** units, and **10** units. Square each side length. If the sum of the two lesser squares equals the third square, then the triangle is a right triangle.

$$6^2 = 36, 8^2 = 64, 10^2 = 100$$
$$36 + 64 = 100, \text{ so } 6^2 + 8^2 = 10^2$$

The triangle is a right triangle.

Using either method, the Pythagorean Theorem is helpful when working with right triangles.

 Use the next page to start a conversation about the Pythagorean Theorem.

Activity Thinking About the Pythagorean Theorem

➤ **Do this activity together to investigate the Pythagorean Theorem in the real world.**

The Pythagorean Theorem is a useful tool whenever precise measurements are needed to create right triangles. For example, builders and carpenters can use a speed square tool, linear measurements, and the Pythagorean Theorem to make sure that floors are level, walls are perpendicular, and corners are square.

 Can you think of other situations where right triangles can be found?

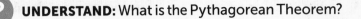

? **UNDERSTAND:** What is the Pythagorean Theorem?

Explore the Pythagorean Theorem

Model It

➤ **Complete the problems about right triangles.**

1 Look at the triangles below.

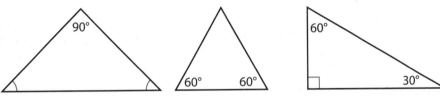

a. Write the missing angle measure(s). Then circle all the right triangles.

b. There are special names for the sides of a right triangle. The side opposite the right angle is the **hypotenuse**. The two sides that meet to form the right angle are called the **legs**. Label each side of any right triangles above as either *hypotenuse* or *leg*.

2 There is an important relationship between the lengths of the sides of a right triangle: for a right triangle with leg lengths a and b and hypotenuse length c, $a^2 + b^2 = c^2$. This relationship is called the **Pythagorean Theorem**.

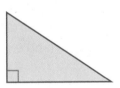

a. Use the information above to label the length of each side of the right triangle with a, b, or c.

b. Write *hypotenuse* or *legs* in each blank to help explain what $a^2 + b^2 = c^2$ means in words:

In a right triangle, when you square the lengths of the _____

and add these squares, the sum is equal to the square of the length of

the _____.

> **DISCUSS IT**
>
> **Ask:** How is a hypotenuse similar to a leg? How is it different?
>
> **Share:** I think the hypotenuse is the longest side in a right triangle because . . .

◎ **Learning Target**   SMP 2, SMP 3, SMP 4, SMP 5, SMP 6, SMP 7
Explain a proof of the Pythagorean Theorem and its converse.

Model It

➤ **Complete the problems about the Pythagorean Theorem.**

3 Here is another way to think about the Pythagorean Theorem:

In a right triangle, the area of a square drawn on the hypotenuse is equal to the combined areas of the squares drawn on the two legs.

You can see an example of this in the diagram to the right.

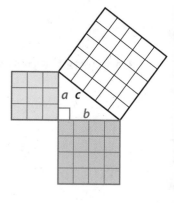

a. Write the length of each side of the right triangle.

a: _____ units

b: _____ units

c: _____ units

b. Write the area of each square.

Square with side length a: _____ square units

Square with side length b: _____ square units

Square with side length c: _____ square units

c. Use your answers from problems 3a and 3b to show that this diagram supports the Pythagorean Theorem. Identify which sides of the right triangle are the legs and which is the hypotenuse in your answer.

DISCUSS IT

Ask: How does a square with side length a represent a^2?

Share: I think it is important to know which side of a right triangle is the hypotenuse because . . .

4 **Reflect** Rodrigo drew this diagram related to the diagram in problem 3. How does Rodrigo's diagram help to support understanding of the Pythagorean Theorem?

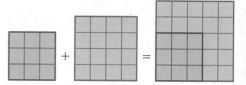

Prepare for The Pythagorean Theorem and Its Converse

1 Think about what you know about triangles. Fill in each box. Use words, numbers, and pictures. Show as many ideas as you can.

In My Own Words	My Illustrations

right triangle

Examples	Non-Examples

2 Circle the groups of angle measures that represent a right triangle.

25°, 90°, 75   40°, 90°, 50°

60°, 60°, 90°   90°, 35°, 55°

➤ **Complete the problems 3–4.**

3 Look at the triangles below.

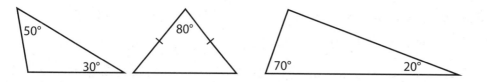

a. Write the missing angle measure(s) for each triangle. Then circle all of the right triangles.

b. Label each side of any right triangles as either *hypotenuse* or *leg*.

4 Explain how the diagram demonstrates the Pythagorean Theorem.

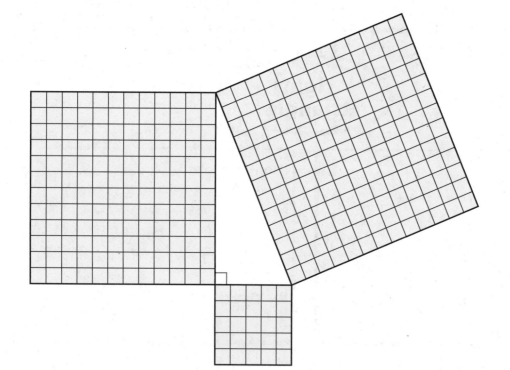

Develop Understanding of the Pythagorean Theorem

Model It: Geometric Proof

➤ **Try these four problems involving a proof of the Pythagorean Theorem.**

1 Figure 1 shows four congruent right triangles forming a square of side length $a + b$. You can prove that the unshaded shape is also a square.

    a. How do you know the sides of the unshaded shape are congruent?

    b. How can you prove that each angle of this shape measures 90°?

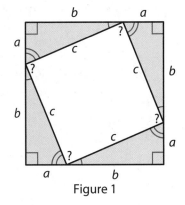

Figure 1

2 Figure 2 shows a different way to arrange the right triangles from Figure 1 to also form a square of side length $a + b$. Explain why each unshaded shape is also a square.

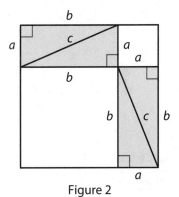

3 Explain why the total area of the two unshaded squares in Figure 2 equals the area of the unshaded square in Figure 1.

Figure 2

4 How do Figures 1 and 2 prove the Pythagorean Theorem?

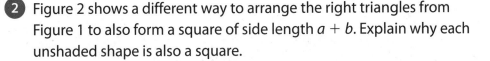

DISCUSS IT

Ask: How are the three unshaded squares important in this proof?

Share: Figures 1 and 2 are alike because . . .

Model It: Algebraic Proof

➤ **Try these three problems about a proof of the Pythagorean Theorem.**

5 What is the total area of all four triangles in Figure 1? What is the area of the unshaded shape? Use your answers to write an expression for the area of the square with side length $a + b$.

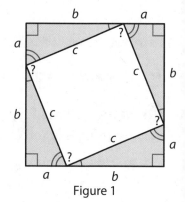

Figure 1

6 **a.** Why can the area of the large square be written as $(a + b) \cdot (a + b)$?

b. The distributive property shows that $(a + b) \cdot (a + b) = a^2 + 2ab + b^2$:

$$(a + b) \cdot (a + b) = a(a + b) + b(a + b)$$
$$= a^2 + ab + ab + b^2$$
$$= a^2 + 2ab + b^2$$

Look at your answers to problem 5. Why is $a^2 + 2ab + b^2 = 2ab + c^2$?

7 Simplify the last equation in problem 6b by subtracting $2ab$ from both sides. How does this prove the Pythagorean Theorem?

> **DISCUSS IT**
>
> *Ask:* How does the distributive property help you to find the area of a square with side length $a + b$?
>
> *Share:* Simplifying the area expressions is important because . . .

CONNECT IT

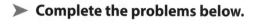

➤ **Complete the problems below.**

8 What do the geometric proof and the algebraic proof have in common?

9 How do both the geometric proof and the algebraic proof show that the Pythagorean Theorem applies to all right triangles?

Practice Understanding of the Pythagorean Theorem

➤ **Study how the Example shows how to begin a proof of the Pythagorean Theorem. Then solve problems 1–5.**

Example

Four congruent right triangles are arranged to form a large quadrilateral as shown. The unshaded shape formed in the middle of this figure is also a quadrilateral. Explain how you know both quadrilaterals are squares.

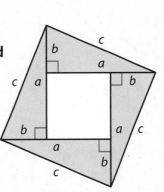

In the large quadrilateral, all sides are the same length, c. Each angle is made up of the two acute angles of a right triangle whose measures sum to 90°.

In the small quadrilateral, all sides are the same length, $a - b$. Each of the right triangles has a 90° angle that forms a linear pair with the angle in the small quadrilateral. So, each angle in the small quadrilateral is also 90°.

Both figures have four congruent sides and four right angles, so they are both squares.

1 Refer to the diagram in the Example to answer these questions.

   a. Write an expression for the area of the large square.

   b. Write an expression for the total area of the 4 triangles.

   c. Write an expression for the area of the small square.

2 The diagram in the Example shows:

   | area of large square | $=$ | area of four triangles | $+$ | area of small square |

   Use your answers to problem 1 to write an equation to show this relationship. Then simplify the equation. (*Hint*: $(a - b)^2 = a^2 - 2ab + b^2$)

3 Suppose you have a right triangle with sides of length x, y, and z where $y^2 = z^2 + x^2$. Which sides are the legs and which is the hypotenuse in the triangle? How do you know?

4 Damita uses the Pythagorean Theorem to write the equation $2k^2 = j^2$ to represent the triangle shown. Is she correct? Explain.

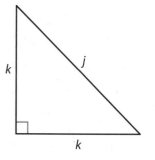

5 Andrew sketches a right triangle with side lengths p, q, and r as shown. He uses the Pythagorean Theorem to write the equation $p^2 + q^2 = r^2$ to represent the triangle. What is a correct equation for the triangle? What mistake might Andrew have made?

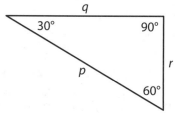

Refine Ideas About the Pythagorean Theorem and Its Converse

Apply It

➤ **Complete problems 1–5.**

1 **Apply** Sketch a right triangle with legs of lengths f and g and hypotenuse of length h. Write an equation relating the lengths of f, g, and h. Now use what you know about squares and square roots to write an expression for the length of the hypotenuse, h. Then choose values for f and g so that h is not a whole number. Find an approximate value for h.

2 **Generalize** What is the length of the hypotenuse for each isosceles right triangle?

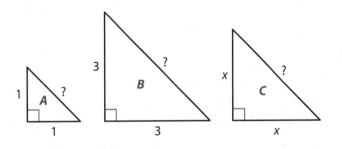

3 **Analyze** A right triangle with leg lengths of 5 and 12 has a hypotenuse of length 13. Show that a triangle with side lengths $5p$, $12p$, and $13p$ is also a right triangle. Explain your reasoning, using what you know about similar triangles.

4 A triangle is a right triangle if the square of one side length equals the sum of the squares of the other two side lengths. This relationship is called the **converse of the Pythagorean Theorem**. You can use congruent triangles to prove this converse.

Start with $\triangle XYZ$ with side lengths a, b, and c as shown. The triangle is drawn so that $a^2 + b^2 = c^2$. The angle measures are unknown. Follow the steps below to show that $\triangle XYZ$ must be a right triangle by proving that $\angle Z$ must be a right angle.

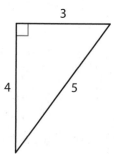

PART A Sketch $\triangle DEF$ with a right angle at F such that $FE = ZY = a$ and $FD = ZX = b$. What is DE, the length of the hypotenuse? Explain.

PART B How do you know that $\triangle XYZ$ and $\triangle DEF$ are congruent triangles?

PART C Explain how you know that $\angle Z$ is a right angle.

5 **Math Journal** Ignacio draws a right triangle with side lengths of 3, 4, and 5. He claims: A) If you add 2 to the length of each side, the new triangle will be a right triangle. B) If you multiply each side length by 2, the new triangle will be a right triangle. Use words and numbers to explain if each claim is true.

End of Lesson Checklist

☐ **INTERACTIVE GLOSSARY** Find the entry for *Pythagorean Theorem*. Add two important things you learned about the Pythagorean Theorem in this lesson.

Dear Family,

This week your student is learning how to apply the Pythagorean Theorem. Previously, students learned the Pythagorean Theorem: In any right triangle, the sum of the squares of the lengths of the legs, a and b, is equal to the square of the length of the hypotenuse, c. So, $a^2 + b^2 = c^2$.

Students will see that the Pythagorean Theorem can be used to find unknown lengths in problems involving right triangles, as in the problem below.

Arturo is buying a flat-screen monitor to hang in a 3-foot high by 4-foot wide area of wall space. He sees an ad for a monitor with a 60-inch diagonal and a 36-inch height. Will the monitor fit in the wall space?

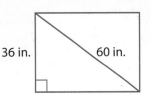

36 in.   60 in.

➤ **ONE WAY** to solve the problem is to find the width of the monitor.

Let the diagonal length of the monitor be c, the length of the hypotenuse of a right triangle. Let the height of the monitor be a, one leg length, and the unknown width be b, the other leg length. Use $a^2 + b^2 = c^2$.

$$36^2 + b^2 = 60^2$$
$$1{,}296 + b^2 = 3{,}600$$
$$b^2 = 2{,}304$$
$$b = \sqrt{2{,}304} = 48$$

> The width of the monitor is 48 in. or 4 ft.

➤ **ANOTHER WAY** is to find the diagonal length of the wall space.

Let a and b be the width and height of the wall space. Find c, the length of the diagonal, using $a^2 + b^2 = c^2$.

$$3^2 + 4^2 = c^2$$
$$9 + 16 = c^2$$
$$25 = c^2$$
$$c = \sqrt{25} = 5$$

> The diagonal length of the wall space is 5 ft or 60 in.

Using either method, the monitor will fit in the wall space.

 Use the next page to start a conversation about applying the Pythagorean Theorem.

Activity Thinking About the Pythagorean Theorem

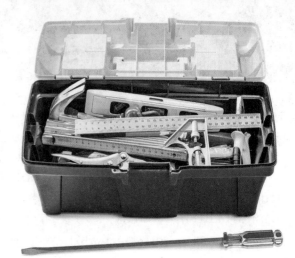

➤ **Do this activity together to investigate applications of the Pythagorean Theorem.**

The Pythagorean Theorem can also help you find an unknown length in a three-dimensional object. For example, will an 11-inch long screwdriver fit in a toolbox that is 8 inches long, 6 inches wide, and 5 inches deep? You can apply the Pythagorean Theorem twice to find out that it will fit!

 In what other situations can it be helpful to find an unknown length of a right triangle?

Explore Applying the Pythagorean Theorem

Previously, you learned about the Pythagorean Theorem. In this lesson, you will learn how to use the Pythagorean Theorem to solve problems involving right triangles.

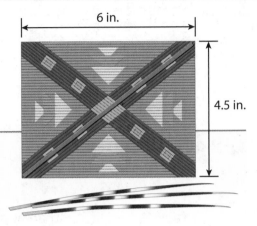

6 in.

4.5 in.

➤ **Use what you know to try to solve the problem below.**

A Mi'kmaq (Mic-mac) artist uses porcupine quills to decorate a rectangular piece of leather. She places a row of porcupine quills extending from one corner to the opposite corner. Each quill measures 1.5 inches long. How many quills does the artist need to make her first diagonal?

TRY IT

Math Toolkit grid paper, rulers, unit tiles

DISCUSS IT

Ask: What did you do first to find the number of quills? Why?

Share: I knew . . . so I . . .

◎ **Learning Targets** SMP 1, SMP 2, SMP 3, SMP 4, SMP 5, SMP 6, SMP 7
• Apply the Pythagorean Theorem to determine unknown side lengths in right triangles in real-world and mathematical problems in two and three dimensions.
• Apply the Pythagorean Theorem to find the distance between two points in a coordinate system.

CONNECT IT

1 **Look Back** How many quills are in the diagonal? How do you know?

2 **Look Ahead**

a. Fill in the blanks to restate the Pythagorean Theorem.

In any _____ triangle, the sum of the squares of the lengths of the

_____ is equal to the square of the length of the _____.

If a and b are the lengths of the legs of a right triangle and c is the length of
the hypotenuse, then the theorem can be represented by the equation

_____.

b. When the side lengths of a right triangle are whole numbers, the lengths are
known as *Pythagorean triples*. For example, the set of lengths 3, 4, 5 is a
Pythagorean triple because $3^2 + 4^2 = 5^2$. Look at each set of three numbers
shown on the right. Circle each set that is a Pythagorean triple.

c. Jason says that if you multiply each length in a Pythagorean triple by the same
factor, you will get another Pythagorean triple. Explain why Jason is correct.

2, 3, 4
4, 5, 6
5, 12, 13
6, 8, 10
8, 15, 17
9, 16, 25

3 **Reflect** Give an example to show that a multiple of a Pythagorean triple is also a
Pythagorean triple.

Name:

Prepare for Applying the Pythagorean Theorem

1 Think about what you know about right triangles. Fill in each box. Use words, numbers, and pictures. Show as many ideas as you can.

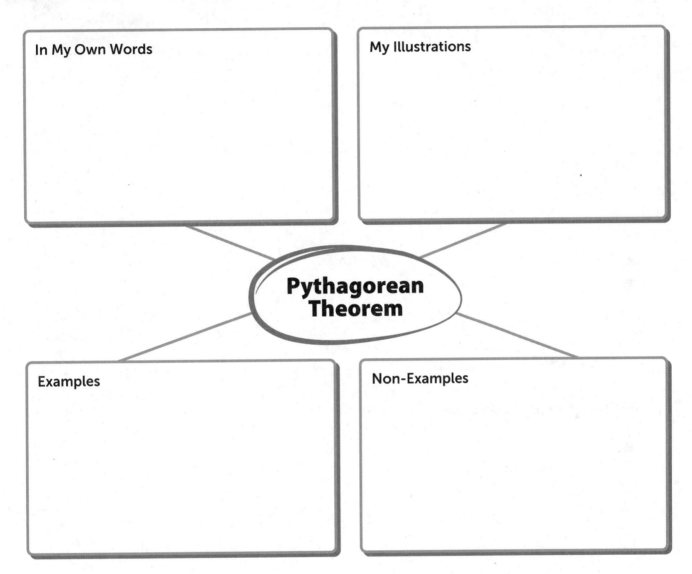

In My Own Words

My Illustrations

Pythagorean Theorem

Examples

Non-Examples

2 Suppose you have a right triangle with side lengths 26, 24, and 10. Which lengths represent the legs and which length represents the hypotenuse of the triangle? Use the Pythagorean Theorem to explain how you know.

3 The flag of Scotland consists of a blue rectangular background with two white diagonals.

a. The dimensions of a Scottish flag are shown. If the flag's diagonals are made of white ribbon, what length of ribbon is needed for both diagonals? Show your work. Round your answer to the nearest foot.

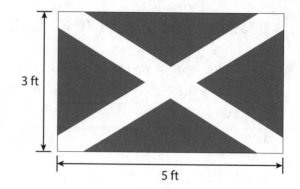

3 ft

5 ft

SOLUTION _____

b. Check your answer to problem 3a. Show your work.

Develop Finding an Unknown Length in a Right Triangle

➤ **Read and try to solve the problem below.**

A firefighter is trying to rescue a kitten from a tree. He leans a 13-foot ladder so its top touches the tree. The base of the ladder is 5 feet from the base of the tree. The tree forms a right angle with the ground. How high up the tree does the ladder reach?

TRY IT

Math Toolkit centimeter grid paper, centimeter ruler, unit cubes

DISCUSS IT

Ask: Where does your model show the leg and the hypotenuse of the right triangle formed by the ground, tree, and ladder?

Share: In my model, . . . represents . . .

➤ **Explore different ways to find how to use the Pythagorean Theorem to find an unknown length.**

A firefighter is trying to rescue a kitten from a tree. He leans a 13-foot ladder so its top touches the tree. The base of the ladder is 5 feet from the base of the tree. The tree forms a right angle with the ground. How high up the tree does the ladder reach?

Picture It

You can draw a picture to show the information you are given and what you still need to find.

Model It

You can use the Pythagorean Theorem.

The ladder represents the hypotenuse of the right triangle formed by the ladder, tree, and ground. Let b be the length you need to find.

$$5^2 + b^2 = 13^2$$
$$25 + b^2 = 169$$
$$b^2 = 169 - 25$$
$$b^2 = 144$$
$$b = \pm\sqrt{144}$$

➤ **Use the problem from the previous page to help you understand how to use the Pythagorean Theorem to find an unknown length.**

1 Look at **Picture It** and **Model It**. Explain how the picture and the equation $5^2 + b^2 = 13^2$ represent this situation.

2 **a.** How high up the tree does the ladder reach? Why do you not need to consider the negative square root of b?

b. When using the Pythagorean Theorem to find an unknown length, do you ever need to consider a negative square root? Explain.

3 A right triangle has leg lengths a and b and hypotenuse length c. Write a subtraction equation that you could use to solve for b. Write a subtraction equation that you could use to solve for a.

4 When might you use one of the equations in problem 3? Why?

5 **Reflect** Think about all the models and strategies you have discussed today. Describe how one of them helped you better understand how to solve the **Try It** problem.

Apply It

➤ **Use what you learned to solve these problems.**

6 A car salesman is stringing banners from the top of the roof to a fence pole 20 feet away. The fence pole is 8 feet high. He uses 29 feet of banner rope to reach from the rooftop to the fence pole. How tall is the roof? Show your work.

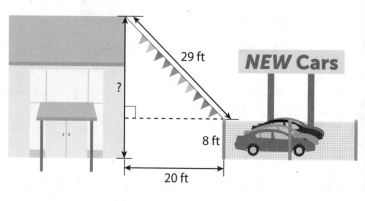

SOLUTION _____

7 Which set of side lengths do not form a right triangle?

A $5, 6, \sqrt{61}$

B $24, 7, 25$

C $14, 7, \sqrt{245}$

D $12, 15, 18$

8 The perimeter of an equilateral triangle is 48 cm. Find the height of the triangle to the nearest whole number. Show your work.

SOLUTION _____

Name:

Practice Finding an Unknown Length in a Right Triangle

➤ Study the Example showing how to find an unknown length in a right triangle. Then solve problems 1–4.

Example

A meteorologist ties a spherical balloon that is 2 feet in diameter to a stake in the ground. The string is 15 feet long. The wind blows the balloon so that the top of it is 8 feet to the right of the stake. What is the distance, b, from the top of the balloon to the ground?

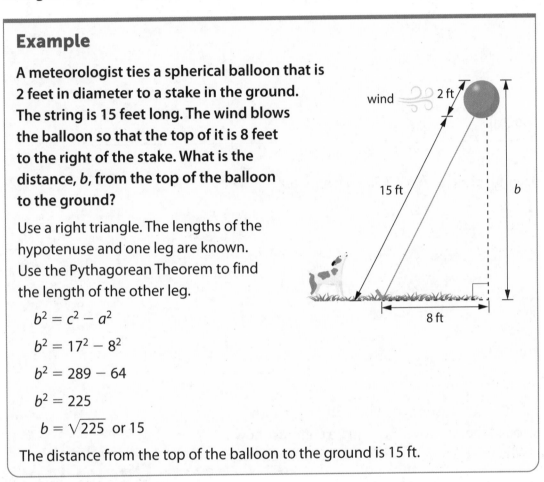

Use a right triangle. The lengths of the hypotenuse and one leg are known. Use the Pythagorean Theorem to find the length of the other leg.

$$b^2 = c^2 - a^2$$
$$b^2 = 17^2 - 8^2$$
$$b^2 = 289 - 64$$
$$b^2 = 225$$
$$b = \sqrt{225} \text{ or } 15$$

The distance from the top of the balloon to the ground is 15 ft.

1 Imani used the equation $8^2 + b^2 = 17^2$ to find the distance from the top of the balloon to the ground in the Example. Why does this equation also work?

2 Kamal said the distance from the top of the balloon to the ground in the Example is $\sqrt{353}$ ft. What mistake might Kamal have made?

3 The diagram shows △*ABC*.

   a. What is the height of △*ABC*? Show your work.

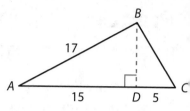

SOLUTION _____

   b. What is the length of $\overline{BC}$ in △*ABC*? Show your work.

SOLUTION _____

4 Alyssa is designing a square wooden deck with side length
c yards. She will build the deck over her square patio, as shown
in the diagram. Find the perimeter of the deck. Show your work.

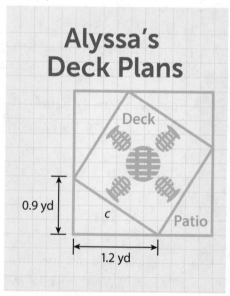

SOLUTION _____

Develop Finding an Unknown Length in a Three-Dimensional Figure

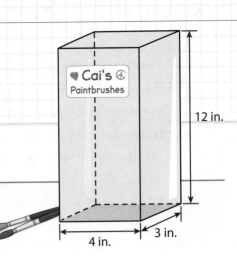

➤ **Read and try to solve the problem below.**

Cai has a box for her paintbrushes. The box is a right rectangular prism. What is the longest paintbrush that will fit in the box?

 Math Toolkit grid paper, rulers

TRY IT

DISCUSS IT

Ask: Why did you choose that strategy to find the longest paintbrush that will fit?

Share: The problem is asking . . .

➤ **Explore different ways to find an unknown length in a right rectangular prism.**

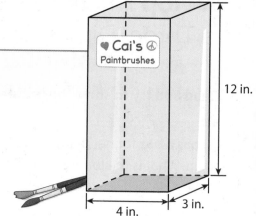

Cai has a box for her paintbrushes. The box is a right rectangular prism. What is the longest paintbrush that will fit in the box?

Picture It

You can draw a diagram to represent the problem.

Look for right triangles that can help you find the length you need.

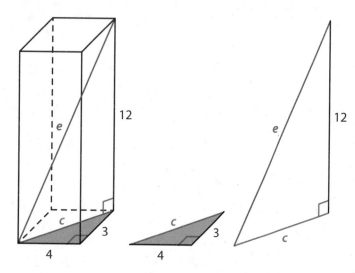

You can use the diagonal length of the base, c, to find the diagonal length of the box, e.

Model It

You can use the Pythagorean Theorem to write equations.

To find the diagonal length of the base: $3^2 + 4^2 = c^2$

To find the diagonal length of the box: $c^2 + 12^2 = e^2$

Substitute to get one equation: $3^2 + 4^2 + 12^2 = e^2$

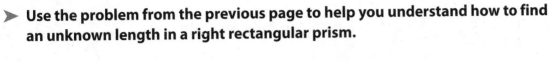

CONNECT IT

➤ **Use the problem from the previous page to help you understand how to find an unknown length in a right rectangular prism.**

1 Look at **Picture It** and **Model It**. How does finding the length of diagonal c help you find the length of diagonal e?

2 Solve the last equation in **Model It** to find e. What is the longest paintbrush that will fit in the box?

3 Tyrone says you can also solve the problem by first solving $3^2 + 4^2 = c^2$ for c and then using this value of c to solve $c^2 + 12^2 = e^2$ for e. Is Tyrone correct? Explain.

4 When can you use the Pythagorean Theorem to find an unknown length in a right rectangular prism?

5 **Reflect** Think about all the models and strategies you have discussed today. Describe how one of them helped you better understand how to solve the **Try It** problem.

Apply It

➤ **Use what you learned to solve these problems.**

6 Find the length of the diagonal from *P* to *Q* in this right rectangular prism. Show your work.

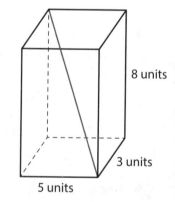

SOLUTION _____

7 What is the distance from one corner of the bottom base to the opposite corner of the top base in this right rectangular prism?

A $\sqrt{34}$ units

B $\sqrt{80}$ units

C $\sqrt{89}$ units

D $\sqrt{98}$ units

8 Anica is shipping a poster to a customer. When the poster is rolled up, it measures 6 feet long. She will use a box that is a right rectangular prism with a base that is 3 feet by 4 feet. What whole number could be the shortest height of the box that will hold the poster? Show your work.

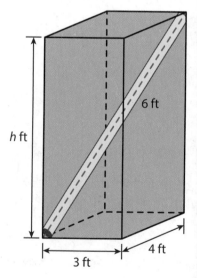

SOLUTION _____

Practice Finding an Unknown Length in a Three-Dimensional Figure

➤ **Study the Example explaining how to find the length of a diagonal in a right rectangular prism. Then solve problems 1–4.**

Example

The diagram shows a diagonal drawn in a right rectangular prism. Explain how you can find d, the length of this diagonal.

Look for right triangles. Side length d is the hypotenuse of the right triangle with leg lengths c and 24. Side length c is the hypotenuse of the right triangle in the base of the prism with leg lengths 6 and 8. Use the Pythagorean Theorem to find c. Then use it again to find d.

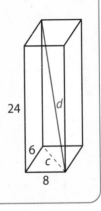

1 **a.** How do you know that the triangle with side lengths 6, 8, and c in the Example is a right triangle?

b. How do you know that the triangle with side lengths c, 24, and d in the Example is a right triangle?

2 What is the length of the diagonal d in the Example? Show your work.

SOLUTION _____

3 Will a 12-inch ruler fit in a box that is a right rectangular prism with a width of 5 inches, a length of 10 inches, and a height of 3 inches? Explain your answer.

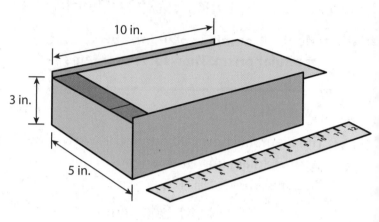

4 In the right rectangular prism, what is the length of the diagonal from M to N to the nearest tenth of a meter? Show your work.

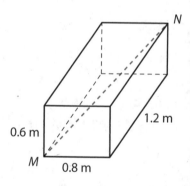

SOLUTION _____

Develop Finding Distance in the Coordinate Plane

➤ **Read and try to solve the problem below.**

Find the shortest distance between the points (0, −6) and (−8, 0).

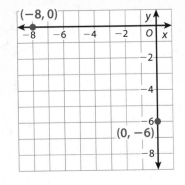

 TRY IT

 Math Toolkit compasses, graph paper, rulers, tracing paper

DISCUSS IT

Ask: How did you get started?

Share: I started by . . .

LESSON 27 Apply the Pythagorean Theorem **647**

➤ **Explore different ways to find the distance between points in the coordinate plane.**

Find the shortest distance between the points $(0, -6)$ and $(-8, 0)$.

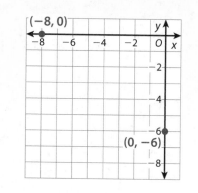

Picture It

You can draw a right triangle.

Draw a line segment between the points. Then draw a right triangle so the distance between the points is the hypotenuse.

In the right triangle, a and b are the lengths of the legs and c is the length of the hypotenuse.

Model It

You can use the Pythagorean Theorem to find the unknown distance.

$a^2 + b^2 = c^2$

$6^2 + 8^2 = c^2$

©Curriculum Associates, LLC   Copying is not permitted.

➤ **Use the problem from the previous page to help you understand how to find the distance between two points in the coordinate plane.**

1 Look at **Picture It**. How do you know the triangle formed by the two points and the origin is a right triangle?

2 Jessica said the lengths of the legs are −6 units and −8 units. What mistake did Jessica make? What are the correct lengths of the legs?

3 Look at **Model It**. What is the distance between $(0, -6)$ and $(-8, 0)$? Why can you use the Pythagorean Theorem to find this distance?

4 Why is it important that the distance between $(0, -6)$ and $(-8, 0)$ be the hypotenuse of the right triangle and not a leg?

5 Explain how to find the distance between any two points in the coordinate plane that do not lie on the same horizontal or vertical line.

6 **Reflect** Think about all the models and strategies you have discussed today. Describe how one of them helped you better understand how to find the distance between two points in the coordinate plane.

Apply It

➤ **Use what you learned to solve these problems.**

7 Hailey plots the first two vertices of a right triangle in the coordinate plane. Where could she plot the third point so the hypotenuse of the triangle has a length of 5 units?

A (1, 5)

B (−3, 4)

C (0, −5)

D (1, −3)

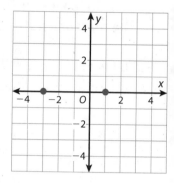

8 Draw a line segment from the origin (0, 0) with length $\sqrt{20}$. Show your work.

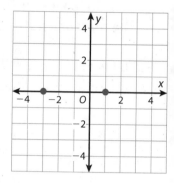

9 Find the distance between the points shown. Show your work.

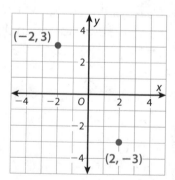

SOLUTION _____

Practice Finding Distance in the Coordinate Plane

➤ Study the Example showing how to find the distance between two points in the coordinate plane. Then solve problems 1–3.

Example

What is the distance between $P(-1, 3)$ and $Q(3, -2)$ in the coordinate plane?

Draw a right triangle with $R(-1, -2)$ as the vertex of the right angle. Then use the Pythagorean Theorem to find the length of the hypotenuse, which is the distance between P and Q.

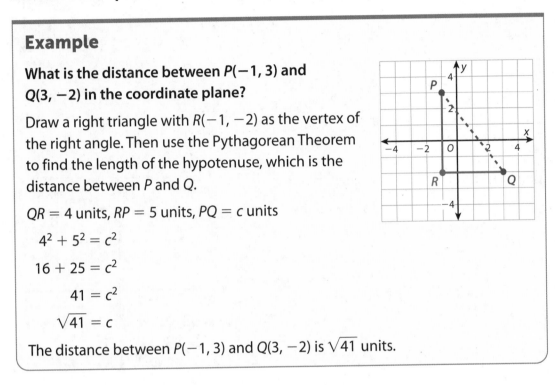

$QR = 4$ units, $RP = 5$ units, $PQ = c$ units

$$4^2 + 5^2 = c^2$$
$$16 + 25 = c^2$$
$$41 = c^2$$
$$\sqrt{41} = c$$

The distance between $P(-1, 3)$ and $Q(3, -2)$ is $\sqrt{41}$ units.

1 Look at the Example.

a. Describe another right triangle you could draw from points $P(-1, 3)$ and $Q(3, -2)$.

b. Will your triangle from problem 1a give you the same distance between points P and Q? Explain.

c. Would drawing a triangle with points $(-1, 3)$, $(3, -2)$, and $(3, 2)$ as vertices help you find the distance between the points? Explain.

2 What is the distance between the points shown? Show your work. Round your answer to the nearest tenth.

$(-1.5, 4)$

$(-5, -3.5)$

SOLUTION _____

3 Dr. Patel plots points *J*, *K*, and *L* in the coordinate plane.

a. What is the distance between points *J* and *K*? Show your work.

K(1, 5)

J(−5, −3)

L(7, −3)

SOLUTION _____

b. What is the distance between points *K* and *L*? Show your work.

SOLUTION _____

c. Is △*JKL* an equilateral triangle? Explain.

Refine Applying the Pythagorean Theorem

➤ **Complete the Example below. Then solve problems 1–8.**

Example

Chase drew a triangle with vertices at $(-2, -1)$, $(-1, 2)$, and $(1, -1)$. Classify Chase's triangle as scalene, isosceles, or equilateral.

Look at how you could use the Pythagorean Theorem.

Draw a right triangle at each nonvertical and nonhorizontal side of the original triangle.

$\overline{AB}$: $1^2 + 3^2 = AB^2$

   $AB^2 = 10$, so $AB = \sqrt{10}$.

$\overline{BC}$: $2^2 + 3^2 = BC^2$

   $BC^2 = 13$, so $BC = \sqrt{13}$.

$\overline{AC}$: $AC = 3$

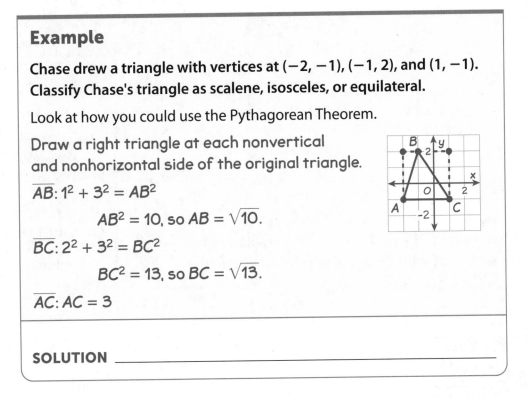

CONSIDER THIS...
An isosceles triangle has at least two congruent sides. A scalene triangle has no congruent sides.

SOLUTION _____

PAIR/SHARE
How else could you solve this?

Apply It

1 Mr. Gaspar wants to store a 12-foot-long pipe in a tool closet. The closet has the shape of a right rectangular prism with the dimensions shown. Will the pipe fit? Show your work.

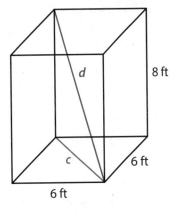

CONSIDER THIS...
This problem takes more than one step to solve.

PAIR/SHARE
Can you find two different paths to the solution? Explain.

SOLUTION _____

2 $\overline{AB}$ is one side of a square. Find the coordinates of the other two vertices of the square and draw the square. Explain your reasoning.

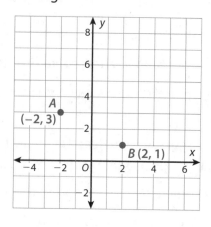

CONSIDER THIS...
How could a right triangle help you find the side length of the square?

PAIR/SHARE
How else could you solve this?

3 Mr. Shaw is building a walkway from the corner of his house out to his vegetable garden in the corner of the yard. The dimensions of the yard and the garden are shown. What is the length of the walkway, w, to the nearest foot?

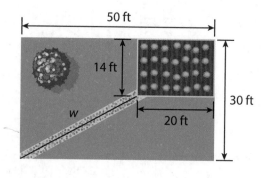

CONSIDER THIS...
Where can you draw a useful right triangle?

A 24 ft

B 34 ft

C 46 ft

D 58 ft

Ummi chose C as the correct answer. How might she have gotten that answer?

PAIR/SHARE
Was there more than one helpful right triangle that would lead to the solution?

4 Draw the reflection of △ABC across the y-axis. Then show that the corresponding sides of the two triangles are congruent.

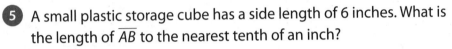

5 A small plastic storage cube has a side length of 6 inches. What is the length of $\overline{AB}$ to the nearest tenth of an inch?

A 6 in.

B 8.5 in.

C 10.4 in.

D 12 in.

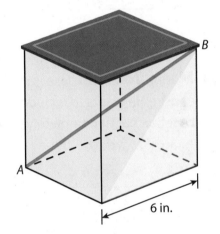

6 in.

6 In △ABC, $\overline{BC}$ is longer than $\overline{AB}$, and $BC = 24$. $\overline{AB}$ and $\overline{CA}$ have whole-number lengths. Tell whether each side length is *Possible* or *Not Possible*.

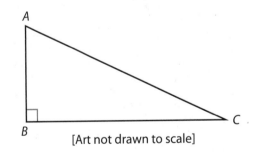

[Art not drawn to scale]

	Possible	Not Possible
a. $AB = 7$	○	○
b. $AB = 9$	○	○
c. $AB = 10$	○	○
d. $CA = 25$	○	○

7 What is the perimeter of parallelogram *ABCD*?

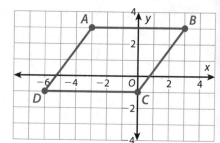

8 **Math Journal** José is mailing some baseball equipment to his cousin. He wants to include a baseball bat that is 33 in. long. Will the baseball bat fit completely in the box? Explain your reasoning.

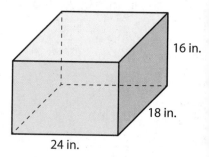

✔ **End of Lesson Checklist**

☐ **INTERACTIVE GLOSSARY** Write a new entry for *consider*. Tell what you do when you consider something.

☐ **SELF CHECK** Go back to the Unit 6 Opener and see what you can check off.

Dear Family,

Previously, your student learned about the volumes of right prisms. Now your student will learn about the volumes of cylinders, **cones,** and **spheres**.

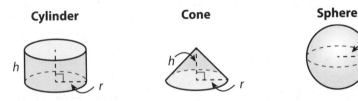

Cylinder　　　　**Cone**　　　　**Sphere**

The volume, V, of a cylinder is $V = \pi r^2 h$, where r is the radius of the base and h is the height of the cylinder.

The volume, V, of a cone is $V = \frac{1}{3}\pi r^2 h$, where r is the radius of the base and h is the height of the cone.

The volume, V, of a sphere is $V = \frac{4}{3}\pi r^3$, where r is the radius of the sphere.

Students will learn to solve volume problems like the one below.

> The volume of a cylinder with radius 6 in. and height 8 in. is 288π in.^{3}. What is the volume of a cone with the same radius and height?

➤ **ONE WAY** to find the volume is to use the relationship between the volume of a cylinder and a cone with the same radius and height.

The volume of the cone is $\frac{1}{3}$ the volume of the cylinder.

$$\frac{1}{3}(288\pi) = 96\pi$$

➤ **ANOTHER WAY** is to use the volume formula for a cone.

$$V = \frac{1}{3}\pi r^2 h$$

$V = \frac{1}{3}\pi(6^2)(8) = 96\pi$　　Using 3.14 for π, the volume of the cone is about 301.44 in.^{3}.

Using either method, the volume of the cone is 96π in.^{3}, or about 301.44 in.^{3}.

 Use the next page to start a conversation about volume.

Activity Thinking About Volume

➤ **Do this activity together to investigate solving problems using volume.**

You can use what you know about the volume of cylinders, cones, and spheres to think about the amount of space inside these figures. For example, if you want a flower vase that can hold a lot of water, you can find the volumes of different-shaped vases to find which one can hold the most water.

 Can you think of other situations where thinking about volume is useful?

Explore Volumes of Cylinders, Cones, and Spheres

Previously, you learned how to find the volumes of prisms. In this lesson, you will learn how to find the volumes of cylinders, cones, and spheres.

➤ **Use what you know to try to solve the problem below.**

The shaded figures shown are a cylinder, a cone, and a sphere. What fraction of the volume of the cylinder is the volume of the cone? What fraction of the volume of the cylinder is the volume of the sphere?

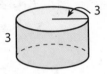
3
3

The volume of the cylinder is the area of the base multiplied by the height.

3
3

The volume of the cone is 9π.

3
3

The volume of the sphere is 36π.

TRY IT

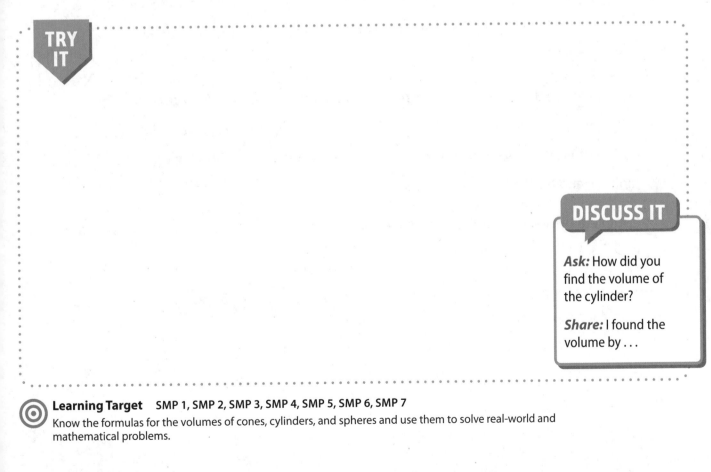

DISCUSS IT

Ask: How did you find the volume of the cylinder?

Share: I found the volume by . . .

◎ **Learning Target**   SMP 1, SMP 2, SMP 3, SMP 4, SMP 5, SMP 6, SMP 7
Know the formulas for the volumes of cones, cylinders, and spheres and use them to solve real-world and mathematical problems.

LESSON 28 Solve Problems with Volumes of Cylinders, Cones, and Spheres   **659**

CONNECT IT

1 **Look Back** What fraction of the volume of the cylinder is the volume of the cone? What fraction of the volume of the cylinder is the volume of the sphere? How did you get your answers?

2 **Look Ahead** The figures in this lesson all have curved surfaces.

a. A cylinder has two parallel circular bases that are the same size. The volume of a cylinder is the area of the base multiplied by the height. Complete the volume formula for a cylinder with radius, r, and height, h.

$V = $ _____

b. A **cone** has one circular base and one vertex. The volume of a cone is $\frac{1}{3}$ the volume of a cylinder with the same radius and height. Complete the volume formula for a cone with radius, r, and height, h.

$V = $ _____

c. Every point on the surface of a **sphere** is the same distance from the center. The volume of a sphere with radius, r, is $\frac{4}{3}$ the volume of a cylinder with radius and height both equal to r. Complete the volume formula for a cylinder with radius, r, and height, h. $V = $ _____

Complete the volume formula for a sphere with radius, r.

$V = $ _____

3 **Reflect** How is the volume formula for a cylinder like the volume formula for a rectangular prism? How are the formulas different?

Prepare for Solving Problems with Volumes of Cylinders, Cones, and Spheres

1 Think about what you know about three-dimensional figures and volume. Fill in each box. Use words, numbers, and pictures. Show as many ideas as you can.

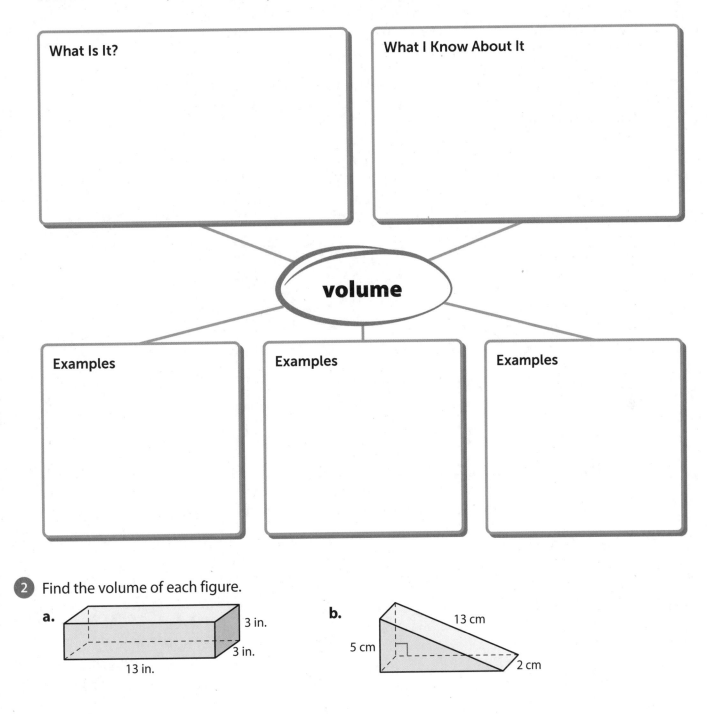

What Is It?

What I Know About It

volume

Examples

Examples

Examples

2 Find the volume of each figure.

a.

3 in.

3 in.

13 in.

b.

13 cm

5 cm

2 cm

The shaded figures shown are a cylinder, a cone, and a sphere.

The volume of the cylinder is the area of the base multiplied by the height.

The volume of the cone is 72π.

The volume of the sphere is 288π.

a. What fraction of the volume of the cylinder is the volume of the cone? What fraction of the volume of the cylinder is the volume of the sphere? Show your work.

SOLUTION _____

_____

b. Check your answer to problem 3a. Show your work.

Develop Finding Volume

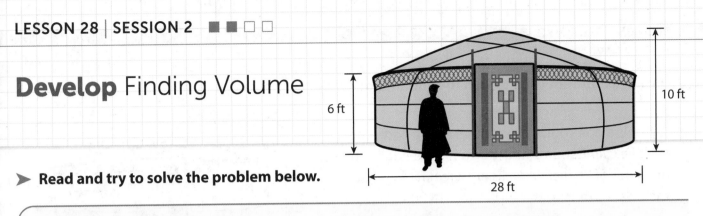

6 ft

10 ft

28 ft

➤ **Read and try to solve the problem below.**

A yurt is a one-room home shaped like a cone on top of a cylinder. The yurt shown above is 10 feet tall with a diameter of 28 feet. Its walls are 6 feet high. What is the total volume of the yurt? Use 3.14 for π.

DISCUSS IT

Ask: How did you find the volume of each part of the yurt?

Share: I found the volume by . . .

➤ **Explore different ways to find the volumes of cylinders and cones.**

A yurt is a one-room home shaped like a cone on top of a cylinder. The yurt shown is 10 feet tall with a diameter of 28 feet. Its walls are 6 feet high. What is the total volume of the yurt? Use 3.14 for π.

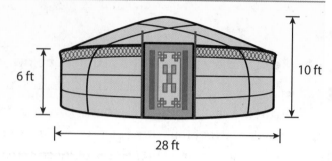

6 ft

10 ft

28 ft

Picture It

You can separate the figure into two parts.

The top is a cone.

$r = 14$ and $h = 4$

$h = 10 - 6$

$r = 28 \div 2$

The bottom is a cylinder.

$r = 14$ and $h = 6$

$h = 6$

$r = 28 \div 2$

Model It

You can find the volume of each part of the figure.

volume of cone $= \frac{1}{3}\pi r^2 h$

$= \frac{1}{3}\pi \cdot 14^2 \cdot 4$

$= 261\frac{1}{3} \cdot \pi$

volume of cylinder $= \pi r^2 h$

$= \pi \cdot 14^2 \cdot 6$

$= 1,176 \cdot \pi$

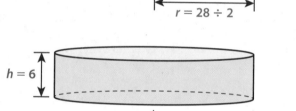

➤ **Use the problem from the previous page to help you understand how to use volume formulas to solve problems.**

1 Look at **Model It**. What is the total volume of the yurt? How did you get your answer? Use 3.14 for π.

2 Look at the figures in **Picture It**. How do you know that the cone and the cylinder have the same radius?

3 Is the volume of the cone $\frac{1}{3}$ the volume of the cylinder? Explain.

4 Bridget combines the volume formulas for the parts of the yurt to write a volume formula for the whole yurt. Her work is shown.

$$V = \frac{1}{3}\pi r^2 h + \pi r^2 h$$

$$= \frac{4}{3}\pi r^2 h$$

Is Bridget correct? Explain.

5 **Reflect** Think about all the models and strategies you have discussed today. Describe how one of them helped you better understand how to solve the **Try It** problem.

Apply It

➤ **Use what you learned to solve these problems.**

6 A cylindrical swimming pool has a radius of 9 feet. Daniel fills the pool with water at a rate of 72 cubic feet per hour. How long will it take for the depth of water in the pool to reach 4 feet? Show your work. Use 3.14 for π.

SOLUTION _____

7 A sphere and a cylinder have the same radius, r, and the same volume. What is the height of the cylinder in terms of r? Show your work.

2.7 in.

SOLUTION _____

8 A tennis ball has a diameter of 2.7 inches. A cylindrical container for tennis balls is shown. When there are three tennis balls in the container, how much empty space is in the container? Show your work. Use 3.14 for π.

8.5 in.

3 in.

SOLUTION _____

Practice Finding Volume

➤ **Study the Example showing how to use formulas to find the volume of a figure. Then solve problems 1–5.**

Example

The figure shows a cone shape removed from a solid cylinder. What is the volume of the figure without the cone? Use 3.14 for π.

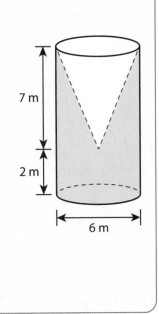

7 m

2 m

6 m

cylinder:

$V = \pi r^2 h$

$= \pi \cdot \left(\dfrac{6}{2}\right)^2 \cdot (7 + 2)$

$= \pi \cdot 3^2 \cdot 9$

$= 81\pi$

cone:

$V = \dfrac{1}{3}\pi r^2 h$

$= \dfrac{1}{3} \cdot \pi \cdot \left(\dfrac{6}{2}\right)^2 \cdot 7$

$= \dfrac{1}{3} \cdot \pi \cdot 3^2 \cdot 7$

$= 21\pi$

difference in volumes: $81\pi - 21\pi = 60\pi \approx 188.4$

The volume of the figure is about 188.4 m³.

---

1 The figure shown is made up of two identical cones and a cylinder. What is the volume of the figure? Show your work. Use 3.14 for π.

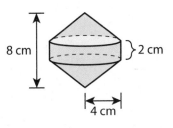

8 cm

2 cm

4 cm

SOLUTION _____

2 What is the volume of each figure? Use 3.14 for π.

a. a cylinder with diameter 20 m and height 7 m

b. a cone with radius 3 yd and height 11 yd

c. a sphere with radius 9 cm

3 Carmen is packing moisturizing bath powder into spherical molds. She has enough powder to fill about 12 spherical molds with a diameter of 4 cm. How many spherical molds with a diameter of 5 cm could she fill with the same amount of powder? Show your work.

SOLUTION _____

4 A sphere has a radius of 4 feet. A cone has a radius of 5 feet and a height of 7 feet. What is the difference in the volumes of the cone and sphere, to the nearest cubic foot? Show your work. Use 3.14 for π.

SOLUTION _____

5 How many cubic inches of soil would it take to fill each planter? Use 3.14 for π.

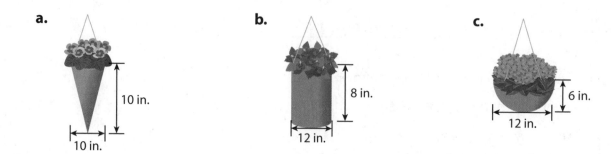

a.

10 in.

10 in.

b.

8 in.

12 in.

c.

6 in.

12 in.

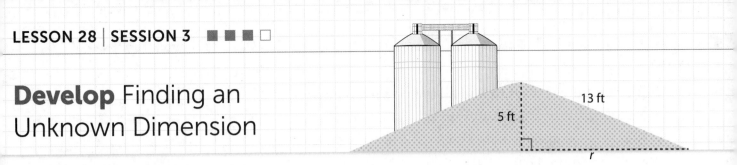

Develop Finding an Unknown Dimension

➤ **Read and try to solve the problem below.**

A cone-shaped pile of corn in a field has a height of 5 feet. The distance from the top of the pile to the edge is 13 feet. What is the volume of the pile of corn? Use 3.14 for π.

TRY IT

DISCUSS IT

Ask: What was your first step?

Share: The first thing I did was . . .

LESSON 28 Solve Problems with Volumes of Cylinders, Cones, and Spheres **669**

➤ **Explore different ways to find an unknown dimension.**

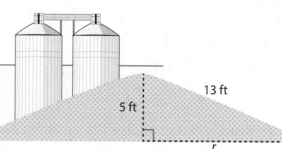

A cone-shaped pile of corn in a field has a height of 5 feet. The distance from the top of the pile to the edge is 13 feet. What is the volume of the pile of corn? Use 3.14 for π.

Picture It

You can use the Pythagorean Theorem to find the radius of the cone.

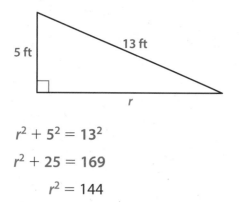

$$r^2 + 5^2 = 13^2$$
$$r^2 + 25 = 169$$
$$r^2 = 144$$
$$r = 12$$

Model It

You can use the formula for the volume of the cone.

$$V = \frac{1}{3}\pi r^2 h$$
$$= \frac{1}{3}\pi \cdot 12^2 \cdot 5$$
$$= \frac{1}{3}\pi \cdot 144 \cdot 5$$

CONNECT IT

➤ **Use the problem from the previous page to help you understand how to find the volume of a figure when a dimension is unknown.**

1 Look at **Picture It**. The third step shows $r^2 = 144$. Do you need to solve this equation for r to find the volume of the cone? Explain.

2 Look at **Model It**. What is the volume of the pile of corn?

3 Suppose you knew the radius of the cone and not the height. How could you find the volume of the cone?

4 What dimension of a cylinder or cone could you find if you know the circumference or area of a base? Explain.

5 How can you use the distance from the vertex of a cone to the edge of its base to help you find an unknown radius or height?

6 **Reflect** Think about all the models and strategies you have discussed today. Describe how one of them helped you better understand how to solve the **Try It** problem.

Apply It

➤ **Use what you learned to solve these problems.**

7 The cone and sphere have equal volumes. What is the radius of the sphere? Show your work.

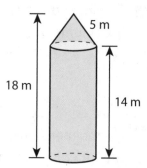

SOLUTION _____

8 The volume of the figure is 138π m³. What is the radius? Show your work. Use 3.14 for π.

SOLUTION _____

9 The circumference of a globe is 16π inches. What is the volume of the globe? Show your work. Use 3.14 for π.

circumference is 16π in.

SOLUTION _____

Practice Finding an Unknown Dimension

➤ **Study the Example showing how to find an unknown dimension to find volume. Then solve problems 1–4.**

Example

A cone is divided into two parts, as shown. The original cone has a height of 14 and a radius of 6. The top part of the divided figure is a cone with a height of 7. Use similar triangles to find the radius of the top part. Then find the volume of the top part. Use 3.14 for π.

$$\frac{r}{6} = \frac{7}{14} \longrightarrow r = 3$$

$$V = \frac{1}{3}\pi r^2 h$$

$$= \frac{1}{3}\pi \cdot 3^2 \cdot 7$$

$$= 21\pi$$

$$21(3.14) = 65.94$$

The volume is about 65.94 cubic units.

1 **a.** What is the volume of the original cone in the Example before it is divided? Use 3.14 for π.

b. What is the volume of the bottom part of the cone after it is divided?

2 What is the radius of each figure described?

a. a sphere with a volume of $\frac{500\pi}{3}$ cm³

b. a cylinder with a height of 3 m and a volume of 147π m³

c. a cone with a height of 12 in. and a volume of 16π in.³

Vocabulary

cone
a three-dimensional figure with one circular base and one vertex, connected by a curved surface.

cylinder
a three-dimensional figure with two parallel curved bases that are the same size.

sphere
a three-dimensional figure in which every point is the same distance from the center.

3 The circumference of the base of the cone shown is 8π mm. What is the volume of the cone? Show your work. Use 3.14 for π.

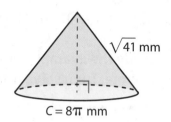

$\sqrt{41}$ mm

C = 8π mm

SOLUTION _____

4 A cylindrical storage bin is filled with sunflower seeds. The seeds form a cone-shaped pile above the bin. How many cubic feet of sunflower seeds are in the bin? Show your work. Use 3.14 for π.

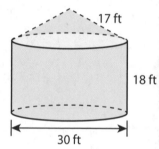

17 ft

18 ft

30 ft

SOLUTION _____

Refine Solving Problems with Volumes of Cylinders, Cones, and Spheres

➤ **Complete the Example below. Then solve problems 1–9.**

Example

The volume formula for a cone is the same whether or not the vertex is directly above the center of the base. What is the volume of this cone?

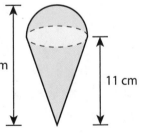

Look at how you could use a volume formula.

$r = 6, h = 5$

$V = \frac{1}{3}\pi r^2 h$

$V = \frac{1}{3}\pi \cdot 6^2 \cdot 5$

SOLUTION _____

Apply It

1 The figure shown is made up of a cone and a half sphere. What is the volume of the figure? Show your work. Use 3.14 for π.

15 cm

11 cm

SOLUTION _____

2 The figure shown is made up of a half sphere and a cylinder. The volume of the figure is about 497 cubic meters. What is the height of the cylinder? Show your work. Use 3.14 for π.

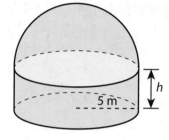

5 m

h

SOLUTION _____

3 A cylinder and a cone have the same radius and the same volume. The height of the cone is 12 cm. What is the height of the cylinder?

A 4 cm

B 9 cm

C 16 cm

D 36 cm

David chose D as the correct answer. How might he have gotten that answer?

4 A laboratory test tube is cylindrical with a half-sphere bottom. The height of the cylindrical part is 6 inches. What is the volume of the test tube? Show your work. Use 3.14 for π.

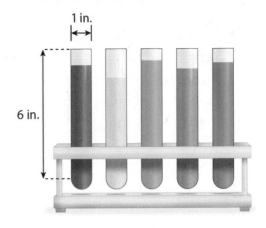

6 in.

1 in.

SOLUTION _____

5 Tell whether each statement is *True* or *False*.

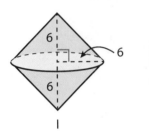 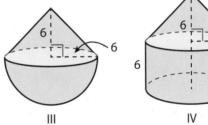 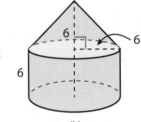

I   II   III   IV

	True	False
a. The volume of Figure II is exactly twice the volume of Figure I.	○	○
b. The volume of Figure IV is equal to the volume of a sphere with radius 6.	○	○
c. The volume of a sphere with radius 6 is exactly twice the volume of Figure I.	○	○
d. The volume of Figure III is exactly one-third the volume of Figure II.	○	○
e. The volume of Figure III is equal to the volume of a cylinder with radius 6 and height 12.	○	○

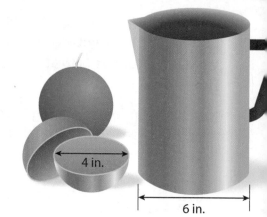

4 in.

6 in.

6 Geraldo is making candles. He melts wax in a cylindrical pitcher and then pours the wax into spherical molds. The pitcher has a diameter of 6 in. The wax in the pitcher is 7 in. deep. How many spherical candles can he make if each mold has a diameter of 4 in.?

7 The volume of a _____ with radius r and height h is $V = \frac{1}{3}\pi r^2 h$.

8 The volume of a sphere is 36π. What is the diameter of the sphere?

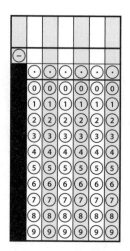

9 **Math Journal** You are designing a cylindrical tank that holds between 200 and 250 cubic feet of water. If the radius and height must be whole numbers, what could the dimensions of the tank be?

✔ End of Lesson Checklist

☐ **INTERACTIVE GLOSSARY** Find the entries for *cylinder*, *cone*, and *sphere*. For each entry, sketch an example of the figure.

☐ **SELF CHECK** Go back to the Unit 6 Opener and see what you can check off.

Math IN Action

SMP 1 Make sense of problems and persevere in solving them.

Study an Example Problem and Solution

➤ **Read this problem involving the Pythagorean Theorem and irrational numbers. Then look at one student's solution to this problem on the following pages.**

Installing a Wind Turbine

Adnan plans to install a wind turbine to help generate electricity for his farm. Steel cables called guy wires will support the tower for the wind turbine. Read the information about the guy wires.

Choose a tower height, and decide how far the anchor points for the guy wires will be from the base of the tower. What is the total length of steel cable Adnan will need for the guy wires?

Guy Wires for the Turbine Tower

- **Use 3 anchor points**. All should be the same distance from the base of the tower.

- **Use 3 guy wires** to connect each anchor point to the tower at three different heights.

- **Plan for an extra 5 feet** of length for attaching each wire to the anchor point and tower.

Tower Height (ft)	Height to A (ft)	Height to B (ft)	Height to C (ft)
70	65	44	22
80	75	50	25
90	85	57	28

Top View

120°

Anchor point

Guy wire

Wind turbine

A

B

Guy wire

Tower →

C

Tower base

Anchor point

$\frac{1}{2}$ to $\frac{3}{4}$ of tower height

One Student's Solution

First, I have to choose a tower height and decide how far the anchor points will be from the base of the tower.

I will choose the shortest tower height from the table, 70 feet.

I will make the distance between the anchor points and the base of the tower $\frac{1}{2}$ of the tower height, or 35 feet.

Next, I will draw pictures to show the given information about the three guy wires from an anchor point.

I know the heights to points A, B, and C for a 70-foot tower.

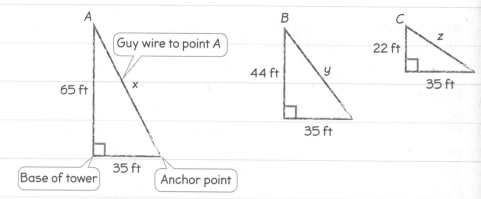

Then, I can use the Pythagorean Theorem to calculate the exact length of each guy wire.

Wire to point A:

$$65^2 + 35^2 = x^2$$
$$4{,}225 + 1{,}225 = x^2$$
$$5{,}450 = x^2$$
$$\sqrt{5{,}450} = x$$

Wire to point B:

$$44^2 + 35^2 = y^2$$
$$1{,}936 + 1{,}225 = y^2$$
$$3{,}161 = y^2$$
$$\sqrt{3{,}161} = y$$

Wire to point C:

$$22^2 + 35^2 = z^2$$
$$484 + 1{,}225 = z^2$$
$$1{,}709 = z^2$$
$$\sqrt{1{,}709} = z$$

Now, I can find a rational approximation of each irrational number.

To make sure there is enough cable, I will round up.

Wire to point A: $x = \sqrt{5,450}$

The length of the wire to point A is between 73 feet and **74 feet**.

x	70	72	73	74
x^2	4,900	5,184	5,329	5,476

NOTICE THAT . . .
You can start to estimate each square root by approximating to the nearest ten. Because $70^2 = 4,900$ and $80^2 = 6,400$, you know that $70 < \sqrt{5,450} < 80$.

Wire to point B: $y = \sqrt{3,161}$

The length of the wire to point B is between 56 feet and **57 feet**.

y	50	52	54	56	57
y^2	2,500	2,704	2,916	3,136	3,249

Wire to point C: $z = \sqrt{1,709}$

The length of the wire to point C is between 41 feet and **42 feet**.

z	40	41	42
z^2	1,600	1,681	1,764

Next, I will add an extra 5 feet to each length to account for attaching the guy wires to the anchor point and tower.

Wire to point A: $74 + 5 = 79$

Wire to point B: $57 + 5 = 62$

Wire to point C: $42 + 5 = 47$

Finally, I will find the total length of the guy wires.

There are 3 anchor points, so I can multiply each of the different lengths by 3 and then add.

$3(79) + 3(62) + 3(47) = 237 + 186 + 141 = 564$

Adnan will need about 564 feet of steel cable if he chooses a 70-foot tower and places the anchor points 35 feet from the base.

NOTICE THAT . . .
You could also add to find the total length of the guy wires to one anchor point and then multiply the sum by 3.

Try Another Approach

➤ **There are many ways to solve problems. Think about how you might solve the Installing a Wind Turbine problem in a different way.**

Installing a Wind Turbine

Adnan plans to install a wind turbine to help generate electricity for his farm. Steel cables called guy wires will support the tower for the wind turbine. Read the information about the guy wires.

Choose a tower height, and decide how far the anchor points for the guy wires will be from the base of the tower. What is the total length of steel cable Adnan will need for the guy wires?

<table>
<tr><td>✓</td><td>**Problem-Solving Checklist**</td></tr>
</table>

☐	Tell what is known.
☐	Tell what the problem is asking.
☐	Show all your work.
☐	Show that the solution works.

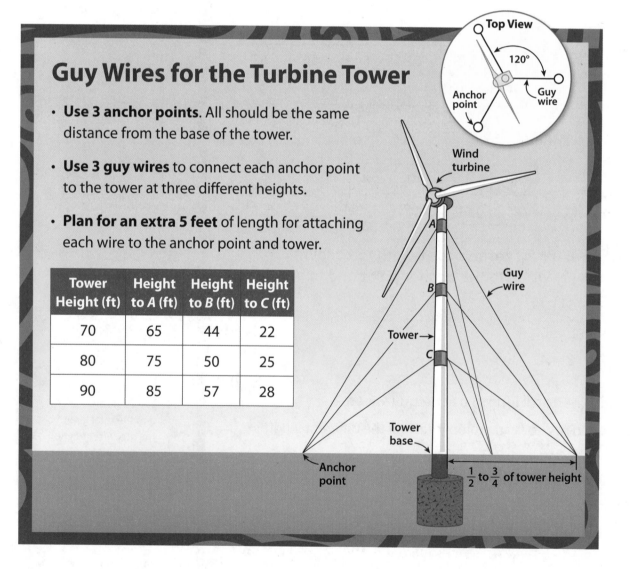

Guy Wires for the Turbine Tower

- **Use 3 anchor points**. All should be the same distance from the base of the tower.

- **Use 3 guy wires** to connect each anchor point to the tower at three different heights.

- **Plan for an extra 5 feet** of length for attaching each wire to the anchor point and tower.

Tower Height (ft)	Height to A (ft)	Height to B (ft)	Height to C (ft)
70	65	44	22
80	75	50	25
90	85	57	28

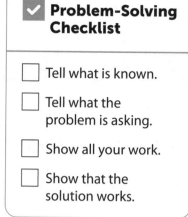

Top View

120°

Anchor point

Guy wire

Wind turbine

A

Guy wire

B

Tower →

C

Tower base

Anchor point

$\frac{1}{2}$ to $\frac{3}{4}$ of tower height

Plan It

➤ **Answer these questions to help you start thinking about a plan.**

  a. What height will you use for the tower of the wind turbine?

  b. How far from the base of the turbine will the anchor points be? How can you show that this distance is between $\frac{1}{2}$ and $\frac{3}{4}$ of the tower height?

Solve It

➤ **Find a different solution for the Installing a Wind Turbine problem. Show all your work on a separate sheet of paper. You may want to use the Problem-Solving Tips to get started.**

PROBLEM-SOLVING TIPS

Math Toolkit grid paper, ruler, unit cubes

Key Terms

right triangle	hypotenuse	Pythagorean Theorem
square root of x	leg	rational number
perfect square	approximation	irrational number

Models You may want to use . . .

- a picture or diagram to organize the information you are given.
- the Pythagorean Theorem to find unknown side lengths of right triangles.
- perfect squares to help you find rational approximations of irrational numbers.

Reflect

Use Mathematical Practices As you work through the problem, discuss these questions with a partner.

- **Make Sense of Problems** How can you tell whether the lengths you calculate for the guy wires are reasonable?

- **Repeated Reasoning** What steps can you use to estimate the square root of a 4-digit number that is not a perfect square?

Discuss Models and Strategies

➤ **Read the problem. Write a solution on a separate sheet of paper. Remember, there can be lots of ways to solve a problem.**

Designing a Food-Waste Digester

A city near Adnan's farm is planning to build a biogas plant. At the plant, food waste from the city and feed waste from local farms, including Adnan's, will be loaded into tanks called digesters. Inside the digesters, bacteria will break down the waste and produce a combination of gases called biogas—a renewable energy source.

A team of engineers is designing the digesters at the biogas plant. Read through their notes, and then help them make a design for the digesters.

Design for Food-Waste Digesters

The digesters will have a cone-shaped portion below ground, a cylinder-shaped portion above ground, and a dome-shaped top.

Requirements:

Measurement	Minimum	Maximum
Volume (not including dome)	1,400 m³	2,000 m³
Diameter of digester	10 m	22 m
Height of cylinder	5 m	12 m
Diameter-to-height ratio for cylinder	2 : 1	4 : 1

Also, the height of the cone should be about $\frac{1}{12}$ of the diameter.

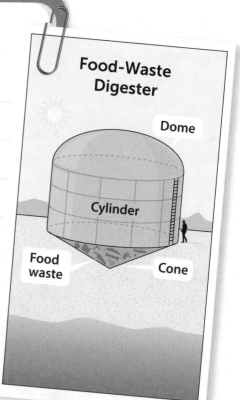

Food-Waste Digester

Dome

Cylinder

Food waste

Cone

WHAT WE NEED TO DO:

- Provide a design that shows the diameter of the digester and the heights of the cylinder and cone. Do not worry about the height of the dome for now.

- Show that the design meets all of the requirements.

Plan It and Solve It

➤ **Find a solution to the Designing a Food-Waste Digester problem.**

Write a detailed plan and support your answer. Be sure to include:

- a design for the food-waste digester that includes its diameter and the heights of the cylinder and cone.

- evidence that your design meets all of the requirements listed in the notes.

PROBLEM-SOLVING TIPS

Math Toolkit compass, grid paper, ruler

Key Terms

cylinder	cone	diameter
radius	volume	irrational number
π	approximation	sum

Sentence Starters

- If I choose . . . for the diameter of the digester, then the height of the cylinder should be between . . . and . . .

- If I choose . . . for the diameter of the digester, then the height of the cone should be about . . .

Reflect

Use Mathematical Practices As you work through the problem, discuss these questions with a partner.

- **Persevere** Does your first design meet all of the requirements? If not, how can you adjust your design?

- **Use Structure** Which dimension has the greatest effect on the volume of the digester—the diameter, the height of the cylinder, or the height of the cone? Explain.

In the United States, the second largest municipal solid waste sent to landfills is food.

Persevere On Your Own

➤ **Read the problem. Write a solution on a separate sheet of paper.**

Fencing a Solar Farm

An energy company is planning to rent part of Adnan's farm. The company will install solar panels on the land to help produce electricity for a nearby city. Read this email between two employees of the energy company, and help complete the assignment.

To: Emily
Subject: Fencing for New Solar Farm

Hi Emily,

We are planning to install 16,000 solar panels on Adnan's farm. We estimate that we can install between 770 and 850 solar panels per acre.

Our rental agreement allows Adnan to graze his sheep underneath the panels, which means we'll need to build a fence suitable for sheep around the land we rent. To keep the cost of fencing down, we are planning to rent a square piece of land. We can spend up to $8,000 for fencing.

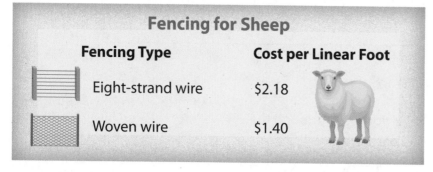

Fencing for Sheep

Fencing Type	Cost per Linear Foot
Eight-strand wire	$2.18
Woven wire	$1.40

YOUR ASSIGNMENT:
- Estimate the number of acres of land we need to rent.
- Estimate our cost to fence the land with each type of fencing.
- Determine which type or types of fencing we can afford.

Thank you!

Kimani

P.S. One acre is equal to 43,560 square feet. You might need this fact for your calculations.

Solve It

➤ **Find a solution to the Fencing a Solar Farm problem.**

- Estimate how many acres of land the energy company needs to rent to have enough space for 16,000 solar panels.

- Estimate the energy company's cost to fence the land with each type of fencing.

- Determine which type or types of fencing the company can afford with their fencing budget of $8,000.

Reflect

Use Mathematical Practices After you complete the problem, choose one of these questions to discuss with a partner.

- **Reason Mathematically** How did you estimate the side length of the square piece of land?

- **Critique Reasoning** How many feet of fencing does your partner suggest the company buy? Will this amount of fencing be enough to enclose the land needed for the solar panels? Explain.

Sheep have rectangular shaped pupils. This helps them have better peripheral vision to view their surroundings.

In this unit you learned to . . .

Skill	Lesson
Recognize numbers as perfect squares and perfect cubes.	23
Take the square root or cube root of a number to solve problems.	23
Know every rational number can be written as a repeating or a terminating decimal.	24
Write repeating decimals as fractions.	24
Find rational approximations of irrational numbers and locate them on the number line.	25
Explain the Pythagorean Theorem and its converse.	26
Apply the Pythagorean Theorem to find an unknown length in a figure or distance between two points in the coordinate plane.	27, 28
Know the volume formulas for cones, cylinders, and spheres and use them to solve problems.	28
Actively participate in discussions by asking questions and rephrasing or building on your classmates' ideas.	23–28

Think about what you have learned.

➤ **Use words, numbers, and drawings.**

1 The most important topic I learned is _____ because . . .

2 The hardest thing I learned to do is _____ because . . .

3 I could use more practice with . . .

➤ **Review the unit vocabulary. Put a check mark by items you can use in speaking and writing. Look up the meaning of any terms you do not know.**

Math Vocabulary   **Academic Vocabulary**

☐ cone   ☐ perfect cube   ☐ approximate
                                                             (verb)
☐ converse of the   ☐ perfect square
   Pythagorean Theorem   ☐ exact
                                ☐ Pythagorean Theorem
☐ cube root of x ☐ integer
                                ☐ real numbers
☐ irrational number   ☐ product
                                ☐ square root of x
☐ legs   ☐ prove
   (of a right triangle)

➤ **Use the unit vocabulary to complete the problems.**

1 How are rational numbers and irrational numbers alike and different? Use at least three math or academic vocabulary terms in your explanation.
Underline each term you use. Give an example of each type of number.

2 Is −5 a square root of 25? Explain.

3 Describe a perfect cube. Use two math or academic vocabulary terms in your answer. Underline each term you use.

4 The answer to a question is *Use the Pythagorean Theorem.* What might the question be?

➤ **Use what you have learned to complete these problems.**

1 A square table has an area of $\frac{49}{64}$ m². What is the perimeter of the table?
Show your work.

SOLUTION _____

2 Decide if each statement about decimals or fractions is true or false.

Choose *True* or *False* for each statement.

	True	False
a. The fractions $\frac{1}{9}$ and $\frac{11}{99}$ are equal to the same repeating decimal.	○	○
b. The fraction $\frac{3}{8}$ is equal to a repeating decimal.	○	○
c. The numbers 0.3 and $0.\overline{3}$ are equal to the same fraction.	○	○
d. The fraction $\frac{2}{11}$ is equal to a repeating decimal.	○	○

3 Consider the values $\frac{\pi}{5}$, $-\sqrt{2}$, $-\sqrt{19}$, and $\pi - 7$. Plot and label the approximate location of each value on the number line. ($\pi \approx 3.14$)

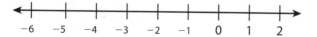

4 Raymond draws a right triangle with side lengths 9, 12, and 15. He says that if he divides each side length by 4, the new triangle will be a right triangle. Is Raymond correct? Explain your reasoning.

SOLUTION _____

_____

_____

5 Maddie is mailing some field hockey equipment to her sister. She wants to use the box shown. Can she close the box with a 30-in. field hockey stick inside it? Explain your reasoning.

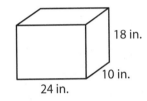

18 in.

10 in.

24 in.

SOLUTION _____

_____

6 A cylinder and a cone have the same radius and the same volume. The height of the cylinder is 9 cm. What is the height of the cone?

A 3 cm   **B** 9 cm   **C** 27 cm   **D** 81 cm

7 What is the distance between the points (3, −3) and (−1, 2)? Round your answer to the nearest tenth. Record your answer on the grid. Then fill in the bubbles.

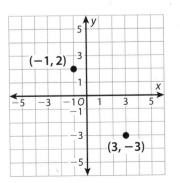

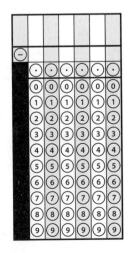

Performance Task

➤ **Answer the questions and show all your work on separate paper.**

In an adventure video game, players collect cubes. Each cube is labeled with its volume:

Red cube: 64 in.^{3}	Gold cube: $\frac{729}{64}$ in.^{3}
Blue cube: 343 in.^{3}	White cube: $\frac{8}{27}$ ft^3
Green cube: $\frac{125}{8}$ in.^{3}	Black cube: $\frac{125}{216}$ ft^3

Players use cubes to solve puzzles to unlock doors to new levels. First, write and solve an equation to find the edge length of each cube. Then solve the puzzles to unlock Doors One and Two. Identify the cubes that will open each door. Explain your reasoning.

At Door One, players have red, blue, green, and gold cubes.

- Two different cubes unlock Door One.

- One of the cubes has a face with an area of $\frac{25}{4}$ in.^{2}.

- The sum of the edge lengths of the cubes is $\frac{13}{2}$ in.

At Door Two, players have blue, green, gold, white, and black cubes.

- Three different cubes unlock Door Two.
- The cubes must be used in order from greatest to least volume.
- The first cube has a volume of 1,000 in.^{3}.
- The last cube has a face with an area of 49 in.^{2}.

Reflect

Use Mathematical Practices After you complete the task, choose one of the following questions to answer.

- **Use Reasoning** How are a cube's edge lengths related to its volume and area of its faces?

- **Be Precise** How could you test your solutions to prove that they solve the puzzles?

Unit 7

Statistics

Two-Variable Data and Fitting a Linear Model

✔ **Self Check** | Before starting this unit, check off the skills you know below.
As you complete each lesson, see how many more skills you can check off!

I can . . .	Before	After
Make and use scatter plots to recognize and describe patterns and associations in two-variable data.	☐	☐
Assess linear models for good fit to a set of data.	☐	☐
Write and interpret equations for linear models that are good lines of fit for data.	☐	☐
Understand and identify associations in two-variable categorical data by displaying frequencies in two-way tables.	☐	☐
Construct and interpret two-way tables with relative frequencies.	☐	☐
Explain my ideas about two-variable data clearly by using models to show why the ideas make sense for the problem.	☐	☐

➤ **You have learned about functions, relationships, and rates of change. Label each graph of a function with the labels below. You may use the same graph of a function for more than one label.**

increasing function	decreasing function	linear function
constant rate of change	varying rate of change	nonlinear function

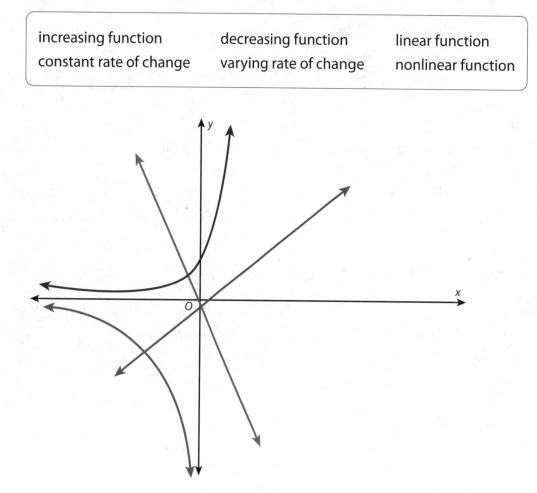

Compare your answers with a partner and explain your thinking. Discuss the answers on which you disagree. You may revise or add to your work.

Dear Family,

This week your student is learning to make and use **scatter plots**. A scatter plot is a graph that shows two-variable data plotted as ordered pairs. Scatter plots are useful tools for revealing relationships between the two variables.

Your student will be learning to recognize different types of relationships in the data sets by describing patterns he or she sees in the graphed data. A scatter plot gives you a visual way to identify if there is a relationship, or an **association**, between the variables.

➤ **ONE WAY** two-variable data can show a relationship is to have a **linear association**.

When there is a linear association, the data points appear to form a line.

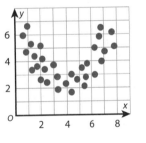

➤ **ANOTHER WAY** is to have a **nonlinear association**.

When there is a nonlinear association, the data points will form a pattern such as a curve, but not a line.

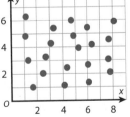

➤ **ANOTHER WAY** is to have **no association**.

When there is no association, the data points are not clustered together in any noticeable pattern.

> ▶ Use the next page to start a conversation about scatter plots.

Activity Thinking About Scatter Plots

➤ **Do this activity together to investigate scatter plots in real life.**

Scatter plots are useful to determine relationships between two variables. They can be used in many real-world contexts! For example, this graph shows the relationship between age and the amount of time spent doing homework.

Homework Time

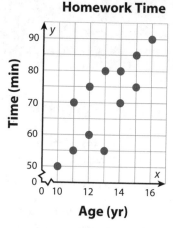

? How would you describe the relationship between these two variables? What other situations in your everyday life would have this same relationship?

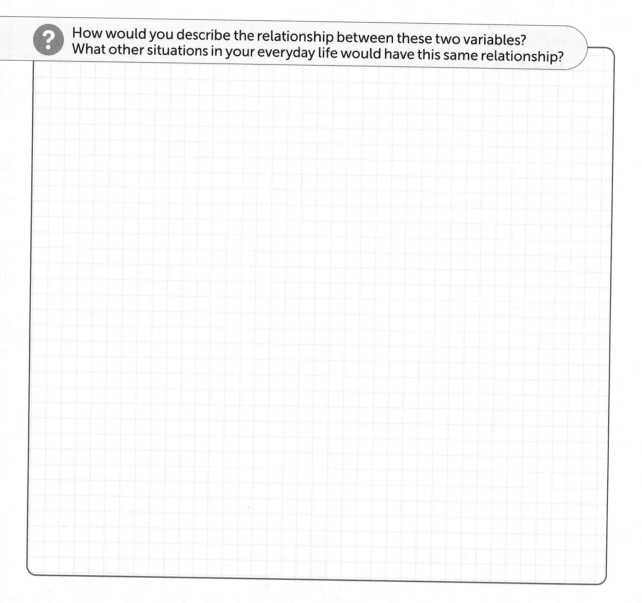

Explore Scatter Plots

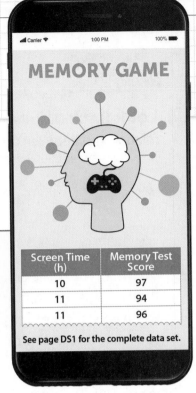

Previously, you learned how to analyze one-variable data in dot plots. In this lesson, you will learn about analyzing two-variable data.

➤ **Use what you know to try to solve the problem below.**

Twenty middle schoolers use an app to play a memory game. The app tracks data for two variables. The first variable is the number of hours per week that the middle schoolers spent on screen time. The second variable is the students' scores on a memory test. Use **Data Set: Memory Game** to plot the data as ordered pairs. Describe the shape of the data.

Screen Time (h)	Memory Test Score
10	97
11	94
11	96

See page DS1 for the complete data set.

 TRY IT

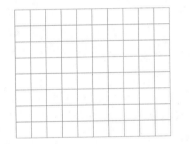 **Math Toolkit** graph paper, graphing calculator

DISCUSS IT

Ask: How did you decide which variable should go on the *x*-axis and which variable should go on the *y*-axis?

Share: I started by . . .

Learning Targets SMP 1, SMP 2, SMP 3, SMP 4, SMP 5, SMP 6
- Construct and interpret scatter plots for bivariate measurement data to investigate patterns such as clustering, outliers, positive or negative association, linear association, and nonlinear association.
- For scatter plots that suggest a linear association, informally fit a straight line, and informally assess the model fit by judging the closeness of the data points to the line.

CONNECT IT

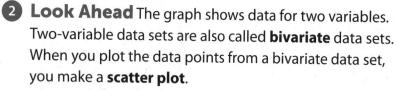

1 **Look Back** Describe the shape of the data. What do you notice about the relationship between the two variables?

2 **Look Ahead** The graph shows data for two variables. Two-variable data sets are also called **bivariate** data sets. When you plot the data points from a bivariate data set, you make a **scatter plot**.

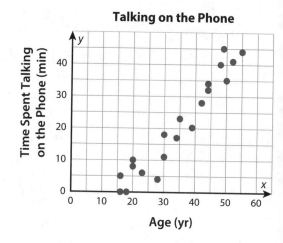

Scatter plots can visually show an **association**, or relationship, between the variables. When the points follow a linear pattern, they can be *modeled* by a straight line and have a **linear association**.

a. How does the scatter plot show that age and time spent talking on the phone have a linear association?

b. Is it possible to draw a line that includes every data point? Explain.

c. Linear association can be positive or negative. A **positive association** occurs when one variable tends to increase while the other increases. A **negative association** occurs when one variable tends to decrease while the other increases. Is there a positive or negative association between age and time spent talking on the phone? Explain.

3 **Reflect** What do you think a scatter plot that does not have a linear association might look like?

Prepare for Analyzing Scatter Plots and Fitting a Linear Model to Data

1 Think about what you know about data and statistics. Fill in each box. Use words, numbers, and pictures. Show as many ideas as you can.

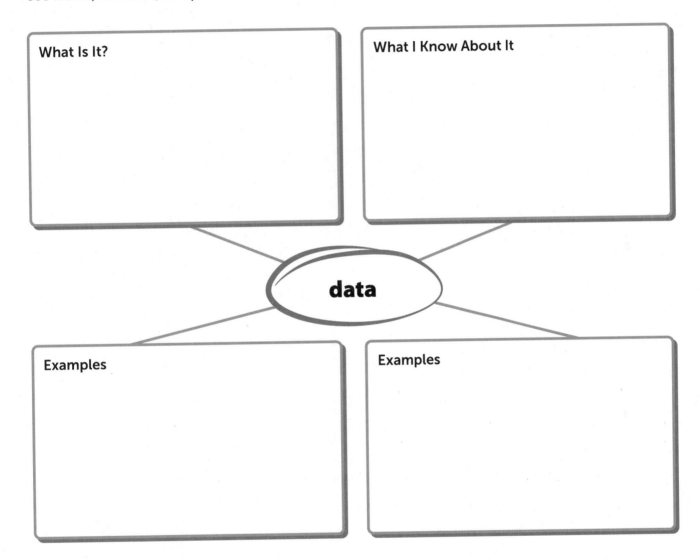

What Is It?

What I Know About It

data

Examples

Examples

2 Name some ways data can be displayed. Explain when each display might be more useful.

3 The table shows the average adult weight and average life expectancy for 12 dog breeds.

a. Plot the data as ordered pairs. Describe the shape of the data. Show your work.

Average Weight (lb)	Life Expectancy (yr)
115	6.5
125	7
90	8.9
57.5	10.3
62.5	12.3
45	12
70	11
4.9	12.4
25	12.7
12	13.4
16	11
5	14.7

SOLUTION _____

_____

b. Check your answer to problem 3a. Show your work.

Develop Using a Scatter Plot to Analyze Data

➤ **Read and try to solve the problem below.**

Year	Number of Attendees		Year	Number of Attendees
2001	149		2009	3,996
2002	1,015		2010	5,894
2003	449		2011	9,771
2004	755		2012	7,999
2005	1,476		2013	14,875
2006	1,390		2014	13,877
2007	2,697		2015	22,312
2008	5,001			

A city hosts an anime festival every year. The number of attendees over a span of 15 years is shown in the table. Describe any relationship between the variables. Is there a linear association between the variables?

TRY IT

Math Toolkit calculator, graph paper, graphing calculator

DISCUSS IT

Ask: How did you determine if there was a linear association?

Share: The strategy I used was . . .

➤ **Explore different ways to understand analyzing data in scatter plots.**

A city hosts an anime festival every year. The number of attendees over a span of 15 years is shown in the table. Describe any relationship between the variables. Is there a linear association between the variables?

Year	Number of Attendees	Year	Number of Attendees
2001	149	2009	3,996
2002	1,015	2010	5,894
2003	449	2011	9,771
2004	755	2012	7,999
2005	1,476	2013	14,875
2006	1,390	2014	13,877
2007	2,697	2015	22,312
2008	5,001		

Picture It

You can make a scatter plot.

Choose the variable for each axis. Plot the data as ordered pairs.

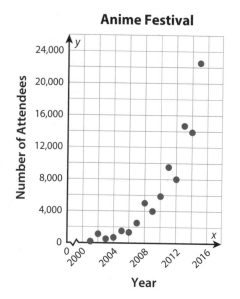

Analyze It

You can analyze the scatter plot to look for patterns in the data.

A data pattern with points that approximate a straight line shows a linear association between the variables.

A data pattern that is not linear shows a **nonlinear association** between the variables.

If there is no pattern at all in the data points, there is **no association** between the variables.

©Curriculum Associates, LLC   Copying is not permitted.

➤ **Use the problem from the previous page to help you understand how to use scatter plots to analyze data.**

 Look at **Picture It** and **Analyze It**. Describe the pattern of the data points in the scatter plot. What association is there between the variables?

2 Describe the relationship between the year and the number of attendees.

3 Would a scatter plot showing the number of attendees on the horizontal axis and the year on the vertical axis show a different association? Explain.

4 The scatter plot shows the ages of 10 attendees at the anime festival and the number of action figures they bought. What association is there between the variables? How do you know?

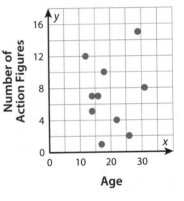

Anime Collectibles

5 How does a scatter plot help you identify the association between the variables in a bivariate data set?

6 **Reflect** Think about all the models and strategies you have discussed today. Describe how one of them helped you better understand how to solve the **Try It** problem.

Apply It

➤ **Use what you learned to solve these problems.**

7 Does the scatter plot show a *linear association*, a *nonlinear association*, or *no association* between the variables? Explain.

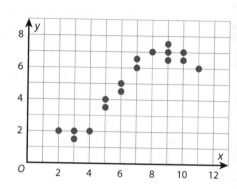

8 Which scatter plot shows a linear association?

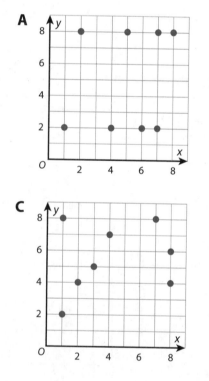

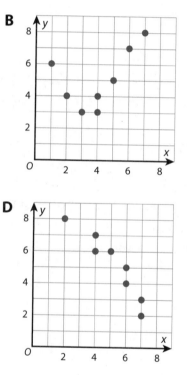

9 The scatter plot shows the gold medal times for the men's Olympic 100-meter dash for several years. Is there a *linear association*, a *nonlinear association*, or *no association* between the year and the winning time? Describe any relationship you see between the variables.

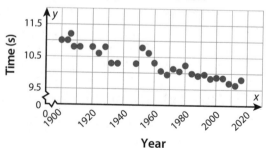

100-Meter Dash

Name:

Practice Using a Scatter Plot to Analyze Data

➤ **Study the Example showing how to describe an association between two variables. Then solve problems 1–4.**

Example

The data compare the amount of time people spent meditating and the number of headaches they got over a one-week period. Describe any association between these two variables.

Meditation and Headaches

Number of Headaches (y-axis): 0, 4, 8, 12, 16
Time (min) (x-axis): 0, 4, 8, 12, 16, 20

Meditation (min)	Number of Headaches
14	5
18	4
0	15
5	11
12	5
10	8
15	4
8	9
4	10
16	6

The points follow a linear pattern. There is a linear association between the two variables.

1 The dimension data for 15 rectangles are recorded. Use **Data Set: Rectangle Dimensions** to make a scatter plot of the data relating each length to its width. Describe any association between the lengths and widths.

Rectangle Dimensions

Length (in.)	Width (in.)
3	3
2	3
4	1

See page DS1 for the complete data set.

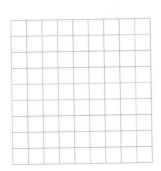

2 The scatter plot shows the pitch speed and hit speed for 10 swings by a certain baseball player. *Pitch speed* is the speed at which a baseball is thrown by the pitcher. *Hit speed* is the speed at which a ball travels after the batter hits it.

Baseball Pitch and Hit

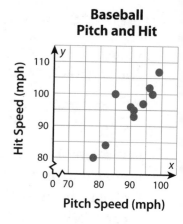

a. Describe any association between these two variables. Explain your reasoning.

b. Would you expect a pitch of 80 mph or a pitch of 90 mph to have a higher hit speed? Explain.

3 How would the rate of change between two variables with a linear association differ from the rate of change between two variables with a nonlinear association?

4 Students at Central Middle School survey their classmates on a number of different topics. Which pair of variables from the survey would be most likely to have no association?

A   test scores and number of missing assignments

B   number of absences and number of missing assignments

C   distance from home to school and number of visits to the doctor's office in one year

D   distance from home to school and driving time

Develop Assessing Linear Models for Good Fit

➤ **Read and try to solve the problem below.**

Avery is saving money to buy her first car. A used car lot nearby has 15 cars for sale. The scatter plot shows a linear association between the price and the age of the 15 cars. Drawing a line that models or follows the pattern of the data can help Avery determine the age of a car she can afford.

Four lines are drawn on the scatter plot. Which line do you think is a good model for the data? Explain your choice.

Used Cars

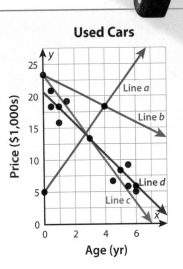

TRY IT

DISCUSS IT

Ask: How did you choose which line you thought was a good model?

Share: At first, I thought . . .

➤ **Explore different ways to decide whether a line is a good fit for data.**

Avery is saving money to buy her first car. A used car lot nearby has 15 cars for sale. The scatter plot shows a linear association between the price and the age of the 15 cars. Drawing a line that models or follows the pattern of the data can help Avery determine the age of a car she can afford.

Four lines are drawn on the scatter plot. Which line do you think is a good fit for the data? Explain your choice.

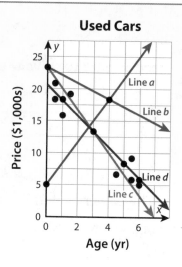

Analyze It

You can look for lines that follow the pattern of most of the data points.

A good **line of fit** closely follows the pattern of the data and models the type of linear association.

The data have a negative association. **Line *a*** does not follow the pattern of most of the data points. The line passes through a point that is far away from the rest of the data. This point is an outlier.

Line *c* follows the pattern of data.

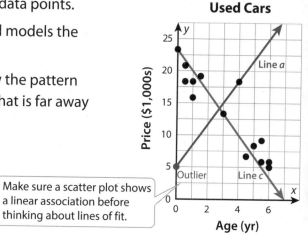

Make sure a scatter plot shows a linear association before thinking about lines of fit.

Analyze It

You can look for lines that go through groups of data points.

Data points grouped close together form a cluster. A good line of fit often passes through the center of clusters.

Line *b* passes through two data points above the clusters.

Line *d* passes through both clusters.

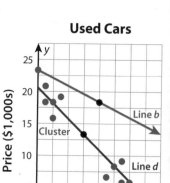

➤ **Use the problem from the previous page to help you understand how to decide whether a line is a good fit for data.**

1 Look at the first **Analyze It**. Is line *a* a good line of fit for the data? Is line *c* a good line of fit? Explain.

2 Look at the second **Analyze It**. Is line *b* a good line of fit for the data? Is line *d* a good line of fit? Explain.

3 A new line *e* is drawn on the scatter plot as shown. Is line *e* a good line of fit for the data? Explain.

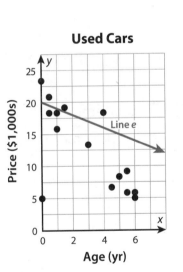

Used Cars

4 How can you tell if a line is a good line of fit for data with a linear association?

5 **Reflect** Think about all the models and strategies you have discussed today. Describe how one of them helped you understand how to decide whether a line is a good fit for data.

Apply It

➤ **Use what you learned to solve these problems.**

6 Describe how to determine whether a point in a data set is an outlier. How does a good line of fit take an outlier into account?

7 This scatter plot shows a linear association between the drop height and the maximum speed for 12 steel roller coasters. Which is a good line of fit for the data? Select all that apply.

A Line *a*

B Line *b*

C Line *c*

D Line *d*

E Line *e*

Roller Coasters

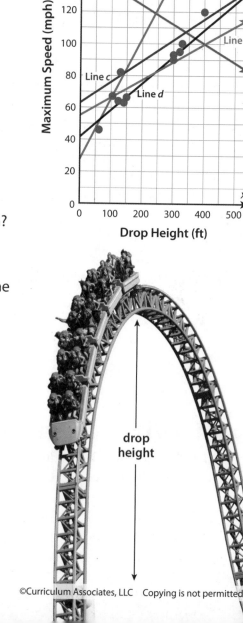

8 Look at the scatter plot in problem 7.

a. Does the scatter plot show a positive or negative association?

b. What does the association suggest about drop height and the maximum speed of the steel roller coasters?

c. Choose one of the data clusters. Explain what the cluster suggests about roller coasters.

drop
height

Practice Assessing Linear Models for Good Fit

➤ **Study the Example showing possible good lines of fit. Then solve problems 1–5.**

Example

Researchers timed 20 children who placed pegs into a peg board. The task tested the children's ability to grasp and manipulate objects. The scatter plot shows the linear association between the age of the child and the time spent to complete the task. Decide whether each line is a good fit for the data. **Explain your reasoning.**

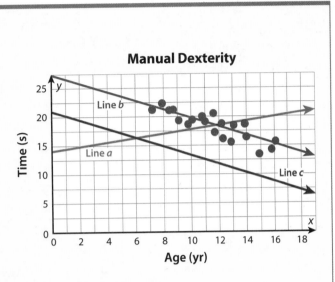

Line *a* is not a good fit because it models a positive association. The data show a negative association.

Line *b* is a good fit because it models a negative association and is close to all the data points.

Line *c* is not a good fit. Although it models a negative association, the line is below all of the data points.

1. Analyze the data in the scatter plot from the Example.

   a. Identify any outliers.

   b. What does the association suggest about a child's age and his or her ability to complete the test?

2. How can you decide whether a line is a good line of fit for data on a scatter plot?

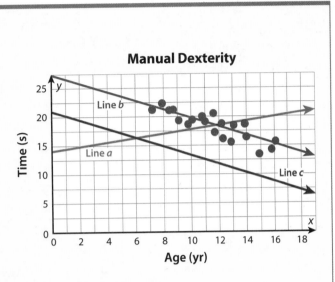

Vocabulary

line of fit
a line drawn on a scatter plot to approximately model the relationship between two sets of data.

outlier
a data value that is much greater or much less than most of the other values in the data set.

3 Ten adults were asked their age and the amount of time they watch cable television news each week. The scatter plot shows the data from the survey. Is line *a* a good line of fit for the data? Explain.

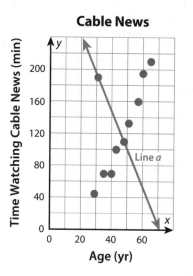

4 Which line is a good line of fit? Explain your choice.

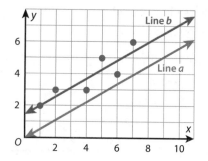

5 Alison says that (6, 4) is an outlier in the scatter plot in problem 4. Do you agree with Alison? Explain.

Develop Fitting a Linear Model Informally

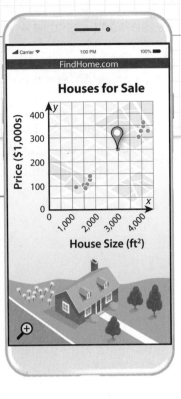

Houses for Sale

House Size (ft²)

➤ **Read and try to solve the problem below.**

The scatter plot shows data for the size and price of 12 houses for sale in a small town. Draw a good line of fit for these data. Explain why you think it is a good fit.

TRY IT

Math Toolkit calculator, straightedges, string

➤ **Explore different ways to informally fit a line to data.**

The scatter plot shows data for the size and price of 12 houses for sale in a small town. Draw a good line of fit for these data. Explain why you think it is a good fit.

Houses for Sale

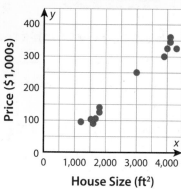

Picture It

You can use data clusters to draw a good line of fit.

If the data have clusters, a good line of fit is likely to pass through the center of the clusters. Use a straightedge to draw a line that goes through the centers of the clusters.

Houses for Sale

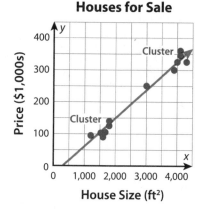

Model It

You can calculate the mean of the data for each variable to find the **balance point**.

Recall that the mean of a data set is the sum of all the data points divided by the number of data points.

mean size of home: $\frac{33,000}{12} = 2,750$

mean price of home: $\frac{2,563}{12} \approx 213.6$

Good lines of fit often pass through or near the balance point. The balance point is usually not a data point.

The balance point for these data is (2750, 213.6).

Houses for Sale

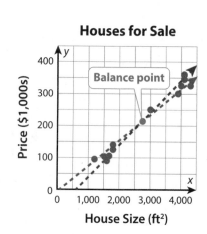

©Curriculum Associates, LLC Copying is not permitted.

CONNECT IT

➤ **Use the problem from the previous page to help you understand how to informally fit a line to data.**

1 Look at **Picture It**. Explain why data clusters can be used to determine a line of fit for the data.

2 Look at **Model It**. You can draw many different lines that would pass through the balance point. Not all would make good lines of fit. What else would you need to consider to draw a good line of fit that passes through the balance point?

3 Did you or any of your classmates use a different method to draw a good line of fit? Explain.

4 Think about data with linear association. Is it possible to draw more than one good line of fit for a scatter plot? Explain.

5 **Reflect** Think about all the models and strategies you have discussed today. Describe how one of them helped you better understand how to solve the **Try It** problem.

Apply It

➤ **Use what you learned to solve these problems.**

6 The table shows average speed and gas mileage for 6 cars.

a. Complete the scatter plot for the data.

Gas Mileage

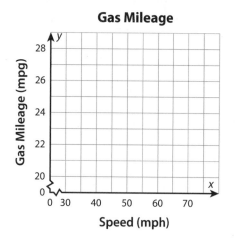

Speed (miles per hour)	Gas Mileage (miles per gallon)
35	27.1
65	25.3
60	25.4
40	26.2
45	26.9
50	25.6

b. Calculate the balance point of the data. Plot the point as a triangle on the scatter plot. Show your work.

SOLUTION _____

c. Draw a good line of fit for the data on the scatter plot. Explain your reasoning.

7 The scatter plot shows the standing long jump distances and heights for 15 middle school students. Draw a good line of fit for the data. Explain your reasoning.

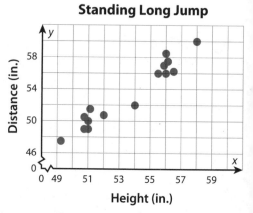

Standing Long Jump

Name:

Practice Fitting a Linear Model Informally

➤ **Study the Example showing how to informally fit a line to data with a linear association. Then solve problems 1–5.**

Example

The scatter plot shows the age and price of 10 cars at a car dealership. Explain how you could use the data set of the scatter plot to find the balance point of the data. Then explain how you could use the balance point to draw a good line of fit for the data.

Find the mean of the x-values and the mean of the y-values in the data set. These means are the coordinates of the balance point. Then plot the balance point on the scatter plot. Draw a line through the balance point that follows the general pattern of the data. It should be close to most of the data points. Ignore any outliers.

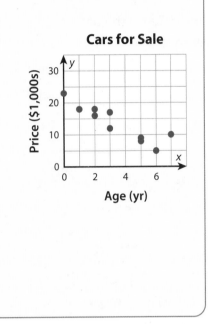

Cars for Sale

1. Is the linear association in the Example data positive or negative? Describe the relationship between the variables.

2. The scatter plot from the Example is repeated below. The data for the scatter plot are given in the table. Find and plot the balance point as a triangle. Use the balance point to draw a good line of fit for the data.

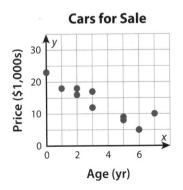

Cars for Sale

Age (yr)	Price ($1,000s)
0	23
1	18
2	18
2	16
3	17
3	12
5	9
5	8
6	5
7	10

③ Alanna says that a good line of fit has to include at least one data point that lies on the line. Explain why Alanna is not correct.

④ Draw a good line of fit for the data in the scatter plot. Describe any clusters or outliers that you notice.

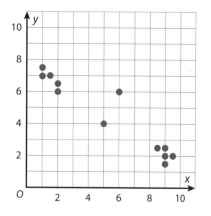

⑤ The scatter plot compares 10 daily high temperatures and the number of frozen fruit bars sold at a snack stand. The line of fit shown takes into account the outlier at (91, 10). Explain why it is not a good line of fit. Then draw a good line of fit.

©Curriculum Associates, LLC Copying is not permitted.

Refine Analyzing Scatter Plots and Fitting a Linear Model to Data

➤ **Complete the Example below. Then solve problems 1–8.**

Example

Mr. Ramírez records the temperature and the number of students who wear a coat to school for 12 Mondays. He makes a scatter plot for the data and draws three lines of fit. Which line is a good line of fit?

Look how you could use clusters and outliers.

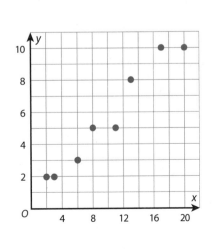

Coats and Temperatures

Line *c* passes through both clusters and is close to all the data points except the outlier. Line *a* goes through the outlier and is far away from many other data points. Line *b* passes through only one cluster and starts to rise away from the data pattern.

CONSIDER THIS . . .
Sometimes it is possible to draw more than one good line of fit.

SOLUTION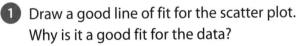

PAIR/SHARE
How does the line change when the outlier is considered?

Apply It

1 Draw a good line of fit for the scatter plot. Why is it a good fit for the data?

CONSIDER THIS . . .
Does a good line of fit have to pass through any data points?

PAIR/SHARE
Are there situations in which there is no good line of fit?

2 The percent of U.S. adults who use at least one social media platform was recorded for each of several years. Use **Data Set: Social Media Users** to determine what type of association the data show. How are the variables related? Show your work.

Social Media Users

Year	U.S. Adults (%)
2005	7
2006	11
2008	25

See page DS1 for the complete data set.

CONSIDER THIS ...
Data can show a linear association, a nonlinear association, or no association.

SOLUTION _____

_____

PAIR/SHARE
How many different ways can you describe a linear association?

3 Which line on the scatter plot is a good line of fit for the data?

A Line *a*

B Line *b*

C Line *c*

D All three lines

Isabella chose B as the correct answer. How might she have gotten that answer?

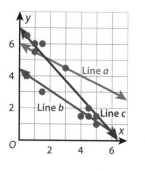

CONSIDER THIS ...
How can clusters of data help determine a good line of fit?

PAIR/SHARE
What do you look for in a good line of fit?

4 Xavier says that the line shown on the scatter plot is a good line of fit because the number of data points above and below the line is the same. Do you agree? Explain.

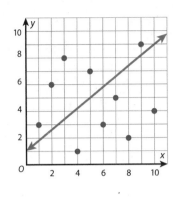

5 Which scatter plot has a linear association?

A
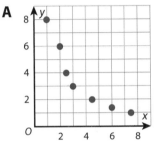

B
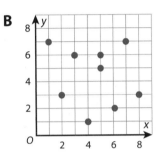

C
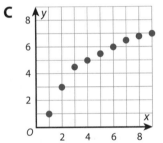

D
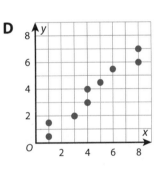

6 Tell whether each statement is *True* or *False*.

	True	False
a. A good line of fit must go through at least one data point.	○	○
b. A line of fit is good if all of the data points are fairly close to it.	○	○
c. A good line of fit almost always goes through the origin (0, 0).	○	○
d. There is always a line of fit for any set of data points.	○	○

7 The scatter plot shows the approximate number of adults and number of voters in the 10 most populous U.S. states in 2016.

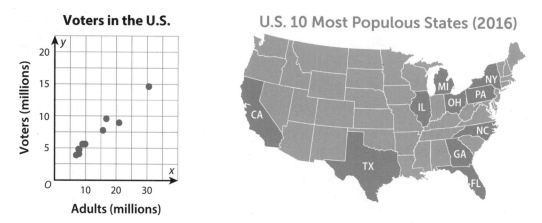

a. Explain how you know that the data have a linear association.

b. Do the data have a positive or negative association? Describe the relationship between the variables.

c. Draw a good line of fit for the data.

8 **Math Journal** Draw four scatter plots: one showing a positive linear association, one showing a negative linear association, one showing a nonlinear association, and one showing no association. Which of your four scatter plots can have good lines of fit for their data? Explain.

✓ End of Lesson Checklist

☐ **INTERACTIVE GLOSSARY** Find the entries for *association* and *line of fit*. Rewrite the definitions in your own words.

☐ **SELF CHECK** Go back to the Unit 7 Opener and see what you can check off.

Dear Family,

This week your student is learning how to write an equation of a good line of fit for data in a scatter plot. Previously, students learned how to informally fit lines to data. In this lesson, students will use the equations of these lines to analyze data.

A good line of fit approximates the data given. By finding an equation of the line, students can make reasonable predictions about data. Students can also interpret what the slope and y-intercept mean in context, like in the problem below.

Book club members record how many hours they spend at a library and how many pages they read on average each week. The data are shown in the scatter plot. Use an equation of the line of fit to predict how many pages a member will read if he spends 6 hours at the library.

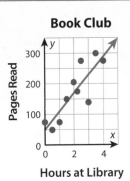

Book Club

Pages Read

Hours at Library

➤ **ONE WAY** to write an equation of the line of fit is to use two points on the line.

The line of fit appears to pass through (**0, 50**) and (**2.5, 200**).

$$\frac{\text{rise}}{\text{run}} = \frac{200 - 50}{2.5 - 0} = \frac{150}{2.5} = 60$$

The y-intercept is 50, so $y = 60x + 50$ is an equation of the line of fit.

➤ **ANOTHER WAY** is to use a point on the line and the y-intercept.

The line of fit goes through the point (**2.5, 200**) and has a y-intercept of **50**.

$$y = mx + b$$
$$200 = m(2.5) + 50$$
$$150 = 2.5m$$
$$m = 60$$

Using either method, the equation is $y = 60x + 50$. Substitute $x = 6$ to predict that the member will read approximately 410 pages if he spends 6 hours at the library.

> ▶ Use the next page to start a conversation about the equations of lines of fit.

Activity Thinking About Equations of Lines of Fit

➤ **Do this activity together to investigate equations of lines of fit in the real world.**

Using an equation of a line of fit can be helpful in many contexts. For example, a city planner could use data comparing time and population to predict the city's population in 50 years.

? What are some other real-world situations where an equation of a line of fit can be useful in making predictions?

Explore Writing an Equation of a Linear Model

Previously, you learned how to make scatter plots and fit lines to data. In this lesson, you will learn about using the equations of lines of fit to solve problems.

➤ **Use what you know to try to solve the problem below.**

Science teachers in 10 middle schools provide data about the time their students spend on hands-on projects throughout the year. The students also take a survey at the end of the year about whether they enjoy science class. The scatter plot shows the data and a good line of fit. Write an equation of the line of fit.

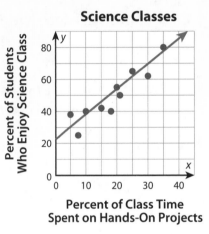

Science Classes

Percent of Students Who Enjoy Science Class (y-axis: 0, 20, 40, 60, 80)

Percent of Class Time Spent on Hands-On Projects (x-axis: 0, 10, 20, 30, 40)

TRY IT  **Math Toolkit** graph paper, graphing calculator

---

DISCUSS IT

Ask: What did you do first to find an equation of the line of fit?

Share: I started by . . .

◎ **Learning Target**   SMP 1, SMP 2, SMP 3, SMP 4, SMP 5, SMP 6
Use the equation of a linear model to solve problems in the context of bivariate measurement data, interpreting the slope and intercept.

1 **Look Back** What is an equation of the line of fit? How did you find the equation?

2 **Look Ahead** A good line of fit represents the data. The equation of the line models the association between the variables. You can use the equation to make reasonable predictions.

    a. What is the relationship between the slope of the line of fit and the rate of change in the equation? What does this suggest about hands-on projects in science classes?

    b. Suppose you know the percent of time a science class spends doing hands-on projects. How could you use your equation to predict the percent of students who enjoy science class?

3 **Reflect** Use your equation to predict the percent of students who will say they enjoy science class if the class does hands-on projects 15% of the time. Is it the same value as the actual data? Explain.

Prepare for Writing and Analyzing an Equation for Fitting a Linear Model to Data

1 Think about what you know about scatter plots that show linear associations. Fill in each box. Use words, numbers, and pictures. Show as many ideas as you can.

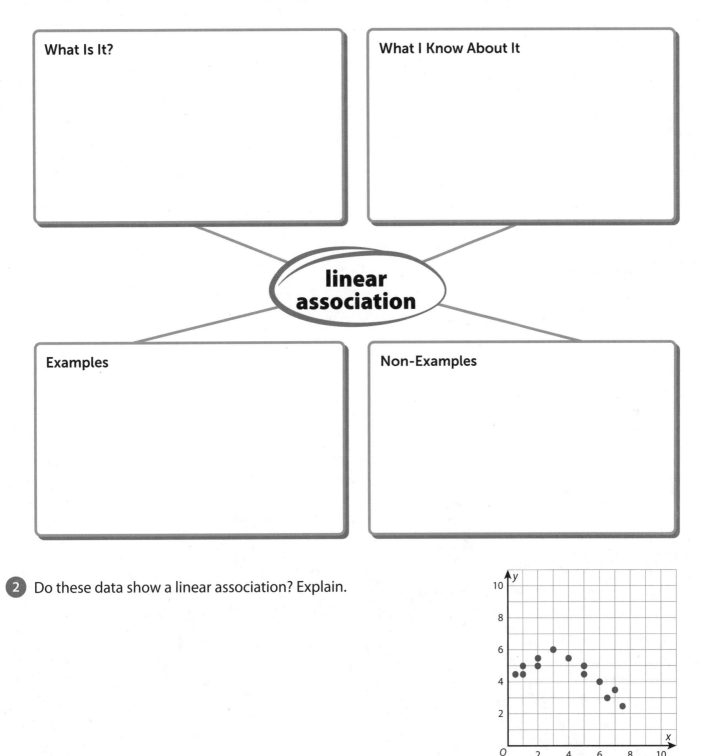

What Is It?

What I Know About It

linear association

Examples

Non-Examples

2 Do these data show a linear association? Explain.

3 This scatter plot shows the number of hours students spend playing outside and playing video games on a Sunday. A good line of fit is drawn through the data.

a. Write an equation of the line of fit. Show your work.

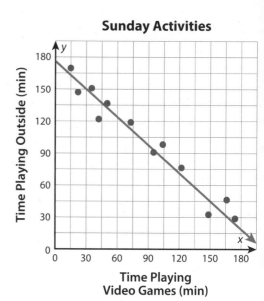

Sunday Activities

SOLUTION _____

b. Check your answer to problem 3a. Show your work.

Develop Writing and Interpreting an Equation of a Linear Model

➤ **Read and try to solve the problem below.**

The scatter plot shows data for 14 women ages 18–25. The graph shows their average resting heart rates and number of hours of physical activity each week. A good line of fit is drawn through the data.

A 20-year-old woman decides to exercise 2 more hours each week. How might this affect her average resting heart rate?

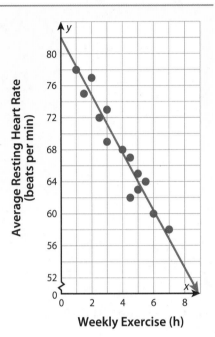

TRY IT

 **Math Toolkit** calculator, graph paper

DISCUSS IT

Ask: Why did you choose that strategy to find the heart rate?

Share: I started by . . .

LESSON 30 Write and Analyze an Equation for Fitting a Linear Model to Data   **729**

➤ **Explore different ways to write and interpret an equation of a linear model.**

The scatter plot shows data for 14 women ages 18–25. The graph shows their average resting heart rates and number of hours of physical activity each week. A good line of fit is drawn through the data.

A 20-year-old woman decides to exercise 2 more hours each week. How might this affect her average resting heart rate?

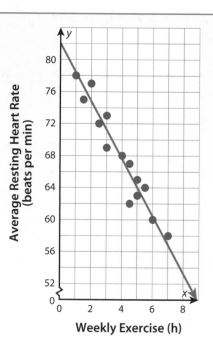

Weekly Exercise (h)

Picture It

You can estimate the slope of the line of fit using $\frac{\text{rise}}{\text{run}}$.

$$\frac{\text{rise}}{\text{run}} = -\frac{11}{3} \approx -3.7$$

The estimated slope of the line of fit is $-\frac{11}{3}$.

The y-intercept is about 82.

Model It

You can estimate the slope of the line of fit using the slope formula.

The line of fit appears to go through the points $(0, 82)$ and $(1, 78)$.

Slope: $\frac{78-82}{1-0} = \frac{-4}{1} = -4$

The estimated slope of the line of fit is -4. The y-intercept is 82.

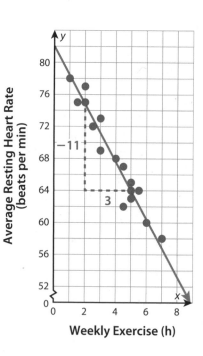

Weekly Exercise (h)

➤ **Use the problem from the previous page to help you understand how to write and interpret an equation of a linear model.**

1 Write the equations of the lines of fit for **Picture It** and for **Model It**. Use each equation to determine how exercising 2 more hours per week will affect the resting heart rate of a 20-year-old woman.

2 The equations of the lines of fit in problem 1 give different answers to the problem. Does this mean that one of the answers is wrong? Explain.

3 Would it be possible to answer the **Try It** problem without using an equation of the line of fit? Explain.

4 For what kinds of data questions would you need to find and use the whole equation of the line of fit?

5 **Reflect** Think about all the models and strategies you have discussed today. Describe how one of them helped you better understand how to write and interpret an equation of a linear model.

Apply It

➤ **Use what you learned to solve these problems.**

6　The scatter plot shows the stride lengths and heights for 10 middle school students. A good line of fit is drawn through data points (57.5, 22.8) and (63, 25). What is the slope of the line of fit? What does the slope say about how stride length changes when height is increased by 1 in.?

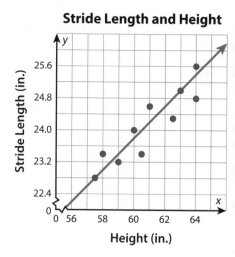

Stride Length and Height

7　Kazuko says that the line of fit for problem 6 is not a good fit because the rates of change between different pairs of data points do not always match the slope of the line of fit. Do you agree with Kazuko? Why or why not?

8　A teacher asks 12 students in his public speaking course the percent of time they feel anxious in class. This scatter plot shows the percent of time a student feels anxious and their current grade. Write an equation of the line of fit. Show your work.

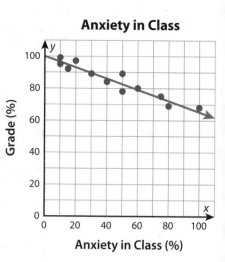

Anxiety in Class

SOLUTION _____

Name:

Practice Writing and Interpreting an Equation of a Linear Model

➤ **Study the Example showing how to write and interpret an equation of a linear model. Then solve problems 1–3.**

Example

The scatter plot shows the foot lengths and the hand lengths of 20 students. The foot length of Student A is 5 cm more than the foot length of Student B. About how much longer would you expect Student A's hand to be than Student B's?

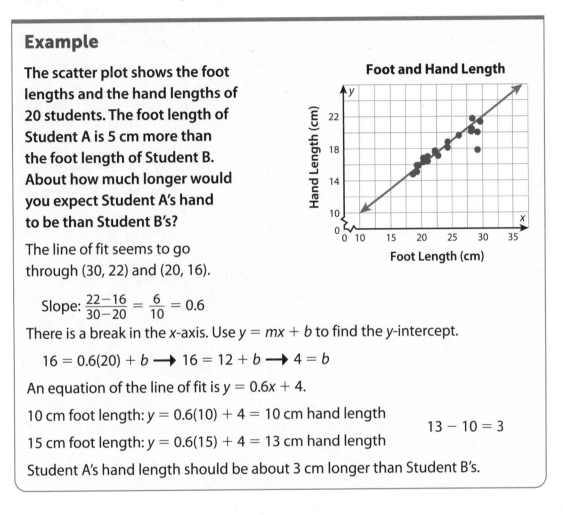

Foot and Hand Length

The line of fit seems to go through (30, 22) and (20, 16).

Slope: $\frac{22-16}{30-20} = \frac{6}{10} = 0.6$

There is a break in the x-axis. Use $y = mx + b$ to find the y-intercept.

$16 = 0.6(20) + b \longrightarrow 16 = 12 + b \longrightarrow 4 = b$

An equation of the line of fit is $y = 0.6x + 4$.

10 cm foot length: $y = 0.6(10) + 4 = 10$ cm hand length

15 cm foot length: $y = 0.6(15) + 4 = 13$ cm hand length

$13 - 10 = 3$

Student A's hand length should be about 3 cm longer than Student B's.

---

1 In the Example, suppose Student A's hand length was 4 cm longer than Student B's. About how much longer would you expect Student A's foot to be?

A 0.6 cm

B 6.7 cm

C 6.4 cm

D 2.4 cm

2 What does the y-intercept of the line of fit in the Example mean in terms of the problem? Does it make sense?

3 A middle school basketball team records the number of minutes they practice free throws before games. Then they record the percent of free throws they make during each game. The scatter plot shows the results. A good line of fit is drawn through the data.

Basketball Free Throws

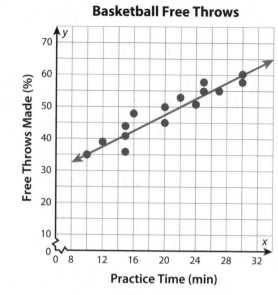

a. Write an equation of the line. Show your work.

SOLUTION _____

b. What can the team expect to happen to the percent of free throws they make during a game if they practice an additional 5 minutes before the game? Explain.

c. The basketball team makes 48% of free throws during a game. Based on the data, about how many minutes would you estimate they practiced before the game? Show your work.

Free throws made
48%

SOLUTION _____

Develop Analyzing a Linear Model to Make Predictions

➤ **Read and try to solve the problem below.**

The scatter plot shows the average amount several companies spend on online advertising and their average monthly sales. A good line of fit is drawn through the data. Suppose a company spends an average of $4,000 on advertising. What would you predict their average monthly sales to be?

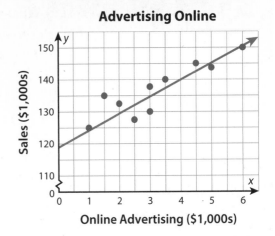

Advertising Online

TRY IT

🖊️ **Math Toolkit** calculator, graph paper

DISCUSS IT

Ask: How do you know your answer is reasonable?

Share: The problem is asking . . .

➤ **Explore different ways to analyze a linear model to make predictions.**

The scatter plot shows the average amount several companies spend on online advertising and their average monthly sales. A good line of fit is drawn through the data. Suppose a company spends an average of $4,000 on advertising. What would you predict their average monthly sales to be?

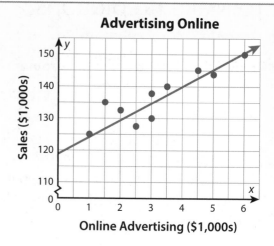

Picture It

You can analyze the line of fit at $x = 4$.

Draw a **vertical line** from $x = 4$ to the line of fit. Then draw a **horizontal line** from the intersection of the vertical line and the line of fit to the y-axis.

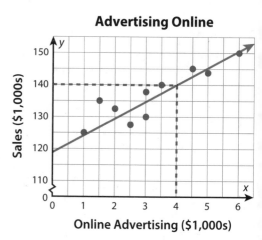

Model It

You can write an equation of the line of fit and substitute $x = 4$.

The y-intercept is about 118.

The line appears to go through (0, 118) and (3, 135).

slope: $\dfrac{135 - 118}{3 - 0} = \dfrac{17}{3} \approx 5.7$

An equation of the line of fit is $y = 5.7x + 118$.

$y = 5.7(4) + 118$

➤ **Use the problem from the previous page to help you understand how to analyze a linear model to make predictions.**

1 Look at **Picture It**. Why analyze the line of fit at $x = 4$? What value of sales is predicted for $4,000 in advertising?

2 Look at **Model It**. What value of sales is predicted for $4,000 in advertising?

3 Are the predictions from **Picture It** and **Model It** far apart? Is one prediction better than the other?

4 Does the **Model It** prediction mean that spending an average of $4,000 on online advertising will definitely result in average monthly sales of $140,800? Explain.

5 Suppose an average of more than $6,000 is spent on online advertising. Can the equation of the line of fit still be used to predict average monthly sales? Explain.

6 **Reflect** Think about all the models and strategies you have discussed today. Describe how one of them helped you better understand how to analyze a linear model to make predictions.

Apply It

➤ **Use what you learned to solve these problems.**

7 A hiking club goes on 10 different hikes. The scatter plot shows the data for the distance of each hike and the time it takes to complete it. The equation of the line of fit is $y = 30.9x + 2$. Which statements are true about the data? Select all that apply.

Hiking Club

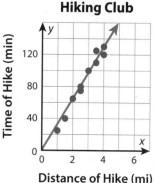

A The line of fit predicts that a 3.25-mile hike will take about 30.9 minutes to complete.

B The line of fit predicts that a 2.75-mile hike will take about 87 minutes to complete.

C If it takes 120 minutes to complete the hike, the line of fit predicts the distance of the hike as exactly 4 miles.

D The line of fit predicts that a hike that takes 45 minutes to complete is about 1.4 miles long.

E In general, the farther the hike, the longer it takes to complete.

8 The hiking club in problem 7 completes a 4-mile hike in 140 min. The equation of the line of fit predicts that the hike will take 125.6 min. Why are the two values different? Is the line of fit a good representation of the data? Explain.

9 The scatter plot shows employees' hourly pay and years of employment at a water park. A good line of fit represented by $y = 0.75x + 7$ is drawn through the data. Aiden predicts that an employee who makes $8.50 an hour has been working at the water park for 2 years. Is Aiden's prediction correct? Show your work.

Water Park Employment

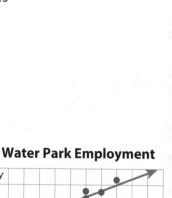

SOLUTION _____

Practice Analyzing a Linear Model to Make Predictions

➤ **Study the Example showing how to use a linear model to make predictions. Then solve problems 1–3.**

Example

Ten students record the time they spend reading each week. At the end of the year, they take a spelling test. The scatter plot shows the average weekly hours of reading time for each student and his or her score on the test. The equation of the line of fit is $y = 3.5x + 53$. Use the equation to predict the test score for a student who reads an average of 2 hours per week.

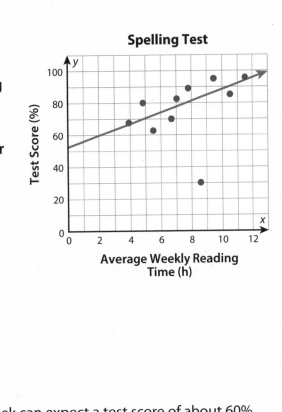

Substitute 2 for x in the equation of the line of fit.

$y = 3.5(2) + 53$

$y = 7 + 53$

$y = 60$

A student who reads 2 hours per week can expect a test score of about 60%.

1 One student in the Example reads an average of 8.6 hours a week outside of class and gets a 30% on the spelling test. The prediction from the line of fit is that the student would get an 83.1%. How can the prediction be so far away from its value?

2 A math teacher asks 20 of her middle school students how much time they spend on a computer after school. This scatter plot shows the amount of time in minutes each student spends on a computer and his or her math grade. The equation of the line of fit is $y = -0.13x + 92$.

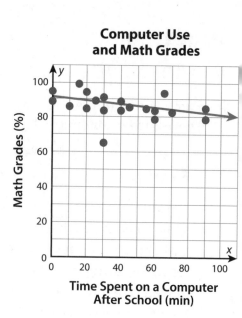

Computer Use and Math Grades

a. A student spends 80 min on a computer after school. What do you predict the student's math grade to be?

b. A student's math grade is 70%. What do you predict for the number of minutes the student spends on a computer after school? Show your work.

SOLUTION _____

3 This scatter plot shows the wait time for a roller coaster at an amusement park on a weekday and the outside temperature.

a. Write an equation of the line of fit. Show your work.

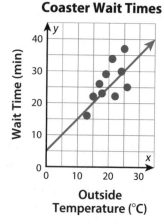

Temperature and Roller Coaster Wait Times

SOLUTION _____

b. Suppose the outside temperature is 0°C. Would you use the equation of the line of fit to predict the waiting time of a roller coaster? Explain.

Refine Writing and Analyzing an Equation for Fitting a Linear Model to Data

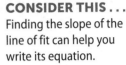

➤ **Complete the Example below. Then solve problems 1–8.**

CONSIDER THIS . . .
Finding the slope of the line of fit can help you write its equation.

Example

The scatter plot shows the lengths and weights of 10 adult corn snakes. A good line of fit passes through (1.4, 28) and (2.4, 36). Predict the likely weight of an adult corn snake that is 38 in. long.

Look at how you could show your work using the slope and y-intercept.

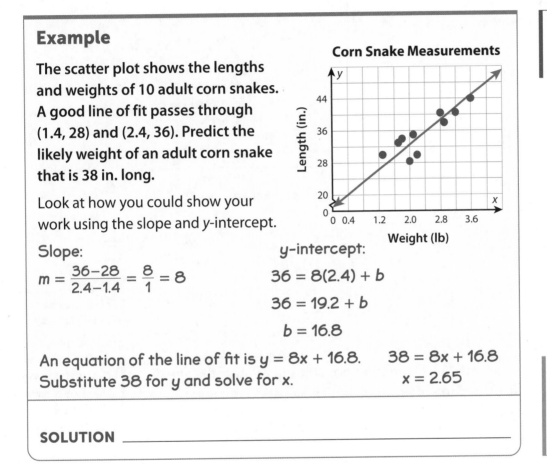

Corn Snake Measurements

Slope:

$$m = \frac{36-28}{2.4-1.4} = \frac{8}{1} = 8$$

y-intercept:

$$36 = 8(2.4) + b$$
$$36 = 19.2 + b$$
$$b = 16.8$$

An equation of the line of fit is $y = 8x + 16.8$. Substitute 38 for y and solve for x.

$$38 = 8x + 16.8$$
$$x = 2.65$$

PAIR/SHARE
How else can you use the scatter plot to make a prediction for the weight of a snake that is 38 in. long?

SOLUTION _____

Apply It

1 Use the information in the Example to predict the length of a corn snake that weighs 1.6 lb. Show your work.

CONSIDER THIS . . .
The equation of a line of fit can be used to make predictions about either variable.

PAIR/SHARE
Will the predicted values from a line of fit always match real data? Why or why not?

SOLUTION _____

2 A food truck vendor records the sales of cups of hot cocoa over a 10-day period. She also records each day's high temperature. The scatter plot shows the data and a good line of fit. Write an equation of the line of fit. Show your work.

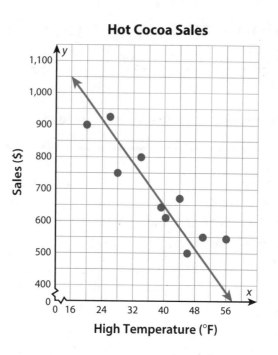

Hot Cocoa Sales

SOLUTION

3 The equation $y = -14.6x + 1,259.2$ is another possible equation of the line of fit in problem 2. What is the slope of the equation and what does it mean?

A The slope is 1,259.2. A temperature rise of 1°F means sales will increase by $1,259.2.

B The slope is −14.6. A temperature decrease of 14.6°F means sales will decrease by $1.00.

C The slope is 1,259.2. A sales increase of $1,259.2 means the temperature will decrease by 14.6°F.

D The slope is −14.6. A temperature increase of 1°F means sales will decrease by $14.60.

Issay chose B as the correct answer. How might he have gotten that answer?

4 The scatter plot shows the percentage of the world's population that used the internet each year between 2008 and 2016. A good line of fit is drawn through the data. Estimate the slope of the line of fit. Can the rate of change indicated by the slope continue forever? Explain.

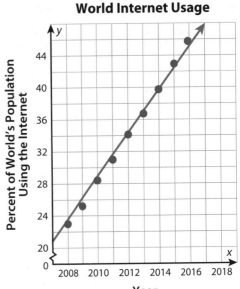

World Internet Usage

5 Tell whether each statement is *True* or *False*.

	True	False
a. A good line of fit can be used to make predictions.	○	○
b. A good line of fit always goes through at least two data points.	○	○
c. The predictions from a good line of fit are exact.	○	○
d. If there is an association between two variables, a good line of fit can always be drawn.	○	○
e. The slope and the *y*-intercept of a line of fit can be found using the same strategies as other graphed lines.	○	○

6 The scatter plot shows the weight in pounds of the world's heaviest giant pumpkin each year since 2008. The equation of the line of fit is $y = 90x + 1,629$.

a. Based on the equation, the heaviest pumpkin in 2025 will weigh _____ pounds.

b. What does the slope of the line of fit tell you about the giant pumpkins in the problem?

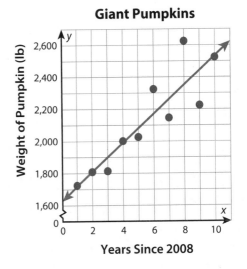

Giant Pumpkins

7 Fernando says that the predictions from good lines of fit are not useful because they are guesses. What could you say to Fernando to convince him that you can make useful predictions from good lines of fit?

8 **Math Journal** A middle school science teacher surveys his students each year. He asks how many families have a landline telephone. This scatter plot shows the percent of families with a landline in each year since 2010. A good line of fit is drawn through the data. Write an equation of the line. Then predict the percent of families that will have a landline in 2020.

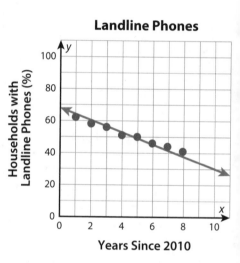

Landline Phones

Households with Landline Phones (%)

Years Since 2010

✔ **End of Lesson Checklist**

☐ **INTERACTIVE GLOSSARY** Write a new entry for *interpret*. Tell what you do when you *interpret* the meaning of the slope and *y*-intercept of a linear model.

☐ **SELF CHECK** Go back to the Unit 7 Opener and see what you can check off.

©Curriculum Associates, LLC Copying is not permitted.

Dear Family,

This week your student is learning about **two-way tables**. Two-way tables display **categorical data**, or data that is divided into different categories. Two-way tables can be used to identify any patterns in the data or describe associations among the categories.

Students will be learning how to make observations about two-way tables, such as in the problem below.

A middle school conducted a survey of 60 students to help determine the event for an assembly. The results of the survey are shown in the two-way table. What do you notice about the data?

	Grade 6	Grade 7	Grade 8	Total
Pep Rally	9	12	14	35
Science Show	11	8	6	25
Total	20	20	20	60

➤ **ONE WAY** to make observations from a two-way table is to analyze the data on the edges of the table.

The **column totals** tell you that 20 students from each grade were surveyed. The **row totals** show that 10 more students voted for a pep rally than a science show. The number where the Total column and row intersect tells you that 60 students were surveyed in all.

➤ **ANOTHER WAY** is to look at the data in the center of the table.

The **center of the table** tells you how the students in each grade voted. For example, more Grade 6 students voted for a science show, but more Grade 7 and 8 students voted for a pep rally.

Using either method, you can analyze categorical data in the table.

 Use the next page to start a conversation about two-way tables.

Activity Thinking About Two-Way Tables

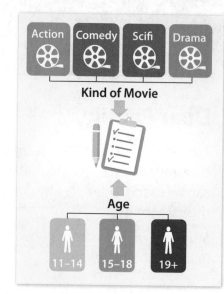

➤ **Do this activity together to investigate two-way tables in the real world.**

Two-way tables can be useful in making decisions based on patterns in data. For example, a local theater can conduct a survey to see how many people in different age groups like different types of movies. One category in the table would be the ages of the people surveyed. The other category would be the types of movies. The survey results can help the theater plan movie festivals that will appeal to different age groups.

? What are some other categories of data that could be used in a survey?

Explore Two-Way Tables

Model It

➤ **Complete the problems about organizing data into tables.**

1 Yukio asks 20 students at her middle school if they like to play fantasy board games. She also asks them their current grade. Her data are shown in the tables.

Yes	No
ⅢⅢ ⅢⅢ ‖	ⅢⅢ ‖‖

Grade 6	Grade 7	Grade 8
ⅢⅢ ‖	ⅢⅢ ‖‖	ⅢⅢ ‖‖

Categorical data are collected in groups, or categories. For these data, the students choose from one category—Grade 6, 7, or 8—that they belong to. They then choose from another category—yes or no—based on the question asked.

a. How many students like to play fantasy board games? How many do not? Complete the table.

Yes	No

b. How many students in each grade responded? Complete the table.

Grade 6	Grade 7	Grade 8

2 Yukio's data can be displayed in a **two-way table**. A two-way table displays data for two categories in a single table. Fill in the values for the row and column totals.

	Grade 6	Grade 7	Grade 8	Total
Yes				
No				
Total				

DISCUSS IT

Ask: Does it matter which category is placed in the rows and which is placed in the columns? Explain.

Share: I cannot fill in all cells in the problem 2 table because . . .

◎ **Learning Target**   SMP 1, SMP 2, SMP 3, SMP 5, SMP 7
Understand that patterns of association can also be seen in bivariate categorical data by displaying frequencies and relative frequencies in a two-way table. Construct and interpret a two-way table summarizing data on two categorical variables collected from the same subjects.

Model It

➤ **Complete the problems about two-way tables.**

3 Below is the two-way table displaying data Yukio collected when she asked 20 students if they like to play fantasy board games. The *Yes* data have been added to Yukio's table.

	Grade 6	Grade 7	Grade 8	Total
Yes	2	6	4	12
No				8
Total	6	7	7	20

a. What does the data value 4 mean in the table?

b. The values in the center cells of a two-way table must add across to equal the row totals, as shown for the *Yes* response. They must also add down to equal the column totals. Complete the table to find how many Grade 6, Grade 7, and Grade 8 students do not like to play fantasy board games.

4 Is it possible for a number in one of the center cells of a two-way table to be greater than the total for that row or column? Explain.

5 **Reflect** Think about the information you get from separate one-way tables and the information you get from a two-way table. What is different? What is the advantage of a two-way table?

Prepare for Two-Way Tables

1 Think about what you know about associations among data. Fill in each box.
Use words, numbers, and pictures. Show as many ideas as you can.

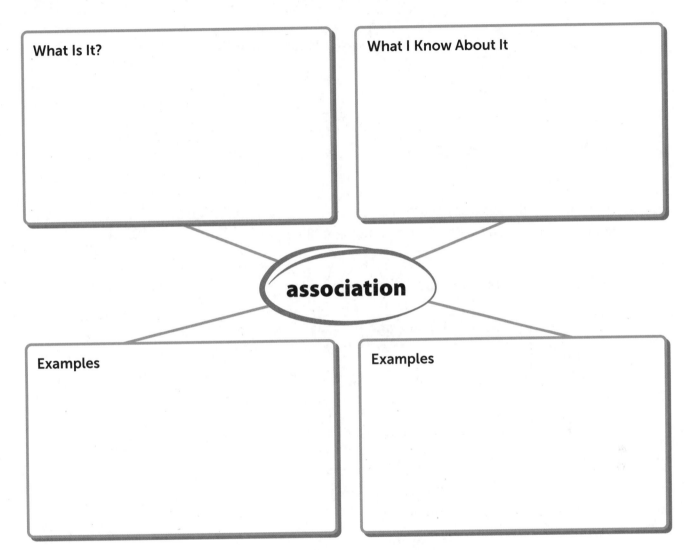

What Is It?

What I Know About It

association

Examples

Examples

2 The scatter plot shows the outside temperature and coffee sales
for a small cafe. Does there appear to be any association between
temperature and sales? Explain.

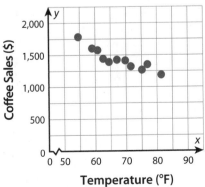

Coffee and Temperature

➤ **Complete problems 3 and 4.**

3 A school district is thinking of having their students wear uniforms. Morgan surveys teachers and students to see whether they are in favor of school uniforms. Morgan shows the data she collected in two tables.

Student	Teacher
卌 卌 |||	卌 ||

In Favor	Not in Favor
||||	卌 卌 卌	

a. How many students did Morgan survey? How many teachers? Complete the table.

Student	Teacher

b. How many of those surveyed are in favor of uniforms? How many are not? Complete the table.

In Favor	Not in Favor

c. Fill in the values for the row totals and column totals.

	In Favor	Not in Favor	Total
Student			
Teacher			
Total			

4 A student collects data about cars in the teachers' parking lot. The student fills in most of the two-way table. Complete the table to find how many of each type of car in the teachers' parking lot are non-hybrid.

		Hybrid	Non-Hybrid	Total
Sedan		6		17
Hatchback		4		12
SUV		3		12
Total		13	28	41

UNDERSTAND: Why are two-way tables useful?

Develop Understanding of Two-Way Tables

Model It: Data on the Edges of the Table

➤ **Try these two problems involving two-way tables.**

1 A city considers building a theater, a small park, or a library on an empty lot. The city planning committee surveys people who rent a home in the city, own a home in the city, or commute from the surrounding area to the city each day. The results of the survey are shown.

Library	Park	Theater
HHT HHT HHT HHT ||	HHT HHT HHT HHT HHT ||||	HHT HHT HHT HHT HHT HHT HHT ||||

Renter	Owner	Commuter
HHT HHT HHT HHT HHT HHT ||||	HHT HHT HHT HHT HHT HHT HHT |	HHT HHT HHT HHT

a. Fill in the values for the row totals and column totals.

b. Which would you recommend building on the lot? Why?

	Library	Park	Theater	Total
Renter				
Owner				
Commuter				
Total				

c. Which group of people surveyed had the fewest responses? Explain.

2 What information would the data in the unfilled center cells of the table in problem 1a provide? Why might the committee want to consider these data?

DISCUSS IT

Ask: How are row and column totals in two-way tables useful for examining categorical data?

Share: The row totals and column totals let you consider . . .

Model It: Data in the Center of the Table

➤ **Try this problem about frequencies in two-way tables.**

3 **a.** Complete the table for the city planning committee's survey data.

	Library	Park	Theater	Total
Renter	10		9	34
Owner		14		36
Commuter		0	20	20
Total	22	29	39	90

DISCUSS IT

Ask: How did you know which numbers to use to complete the table?

Share: I know that 90 represents . . . because . . .

b. Which group of people will be most unhappy if the planning committee recommends building a library? How do you know?

CONNECT IT

➤ **Complete the problems below.**

4 Look at the data in the center cells of the table in problem 3a above. Do these data change your recommendation for which facility the city should build on the lot from problem 1b? Explain.

5 Brownstown Middle School's principal asks students the language they plan to study in high school. Complete the two-way table. Describe any association between grade and the language students plan to study.

	Spanish	German	French	Total
Grade 6	18		24	64
Grade 7		20		75
Grade 8	46			73
Total	101	57	54	212

Name:

Practice Understanding of Two-Way Tables

➤ **Study how the Example shows how to analyze data in a two-way table. Then solve problems 1–4.**

Example

Residents of a city answer a question about how they get to work. They also answer a question about whether they work full time or part time. The two-way table shows the data collected. City leaders want to advertise to increase the number of bus riders. What type of worker should the ads target? Explain.

	Bus	Walk	Car	Subway	Other	Total
Part Time	43	37	12	47	3	142
Full Time	25	31	57	28	44	185
Total	68	68	69	75	47	327

Fewer full-time workers ride the bus, so the program should target them.

1 Use the table in the Example to answer the following questions.

a. Is the most common form of transportation for the full-time workers the same as the most common form of transportation overall? Why or why not?

b. Is there an association between the type of worker and the form of transportation? Explain.

Vocabulary

two-way table
a table that displays two-variable categorical data.

2 Thirty middle school students are asked if they have at least one sibling. The data collected are shown in the table. In which grade would you expect the fewest students to have a sister? Explain.

	Grade 6	Grade 7	Grade 8	Total
Sibling(s)	3	9	7	19
No Siblings	7	2	2	11
Total	10	11	9	30

3 A swimming pool manager is planning an activity for the Fourth of July. He surveys some of the kids at the pool to see what they would prefer.

	Cannonball Contest	Coin Dive	Relay Races	Total
8–10 Years Old	8			46
11–13 Years Old		8		40
Total	22	33	31	86

a. Complete the table.

b. Which activity should the manager choose? Explain.

4 Platon makes a two-way table that shows the favorite activities at a summer camp. He sorts the data for different age groups. Jordan says Platon made an error. Do you agree with Jordan? Explain.

	Art	Swimming	Kickball	Total
6–8	15	18	8	31
9–11	9	21	12	42
12–14	12	24	6	42
Total	36	63	26	125

Refine Ideas About Two-Way Tables

Apply It

➤ **Complete problems 1–5.**

1 **Translate** Measurement data can also be separated into categories and displayed in two-way tables. The Spanish club is selling bags of trail mix to raise money for a trip. The number of hours each member works and the bags of trail mix they sell are recorded. Use **Data Set: Trail Mix Sales** to complete the two-way table.

Trail Mix Sales

Hours	Bags Sold
1	13
1	15
1	21

See page DS2 for the complete data set.

	0–25 Bags Sold	26–50 Bags Sold	Total
0–5 Hours			
6–10 Hours			
Total			

2 **Interpret** A survey is given to 120 people ages 21–60. The people are asked how many packages they received in the past month. The table shows the results. Is there an association between the number of packages and age? Explain.

	1–2 Packages	3–4 Packages	5+ Packages	Total
Age 21–40	22	26	9	57
Age 41–60	41	14	8	63
Total	63	40	17	120

3 **Analyze** Based on this incomplete table, Badru says 47 students do not have pets. Is Badru correct? How do you know?

	Summer Job	No Summer Job	Total
No Pets		34	
Pets	103		180
Total	150		

4 Francisca owns a food truck that serves Mexican food. She wants to know whether she should include rice with a taco or burrito order. One Saturday, she records whether customers who buy a taco or burrito also order rice.

SPECIAL
Taco or
Burrito
with
rice/no rice

PART A Complete the two-way table for the data.

	Rice	No Rice	Total
Taco	47		
Burrito		31	128
Total		119	

PART B Should Francisca include rice with a taco or burrito order? Explain.

5 **Math Journal** A piano teacher asks her students the amount of time they spend practicing each day. She then notes the number of mistakes they make in a recital. What association can you see from the data in the table? What might the piano teacher recommend to her students?

	0–30 Minutes	31–60 Minutes	Total
0–25 Mistakes	1	8	9
26–60 Mistakes	13	2	15
Total	14	10	24

✔ **End of Lesson Checklist**

☐ **INTERACTIVE GLOSSARY** Find the entry for *two-way table*. Rewrite the definition in your own words.

Dear Family,

This week your student is learning about two-way tables with relative frequencies. **Relative frequency** is the quotient of how many times a particular response is given to the total number of responses. Students will solve problems like the one below.

Two teams of 10 campers each choose their favorite activity as shown in the table. What percent of campers choose crafts?

	Swimming	Kickball	Crafts
Team 1	3	1	6
Team 2	6	2	2

➤ **ONE WAY** to find the percentage is to calculate whole-table relative frequencies.

	Swimming	Kickball	Crafts
Team 1	$\frac{3}{20} = 15\%$	$\frac{1}{20} = 5\%$	$\frac{6}{20} = 30\%$
Team 2	$\frac{6}{20} = 30\%$	$\frac{2}{20} = 10\%$	$\frac{2}{20} = 10\%$

Add 30% + 10% to find the total.

➤ **ANOTHER WAY** is to calculate relative frequencies using row or column totals.

	Swimming	Kickball	Crafts	Total
Team 1	$\frac{3}{20} = 15\%$	$\frac{1}{20} = 5\%$	$\frac{6}{20} = 30\%$	$\frac{10}{20} = 50\%$
Team 2	$\frac{6}{20} = 30\%$	$\frac{2}{20} = 10\%$	$\frac{2}{20} = 10\%$	$\frac{10}{20} = 50\%$
Total	$\frac{9}{20} = 45\%$	$\frac{3}{20} = 15\%$	$\frac{8}{20} = 40\%$	$\frac{20}{20} = 100\%$

Using either method, 40% of campers choose crafts as their favorite activity.

▶ Use the next page to start a conversation about two-way tables with relative frequencies.

Activity Thinking About Two-Way Tables with Relative Frequencies

➤ **Do this activity together to investigate two-way tables with relative frequencies.**

A student conducts a survey of 100 students in her middle school. She asks them whether they prefer baseball or soccer. She displays the data in a table. Can you match the percentage to the true statement?

	Baseball	Soccer	Total
Grade 6	$\frac{11}{100} = 11\%$	$\frac{28}{100} = 28\%$	$\frac{39}{100} = 39\%$
Grade 7	$\frac{16}{100} = 16\%$	$\frac{20}{100} = 20\%$	$\frac{36}{100} = 36\%$
Grade 8	$\frac{12}{100} = 12\%$	$\frac{13}{100} = 13\%$	$\frac{25}{100} = 25\%$
Total	$\frac{39}{100} = 39\%$	$\frac{61}{100} = 61\%$	$\frac{100}{100} = 100\%$

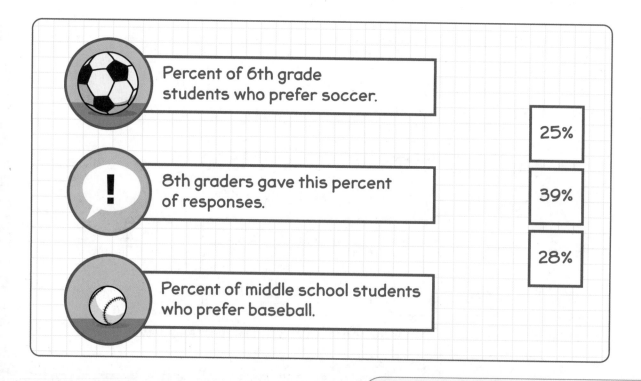

Percent of 6th grade students who prefer soccer.

8th graders gave this percent of responses.

Percent of middle school students who prefer baseball.

25%

39%

28%

? How did you decide which percentage matched each statement?

Explore Whole-Table Relative Frequencies

Johnson City
Public
Library

books, programs, classes, and more

Previously, you learned about two-way tables. In this lesson, you will learn to use two-way tables with relative frequencies.

➤ **Use what you know to try to solve the problem below.**

Middle school students were asked if they visited a public library in the past month. Use **Data Set: Public Library Visits** to answer this question. What percent of the students live in a suburban community and visited a public library in the past month?

Public Library Visits

Community	Visited a Library
urban	yes
suburban	no
urban	yes

See page DS2 for the complete data set.

TRY IT

DISCUSS IT

Ask: Why did you choose that strategy to find the percentage?

Share: I knew . . . so I . . .

◎ **Learning Target**   SMP 1, SMP 2, SMP 3, SMP 4, SMP 5, SMP 6, SMP 7
Understand that patterns of association can also be seen in bivariate categorical data by displaying frequencies and relative frequencies in a two-way table. Construct and interpret a two-way table summarizing data on two categorical variables collected from the same subjects. Use relative frequencies calculated for rows or columns to describe possible association between the two variables.

LESSON 32 Construct and Interpret Two-Way Tables

CONNECT IT

1 **Look Back** What percent of the students live in a suburban community and visited a public library in the past month? Explain how you know.

2 **Look Ahead** A **relative frequency** is the quotient of the number of times a response occurs to the total number of responses in a category or in a whole survey. You have seen two-way tables showing frequencies, or counts. A two-way table can also show relative frequencies. Relative frequencies can be shown as fractions, decimals, or percentages. Consider this two-way table with frequencies.

	Prefer Reading	Prefer Playing Outside	Total
Grade 6	6	18	24
Grade 8	22	4	26
Total	28	22	50

The relative frequency of students surveyed who are in Grade 8 and prefer reading is $\frac{22}{50}$, or 44%.

a. What is the relative frequency of all the students surveyed who are in Grade 6 and prefer playing outside?

b. What is the relative frequency of all the students surveyed who prefer reading?

3 **Reflect** How can relative frequencies be helpful when looking at data?

Prepare for Constructing and Interpreting Two-Way Tables

1 Think about what you know about ratios and percentages. Fill in each box. Use words, numbers, and pictures. Show as many ideas as you can.

In My Own Words	My Illustrations

percent

Examples	Non-Examples

2 Teenagers were asked what type of book they prefer to read. There were 18 teenagers who prefer e-books and 7 teenagers who prefer paperback or hardcover books. Anne says 72% of the teenagers prefer to read an e-book. Is Anne correct? Explain.

3 Students at a high school take a survey. One question asks if they have ever gone horseback riding. Use **Data Set: Horseback Riding** to answer problem 3a.

Horseback Riding

Grade	Horseback
11	yes
11	yes
12	no

See page DS3 for the complete data set.

a. What percent of the students surveyed are in Grade 11 and have gone horseback riding? Show your work.

SOLUTION _____

_____

b. Check your answer to problem 3a. Show your work.

Develop Constructing Two-Way Tables with Relative Frequencies

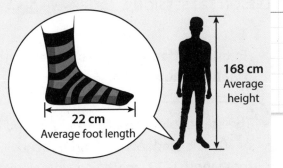

22 cm
Average foot length

168 cm
Average height

➤ **Read and try to solve the problem below.**

The scatter plot shows the heights and foot lengths of 30 male students at a middle school. Their average foot length is 22 cm. Their average height is 168 cm.

What percent of the students with above-average height have at- or below-average foot length?

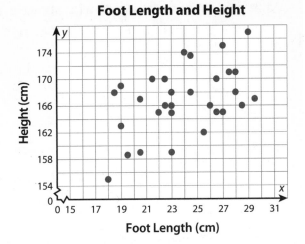

Foot Length and Height

Height (cm) / Foot Length (cm)

TRY IT

©Curriculum Associates, LLC   Copying is not permitted.

➤ **Explore different ways to understand constructing two-way tables with relative frequencies.**

The scatter plot shows the heights and foot lengths of 30 male students at a middle school. Their average foot length is 22 cm. Their average height is 168 cm.

What percent of the students with above-average height have at- or below-average foot length?

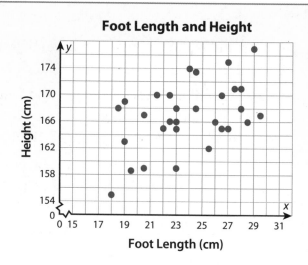

Foot Length and Height

Model It

You can start by making a two-way table with frequencies.

	Foot Length ≤ 22 cm	Foot Length > 22 cm	Total
Height ≤ 168 cm	7	13	20
Height > 168 cm	2	8	10
Total	9	21	30

Model It

You can then make a two-way table with relative frequencies using row totals.

The rows represent the categories for height. The question is asking about a percentage of students in one of the height categories. The row totals are height totals and are the *wholes* in your relative frequencies.

	Foot Length ≤ 22 cm	Foot Length > 22 cm	Total
Height ≤ 168 cm	$\frac{7}{20} = 0.35 = 35\%$	$\frac{13}{20} = 0.65 = 65\%$	$\frac{20}{20} = 1.00 = 100\%$
Height > 168 cm	$\frac{2}{10} = 0.20 = 20\%$	$\frac{8}{10} = 0.80 = 80\%$	$\frac{10}{10} = 1.00 = 100\%$
Total	$\frac{9}{30} = 0.30 = 30\%$	$\frac{21}{30} = 0.70 = 70\%$	

➤ **Use the problem from the previous page to help you understand how to construct two-way tables with relative frequencies.**

1 Look at the second **Model It**. What percent of the students with above-average height have at- or below-average foot length? Explain.

2 **a.** Complete the two-way table with relative frequencies using column totals.

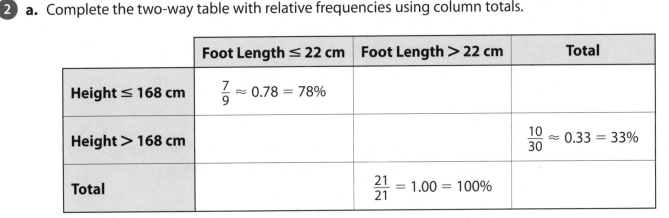

	Foot Length ≤ 22 cm	Foot Length > 22 cm	Total
Height ≤ 168 cm	$\frac{7}{9} \approx 0.78 = 78\%$		
Height > 168 cm			$\frac{10}{30} \approx 0.33 = 33\%$
Total		$\frac{21}{21} = 1.00 = 100\%$	

b. The column totals are the *wholes* in your relative frequencies. What do the column totals represent?

c. Write and answer a question that can be answered using the table you completed in problem 2a.

3 You can calculate relative frequencies using row totals, column totals, or the entire table total. What determines which method you should use?

4 **Reflect** Think about all the models and strategies you have discussed today. Describe how one of them helped you better understand how to solve the **Try It** problem.

Apply It

➤ **Use what you learned to solve these problems.**

5 One hundred adults are asked whether they prefer listening to podcasts or audiobooks. The table shows the results. An audiobook company needs to know what age group to target in advertising. What method should the company use to calculate relative frequencies? Explain.

Listen to

Audiobooks   Podcasts

	Podcast	Audiobook	Total
Younger than 30	39	12	51
30 and Older	22	27	49
Total	61	39	100

6 A company specializes in online content for people 30 and older. Should they use the same relative frequencies used by the company in problem 5? Explain.

7 Amata counts the number of jumping jacks each of 25 high school students do in one minute. Her data are shown in the table. What percent of high school students younger than 17 did more than 50 jumping jacks in a minute? Show your work.

	Younger than 17	17 and Older	Total
≤ 50 Jumping Jacks	11	7	18
> 50 Jumping Jacks	3	4	7
Total	14	11	25

SOLUTION _____

Name:

Practice Constructing Two-Way Tables with Relative Frequencies

➤ Study the Example showing how to construct a two-way table with relative frequencies. Then solve problems 1–3.

Example

A doctor collects the data below on 50 patients involved in bicycle accidents. Which age group may need a stronger reminder to wear helmets?

	Younger than 10	10 and Older	Total
Helmet	13	20	33
No Helmet	3	14	17
Total	16	34	50

Calculate relative frequencies using column totals.

	Younger than 10	10 and Older	Total
Helmet	$\frac{13}{16} \approx 0.81 = 81\%$	$\frac{20}{34} \approx 0.59 = 59\%$	$\frac{33}{50} \approx 0.66 = 66\%$
No Helmet	$\frac{3}{16} \approx 0.19 = 19\%$	$\frac{14}{34} \approx 0.41 = 41\%$	$\frac{17}{50} = 0.34 = 34\%$
Total	$\frac{16}{16} = 1.00 = 100\%$	$\frac{34}{34} = 1.00 = 100\%$	

patients ages 10 and older; About 41% of patients 10 and older did not wear a helmet compared to 19% of patients younger than 10.

① The relative frequencies in the table below are calculated by row using the Example data. Write and answer a question that can be answered using this table.

	Younger than 10	10 and Older	Total
Helmet	0.39	0.61	1.00
No Helmet	0.18	0.82	1.00
Total	0.32	0.68	

Vocabulary

relative frequency
the quotient that compares the number of times a data value occurs and the total number of data values.

2 Hiroaki asked students whether they prefer to watch football, basketball, or soccer. The table shows the results. Hiroaki thinks that basketball is more popular for seventh graders than for sixth graders. To show this, he makes a table with relative frequencies calculated using column totals. Do you agree with Hiroaki? Explain.

	Football	Basketball	Soccer	Total
Grade 6	44	35	13	92
Grade 7	37	41	18	96
Grade 8	32	48	15	95
Total	113	124	46	283

3 High school seniors are asked two questions. Do you plan to go to college? Do you play a musical instrument? The table shows the data.

	No Instrument	Instrument	Total
No College	24	17	41
College	63	77	140
Total	87	94	181

a. Complete the two-way table with relative frequencies, either by row or by column. Round to hundredths.

	No Instrument	Instrument	Total
No College			
College			
Total			

b. Write and answer a question that can be answered by your table.

Develop Interpreting and Analyzing Two-Way Tables

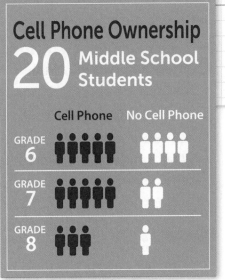

Cell Phone Ownership

20 Middle School Students

| | Cell Phone | No Cell Phone |

➤ **Read and try to solve the problem below.**

Twenty middle school students are asked whether they own cell phones. The table shows their responses and grade levels. Which grade has the highest percentage of students who own cell phones?

TRY IT

DISCUSS IT

Ask: How is your strategy similar to mine? How is it different?

Share: My strategy shows . . .

➤ **Explore different ways to understand interpreting and analyzing two-way tables.**

Twenty middle school students are asked whether they own cell phones. The table shows their responses and grade levels. Which grade has the highest percent of students who own cell phones?

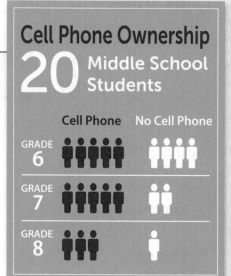

Cell Phone Ownership
20 Middle School Students

Model It

You can make a two-way table with relative frequencies calculated using row totals.

	Cell Phone	No Cell Phone	Total
Grade 6	$\frac{5}{9} \approx 0.56$	$\frac{4}{9} \approx 0.44$	$\frac{9}{9} = 1.00$
Grade 7	$\frac{5}{7} \approx 0.71$	$\frac{2}{7} \approx 0.29$	$\frac{7}{7} = 1.00$
Grade 8	$\frac{3}{4} = 0.75$	$\frac{1}{4} = 0.25$	$\frac{4}{4} = 1.00$
Total	$\frac{13}{20} = 0.65$	$\frac{7}{20} = 0.35$	

Analyze It

You can analyze the relative frequencies in the table.

Look at the *Cell Phone* column. Compare the decimals for each grade.

Grade 6: 0.56 = 56%

Grade 7: 0.71 = 71%

Grade 8: 0.75 = 75%

➤ **Use the problem from the previous page to help you understand how to interpret and analyze two-way tables.**

1 Look at **Analyze It**. Which grade has the highest percent of students who own cell phones? How do you know?

2 Look at the table in **Model It**. Why are the relative frequencies calculated by row?

3 The tallies in the original table show that fewer students in Grade 8 have cell phones than in either of the other two grades. Why do you use relative frequencies to make a comparison?

4 How can you find and interpret associations in categorical data using a two-way table?

5 **Reflect** Think about all the models and strategies you have discussed today. Describe how one of them helped you better understand how to interpret and analyze two-way tables.

Apply It

➤ **Use what you learned to solve these problems.**

 A restaurant manager collects data from 350 diners who order tacos. She records the type of taco each diner orders. She also notes whether diners add guacamole to their tacos. The table shows her data.

	Steak Taco	Chicken Taco	Total
Guacamole	$\frac{92}{179} \approx 51.4\%$	$\frac{87}{179} \approx 48.6\%$	$\frac{179}{179} = 100\%$
No Guacamole	$\frac{86}{171} \approx 50.3\%$	$\frac{85}{171} \approx 49.7\%$	$\frac{171}{171} = 100\%$
Total	$\frac{178}{350} \approx 50.9\%$	$\frac{172}{350} \approx 49.1\%$	

a. The manager is considering adding guacamole to all tacos. Do you think this is a good plan? Explain your reasoning.

b. Did the diners prefer steak tacos or chicken tacos overall? Explain.

⑦ Tamera asks 500 people in her town if they recycle. The table shows her data. Of those who recycle, which age group tends to recycle the least? Show your work.

	30 and Younger	31–50	Older than 50	Total
Recycle	176	168	57	401
Do Not Recycle	13	38	48	99
Total	189	206	105	500

SOLUTION _____

Practice Interpreting and Analyzing Two-Way Tables

➤ **Study the Example showing how to interpret and analyze a two-way table. Then solve problems 1–3.**

Example

A random sample of adults is asked whether they have cable TV. The table shows the responses. Explain how to use the table to determine if there is an association between age and having cable TV.

	Cable TV	No Cable TV	Total
Younger than 35	66	247	313
35 and Older	59	72	131
Total	125	319	444

You can make a two-way table with relative frequencies calculated by rows to determine if there is an association.

	Cable TV	No Cable TV	Total
Younger than 35	$\frac{66}{313} \approx 0.21$	$\frac{247}{313} \approx 0.79$	$\frac{313}{313} = 1.00$
35 and Older	$\frac{59}{131} \approx 0.45$	$\frac{72}{131} \approx 0.55$	$\frac{131}{131} = 1.00$
Total	$\frac{125}{444} \approx 0.28$	$\frac{319}{444} \approx 0.72$	

1 Use the data from the tables in the Example.

a. A video subscription service is running a *cut the cord* campaign to get people to give up cable. What age group should they target? Explain.

b. Which age group has the higher percentage of people with no cable TV? Explain.

2 A store recorded whether 100 customers requested paper receipts, email receipts, or both. What percent of people who received paper receipts were 45 and older? Explain.

	Paper Only	Email Only	Both	Total
Younger than 45	10	25	5	40
45 and Older	40	5	15	60
Total	50	30	20	100

3 The table shows the results of a survey of skateboarders at a skate park. Nathan thinks that more beginner skateboarders than veteran skateboarders prefer doing a Heelflip trick.

	Prefer Ollie Trick	Prefer Heelflip Trick	Total
Beginner	40	15	55
Veteran	6	9	15
Total	46	24	70

a. Explain how Nathan can be correct.

b. Explain how Nathan can be incorrect.

Heelflip Trick

Refine Constructing and Interpreting Two-Way Tables

➤ **Complete the Example below. Then solve problems 1–7.**

Example

Students at a middle school are asked whether they prefer an individual project, a partner project, or a group project. The table shows the results. What is the likelihood that a randomly selected student in Grade 7 will prefer a partner project?

	Individual Project	Partner Project	Group Project	Total
Grade 6	32	20	40	92
Grade 7	22	24	31	77
Grade 8	20	15	46	81
Total	74	59	117	250

Look at how you could show your work using relative frequency.

There are 77 students in Grade 7. There are 24 students in Grade 7 who prefer a partner project. $\frac{24}{77} \approx 0.312$

SOLUTION _____

> **CONSIDER THIS ...**
> Rows in the table for Grade 6, Grade 8, and the total can be covered up so that only the row for Grade 7 is showing.

> **PAIR/SHARE**
> Explain why the denominator is 77.

Apply It

1 Look at the table in the Example. What is the likelihood that a student who prefers a group project is in Grade 8? Show your work.

SOLUTION _____

> **CONSIDER THIS ...**
> The column totals are for the different types of projects that the students prefer.

> **PAIR/SHARE**
> What is the likelihood a student who is in Grade 8 will prefer a group project?

2 There are 255 students at Brownsville Middle School. The students are asked whether they prefer art or music class and whether they prefer science or math class. The table shows the results. Which is greater: the percent of students who prefer science and art classes or the percent of students who prefer math and music classes? Show your work.

CONSIDER THIS . . .
What is the *whole* here?

	Art Class	Music Class	Total
Science Class	51	56	107
Math Class	73	75	148
Total	124	131	255

PAIR/SHARE
What calculations did you use to make your conclusion?

SOLUTION _____

3 The table shows data for students at a middle school. What is the relative frequency of students in Grade 8 who wear glasses?

CONSIDER THIS . . .
The question is asking only about the data for Grade 8 students.

	Glasses	Contacts	Neither	Total
Grade 7	11	21	12	44
Grade 8	5	29	22	56
Total	16	50	34	100

A 5%

B 8.93%

C 16%

D 31.25%

Angela chose D as the correct answer. How might she have gotten that answer?

PAIR/SHARE
How did you know what column or row to use?

4 A veterinarian collects data on the weights of newborn puppies in several litters. The table shows her data.

	Smallest	Not the Smallest	Total
Male	0.44	0.61	0.58
Female	0.56	0.39	0.42
Total	1.00	1.00	1.00

a. What method was used to calculate the relative frequencies in the table? How do you know?

b. What does 0.56 represent? Explain.

5 Tell whether each statement about the table is *True* or *False*.

	School Bus Early	School Bus on Time	School Bus Late	Total
Rainy Day	11.6%	36.2%	52.2%	100%
Sunny Day	33.3%	36.4%	30.3%	100%
Total	22.2%	36.3%	41.5%	

	True	False
a. The school bus is mostly on time.	○	○
b. The relative frequencies are for the whole table.	○	○
c. The school bus tends to be early on sunny days more so than on rainy days.	○	○
d. The relative frequencies are by row.	○	○

6 Neva asks 50 students at her school whether they prefer an early or a late lunch. She surveys 27 athletes and 21 of them prefer a late lunch. The remaining students she surveys are nonathletes. 16 of the nonathletes prefer an early lunch.

a. Complete the two-way table with the relative frequencies calculated by row.

	Early Lunch	Late Lunch	Total
Athlete			
Nonathlete			
Total			

b. Currently, most of the students in the first lunch period are athletes. Should the school consider changing schedules? Explain.

7 **Math Journal** Make a two-way table with relative frequencies for the data shown. Write and answer a question that can be answered using your table.

	Grade 6	Grade 7	Grade 8	Total
Plays Chess	35	45	68	148
Does Not Play Chess	56	86	59	201
Total	91	131	127	349

✓ End of Lesson Checklist

☐ **INTERACTIVE GLOSSARY** Find the entry for *relative frequency*. Tell how relative frequency is different from frequency.

☐ **SELF CHECK** Go back to the Unit 7 Opener and see what you can check off.

Math IN Action

SMP 1 Make sense of problems and persevere in solving them.

Study an Example Problem and Solution

➤ **Read this problem involving scatter plots and two-way tables. Then look at one student's solution to this problem on the following pages.**

Internet Users

Brett and Darius are working together on a research project involving several different countries. They have collected data on several variables for each country. Read the email from Darius. Then complete Brett's deliverables.

Delete   Archive   Reply   Reply All   Forward

To: Brett
Subject: Data displays for research project

Hi Brett,

There are 25 countries in our project. I wonder if the percent of the population using the internet is related to any of the other variables. I have attached data for the population using the internet and data for several other variables.

DELIVERABLES:

• Choose a variable to analyze along with the population using the internet.
• Make a scatter plot to show the relationship.
• Make a two-way table to show the percent of the countries in our project that have above-average usage of the internet and an above-average value for the variable you chose.
• Describe any association between the variables.

Thanks, Darius

Be sure to place your router away from fish tanks! Water can block WiFi signals and slow down your internet connection.

Attachments:

Country	Population using the internet (%)	CO₂ Emissions per capita (metric tons)	Total population (thousands)	Life expectancy at birth (years)	Population under age 15 (%)
Afghanistan	11.4	0.3	32,358	62.3	47.42
Argentina	69.7	4.7	40,765	75.7	24.42
Australia	86.5	15.3	22,606	82.4	18.95

See page DS4 for the complete data set.

One Student's Solution

First, I have to choose a variable to analyze.

I think that countries that have a higher percent of the population using the internet may also have higher life expectancy. So, I will investigate the relationship between those two variables.

Next, I need to make a scatter plot.

There is no clear independent or dependent variable. I will put population using the internet on the *x*-axis and life expectancy on the *y*-axis.

The average percent of the population using the internet is 52.8%. I can draw a vertical line through this value. The average life expectancy is 70.8 years. I can draw a horizontal line through this value.

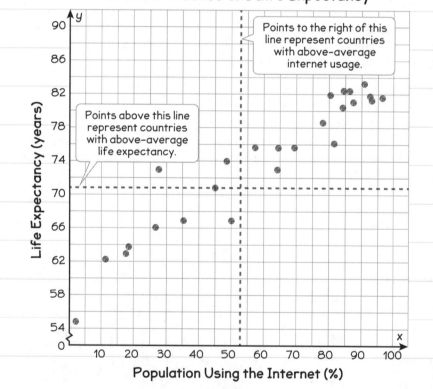

Internet Access and Life Expectancy

I could model the pattern in the data with a straight line with a positive slope, so the variables have a positive, linear association.

NOTICE THAT . . .
The averages for each variable in the data table are located in the last row of the table. See the full data set on page DS4.

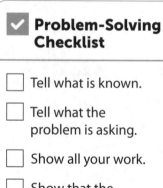

Problem-Solving Checklist

☐ Tell what is known.

☐ Tell what the problem is asking.

☐ Show all your work.

☐ Show that the solution works.

Then, I can count the number of points in each section of the graph to make a two-way table showing frequencies.

	Life expectancy ≤ 70.8	Life expectancy > 70.8	Total
Population using the internet ≤ 52.8%	8	2	10
Population using the internet > 52.8%	0	15	15
Total	8	17	25

> **NOTICE THAT...**
> There are no countries in Brett and Darius's project that have above-average internet usage and below-average life expectancy.

Now, I can calculate whole-table relative frequencies to show the percent of countries in our project with above-average internet usage and above-average life expectancy.

	Life expectancy ≤ 70.8	Life expectancy > 70.8	Total
Population using the internet ≤ 52.8%	$\frac{8}{25} = 32\%$	$\frac{2}{25} = 8\%$	40%
Population using the internet > 52.8%	$\frac{0}{25} = 0\%$	$\frac{15}{25} = 60\%$	60%
Total	32%	68%	100%

I can see that there is association between population using the internet and life expectancy. 60% of countries in the project have above-average internet usage and have above-average life expectancy.

Finally, I can check my solution by comparing the scatter plot and the two-way table.

Both data displays show association: as the percent of the population using the internet increases, life expectancy increases.

Try Another Approach

➤ **There are many ways to solve problems. Think about how you might solve the Internet Users problem in a different way.**

Internet Users

Brett and Darius are working together on a research project involving several different countries. They have collected data on several variables for each country. Read the email from Darius. Then complete Brett's deliverables.

Delete   Archive | Reply   Reply All   Forward

To: Brett
Subject: Data displays for research project

Hi Brett,

There are 25 countries in our project. I wonder if the percent of the population using the internet is related to any of the other variables. I have attached data for the population using the internet and data for several other variables.

DELIVERABLES:
• Choose a variable to analyze along with the population using the internet.
• Make a scatter plot to show the relationship.
• Make a two-way table to show the percent of the countries in our project that have above-average usage of the internet and an above-average value for the variable you chose.
• Describe any association between the variables.

Thanks, Darius

Attachments:

Country	Population using the internet (%)	CO₂ Emissions per capita (metric tons)	Total population (thousands)	Life expectancy at birth (years)	Population under age 15 (%)
Afghanistan	11.4	0.3	32,358	62.3	47.42
Argentina	69.7	4.7	40,765	75.7	24.42
Australia	86.5	15.3	22,606	82.4	18.95

See page DS4 for the complete data set.

Plan It

➤ **Answer these questions to help you start thinking about a plan.**

a. Which variable do you think will be interesting to analyze along with the population using the internet? Why?

b. Will your two-way table show frequencies or relative frequencies? Why?

Solve It

➤ **Find a different solution for the Internet Users problem. Show all your work on a separate sheet of paper. You may want to use the Problem-Solving Tips to get started.**

PROBLEM-SOLVING TIPS

Math Toolkit graph paper, graphing calculator, straightedge, string

---

Key Terms

scatter plot	relative frequency	nonlinear association
bivariate	no association	positive association
two-way table	linear association	negative association

Sentence Starters

- As the percent of the population using the internet increases . . .
- The percent of countries with above-average internet usage . . .

Reflect

Use Mathematical Practices As you work through the problem, discuss these questions with a partner.

- **Be Precise** How will you scale the axes for your scatter plot? Why?

- **Make Sense of Problems** How is the information in the "Worldwide Average" row of the data table different from the information in the other rows? How will you use this information in your scatter plot and in your two-way table?

Discuss Models and Strategies

➤ **Read the problem. Write a solution on a separate sheet of paper. Remember, there can be lots of ways to solve a problem.**

Age Groups

Brett and Darius have collected data on the size of two age groups in each country in their project. Read an email from Brett. Then complete Darius's deliverables.

Delete Archive Reply Reply All Forward

To: Darius
Subject: Two-way tables for research project

Hi Darius,

I would like to include two-way tables showing some of our data in our report. I have attached data on populations for different age groups for each country in our project.

DELIVERABLES:

- Choose two or three countries from our project.
- Make a two-way table to display the percent of the population in each age group.
- Make a second two-way table to display the number of people in each age group.
- Describe any association you see in the tables.

Thanks!

Brett

Attachments:

Country	Total Population (thousands)	Population under age 15 (%)	Population over age 60 (%)
Afghanistan	32,358	47.42	3.82
Argentina	40,765	24.42	14.97
Australia	22,606	18.95	19.46

See page DS5 for the complete data set.

Population growth is caused by more children being born and by individuals living longer lives.

Plan It and Solve It

➤ **Find a solution to the Age Groups problem.**

Write a detailed plan and support your answer. Be sure to include:

- two or three countries from the project.
- a two-way table displaying relative frequencies.
- a two-way table displaying frequencies, or counts.
- a description of any association you see in the tables.

PROBLEM-SOLVING TIPS

Math Toolkit calculator, graph paper, straightedge

Key Terms

relative frequency	two-way table	bivariate
percent	data	association
column	row	frequency

Questions

- How many people are under age 15 in each of the countries you have chosen? How many total people are under age 15 in these countries?
- What percent of people are between ages 15 and 60 in each of the countries you have chosen?

Reflect

Use Mathematical Practices As you work through the problem, discuss these questions with a partner.

- **Make Sense of Problems** Which two-way table will you make first? Why?

- **Use Structure** Write a question that could be answered using a table showing frequencies. Write a question that could be answered using a table showing relative frequencies.

The oldest documented human lived to be 122 years and 164 days old!

Persevere On Your Own

➤ **Read the problem. Write a solution on a separate sheet of paper.**

Emissions, GDP, and Urban Population

Brett wonders if there are any relationships among the following for the countries in his project: CO_2 emissions, GDP (gross domestic product, or the total value of goods and services produced in one year), and urban population. Look at the data and read his notes. Then make and use a scatter plot to predict as many missing values as you can.

We are missing three values:

Ecuador: GDP

Finland: Urban Population

Lebanon: CO_2 Emissions

I could use a line of fit to predict these values.

Country	Total CO_2 Emissions (million metric tons)	GDP (billions of U.S. dollars)	Urban Population (millions)
Afghanistan	10	22.0	8
Argentina	204	637.5	37
Australia	361	1,408.7	19
Canada	537	1,647.1	28
Ecuador	44		9
Egypt	202	195.1	35
Ethiopia	12	75.6	18
Fiji	1	4.9	0.488
Finland	47	252.2	
France	303	2,582.5	51
Germany	720	3,693.2	64
Jamaica	7	14.8	2
Japan	1,214	4,872.4	116
Kenya	14	74.9	11
Lebanon		53.4	4
Micronesia	0.15	0.3	0.025
Netherlands	167	830.6	15
Nicaragua	5	13.8	3
Norway	48	399.5	4
Slovakia	31	95.6	3
Somalia	0.6	1.5	4
Spain	234	1,314.3	37
Turkey	346	851.5	55
Venezuela	185	255.1	26
Yemen	23	28.0	9

Solve It

➤ **Find a solution to the Emissions, GDP, and Urban Population problem.**

- Make a scatter plot to show the relationship between the two variables you selected.

- Describe any association shown in the scatter plot.

- Draw a line of fit and write an equation for your line.

- Use your line of fit to predict two of the values that are missing in the table.

Reflect

Use Mathematical Practices After you complete the problem, choose one of these questions to discuss with a partner.

- **Critique Reasoning** Do you agree with your partner's placement of the line of fit and the equation your partner wrote to model it? Explain.

- **Reason Mathematically** What does the slope of your line of fit suggest about the data?

In this unit you learned to . . .

Skill	Lesson
Make and use scatter plots to recognize and describe patterns and associations in two-variable data.	29
Assess linear models for good fit to a set of data.	29
Write and interpret equations for linear models that are good lines of fit for data.	30
Understand and identify associations in two-variable categorical data by displaying frequencies in two-way tables.	31, 32
Construct and interpret two-way tables with relative frequencies.	32
Explain your ideas about two-variable data clearly by using models to show why the ideas make sense for the problem.	29–32

Think about what you have learned.

➤ **Use words, numbers, and drawings.**

1 The most important math I learned was _____ because . . .

2 I am proud that I can . . .

3 I would like to learn more about how to . . .

Vocabulary Review

➤ **Review the unit vocabulary. Put a check mark by items you can use in speaking and writing. Look up the meaning of any terms you do not know.**

Math Vocabulary		Academic Vocabulary
☐ categorical data	☐ nonlinear association	☐ analyze
☐ cluster	☐ outlier	☐ likelihood
☐ line of fit	☐ relative frequency	☐ random
☐ linear association	☐ scatter plot	☐ survey (verb)
☐ no association	☐ two-way table	

➤ **Use the unit vocabulary to complete the problems.**

1 Use as many math vocabulary terms as you can to describe each graph.

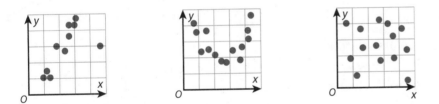

2 Use at least three math or academic vocabulary terms to describe the display of data below. Underline each term you use.

	Grade 6	Grade 7	Grade 8
Buy Lunch	23	45	76
Bring Lunch	72	56	16
Total	95	101	92

Unit Review

➤ **Use what you have learned to complete these problems.**

1. Researchers timed 20 children reading a page of text. The scatter plot shows the age of the child and the total time spent reading the page. Draw a good line of fit. Explain your reasoning.

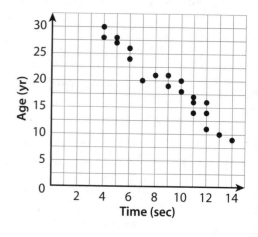

SOLUTION _____

_____

_____

2. This scatter plot shows sales of winter coats at a store and the outside temperature. Which statements describe the scatter plot and line of fit? Choose all the correct answers.

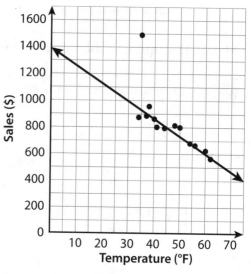

A   A possible equation of the line of fit is $y = 13x + 1{,}382$.

B   The line of fit can be used to predict winter coat sales when the temperature is 70°F.

C   The line of fit shows a negative association.

D   An increase in temperature most likely means an increase in sales.

E   If the temperature is less than 40°F, then the estimated sales will be over $800.

3. A survey is given to 228 people aged 11–70. The people are asked how they most commonly read a book. The table shows the results. Is there an association between the method of reading a book and age? Explain your reasoning.

	Audiobook	Electronic Device	Paperback/Hardcover	Total
Ages 11–30	4	76	7	87
Ages 31–50	21	25	24	70
Ages 51–70	24	21	26	71

SOLUTION _____

_____

4 Students in Grades 7 and 8 are asked whether they prefer earning money completing indoor chores, completing outdoor chores, or babysitting. The table shows the results. What is the likelihood that a randomly selected student in Grade 8 prefers babysitting? Record your answer on the grid. Then fill in the bubbles.

	Indoor Chores	Outdoor Chores	Babysitting	Total
Grade 7	22	60	16	98
Grade 8	32	46	26	104
Total	54	106	42	202

5 Which statements are true about the scatter plot? Choose all the correct answers.

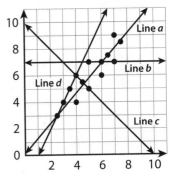

A Line *a* is a good fit because it models a positive association and is close to all the data points.

B Line *b* is a good fit because it goes through three of the data points.

C Line *c* is not a good fit because it models a negative association.

D Line *d* is not a good fit; although it models a positive association, it is above most of the data points.

E Lines *a* and *d* are equally good lines of fit for the data.

6 A survey is given to 189 people aged 11–30. The people are asked how they prefer to watch a movie. The incomplete table shows the results. Complete the table to show how to find how many people aged 11–20 prefer going to the movie theater. Write your answers in the blanks.

	Movie Theater	At Home	Total
Ages 11–20	56		87
Ages 21–30		84	
Total	74		189

Performance Task

➤ **Answer the questions and show all your work on separate paper.**

Student Council gave a survey to middle school students. The table shows how many students in each grade were surveyed.

Grade 6	Grade 7	Grade 8
50	52	54

The students were asked how they prefer to raise money for a new school garden. The table below shows how many students preferred each possible fundraiser.

Dance-a-thon	Walkathon	Swim-a-thon
68	51	37

Of the students surveyed:

- 22 Grade 6 students prefer a dance-a-thon.

- 18 Grade 7 students prefer a walkathon.

- 32 Grade 8 students prefer a dance-a-thon

- 5 Grade 8 students prefer a swim-a-thon.

Student Council asks you to analyze the data to help them choose the fundraiser that will have the greatest participation so the most money will be raised. Create a two-way table that includes the information gathered from the survey. Then answer the following questions submitted by Student Council:

- What percent of Grade 8 students surveyed prefer a walkathon?

- What percent of students surveyed who prefer a dance-a-thon are Grade 6 students?

- What percent of students surveyed prefer a swim-a-thon?

- Which fundraiser do you recommend? Explain your reasoning.

Reflect

Use Mathematical Practices After you complete the task, choose one of the following questions to answer.

- **Be Precise** Will calculating relative frequencies by rows or columns influence your data?

- **Argue and Critique** What mathematical evidence supports your recommendation?

Data Sets

Unit 7

LESSON 29 | SESSION 1 ■ ☐ ☐ ☐ ☐

Try It

Memory Game	
Screen Time (h)	Memory Test Score
10	97
11	94
11	96
13	93
14	94
14	91
15	90
16	89
17	86
18	85
19	82
19	83
20	80
20	81
20	83
21	79
24	75
24	76
25	75
25	72

LESSON 29 | SESSION 2 ■ ■ ☐ ☐ ☐

Practice ①

Rectangle Dimensions	
Length (in.)	Width (in.)
3	3
2	3
4	1
3	4
4	4
2	5
5	3
3	6
5	6
3	7
7	5
2	8
8	4
7	8
5	8

LESSON 29 | SESSION 5 ■ ■ ■ ■ ■

Refine ②

Social Media Users	
Year	U.S. Adults (%)
2005	7
2006	11
2008	25
2009	38
2010	46
2011	50
2012	55
2013	62
2014	62
2015	65
2016	69
2018	69

LESSON 31 | SESSION 3 ■ ■ ■

Apply It ①

Trail Mix Sales	
Hours	Bags Sold
1	13
1	15
1	21
2	20
2	24
3	11
3	23
3	28
4	22
4	28
5	11
5	15
5	19
6	34
7	28
7	43
8	20
8	28
9	15
9	49

LESSON 32 | SESSION 1 ■ □ □ □

Try It

Public Library Visit	
Community	Visited a Library
urban	yes
suburban	no
urban	yes
urban	no
urban	yes
suburban	no
suburban	yes
urban	no
suburban	yes
urban	yes
urban	yes
suburban	yes
suburban	no
suburban	no
urban	yes
urban	no
suburban	yes
urban	yes
urban	yes
suburban	no
suburban	yes
suburban	no
urban	yes
suburban	no
urban	yes
suburban	no
urban	yes
urban	no
urban	no
suburban	yes

Data Sets

Unit 7

LESSON 32 | SESSION 1 ■ □ □ □

Prepare for ③

Horseback Riding	
Grade	**Horseback**
11	yes
11	yes
12	no
12	yes
12	no
12	no
11	yes
11	no
12	yes
11	yes
11	yes
12	no
11	no
12	yes
11	yes
11	yes
12	no
11	yes
12	no
11	yes
11	no
11	yes
11	yes
12	yes
12	no
11	no
12	yes
12	no
12	no
11	yes

Data Sets

Unit 7

MATH IN ACTION | SESSION 1 ■ □

Internet Users

Country	Population using the internet (%)	CO$_2$ Emissions per capita (metric tons)	Total Population (thousands)	Population under age 15 (%)	Life expectancy at birth (years)
Afghanistan	11.4	0.3	32,358	47.42	62.3
Argentina	69.7	4.7	40,765	24.42	75.7
Australia	86.5	15.3	22,606	18.95	82.4
Canada	92.7	15.1	34,350	16.37	81.8
Ecuador	57.3	2.8	14,666	30.29	75.6
Egypt	45.0	2.2	82,537	31.25	70.8
Ethiopia	18.6	0.1	84,734	43.29	63.7
Fiji	50.0	1.3	868	28.88	66.9
Finland	87.5	8.6	5,385	16.42	80.7
France	80.5	4.7	63,126	18.26	81.9
Germany	84.4	8.9	82,163	13.17	80.4
Jamaica	48.8	2.7	2,751	27.78	74.0
Japan	90.9	9.6	126,497	13.12	83.3
Kenya	17.8	0.3	41,610	42.37	62.9
Lebanon	78.2	4.3	4,259	21.64	78.6
Micronesia	35.3	1.4	112	35.81	66.9
Netherlands	93.2	9.9	16,665	17.21	81.3
Nicaragua	27.9	0.8	5,870	33.37	73.1
Norway	96.5	9.2	4,925	18.64	81.6
Slovakia	81.6	5.6	5,472	15.00	76.2
Somalia	2.0	0.1	9,557	47.35	54.9
Spain	84.6	5.1	46,455	15.20	82.5
Turkey	64.7	4.5	73,640	26.00	75.6
Venezuela	64.3	6.1	29,437	28.84	73.1
Yemen	26.7	0.9	24,800	40.72	66.0
Worldwide Average	52.8	5.1	16,348	28.80	70.8

Data Sets

Unit 7

MATH IN ACTION | SESSION 2 ■ ■

Age Groups

Country	Total Population (thousands)	Population under age 15 (%)	Population over age 60 (%)
Afghanistan	32,358	47.42	3.82
Argentina	40,765	24.42	14.97
Australia	22,606	18.95	19.46
Canada	34,350	16.37	20.82
Ecuador	14,666	30.29	9.21
Egypt	82,537	31.25	8.62
Ethiopia	84,734	43.29	5.17
Fiji	868	28.88	8.38
Finland	5,385	16.42	25.90
France	63,126	18.26	23.82
Germany	82,163	13.17	26.72
Jamaica	2,751	27.78	10.98
Japan	126,497	13.12	31.92
Kenya	41,610	42.37	4.25
Lebanon	4,259	21.64	12.03
Micronesia	112	35.81	6.67
Netherlands	16,665	17.21	23.02
Nicaragua	5,870	33.37	6.59
Norway	4,925	18.64	21.41
Slovakia	5,472	15.00	18.60
Somalia	9,557	47.35	4.46
Spain	46,455	15.20	22.86
Turkey	73,640	26.00	10.56
Venezuela	29,437	28.84	9.17
Yemen	24,800	40.72	4.54

Set 1 Functions

➤ **Fill in the blanks for problem 1.**

1 The table shows inputs and outputs.

Input (x)	1	2	3	4	5
Output (y)	1	1	2	2	3

In the table, y _____ a function of x, because each _____ has only

one _____ .

➤ **Solve problem 2.**

2 Complete the graph by plotting the (input, output) pairs in the table.
Use the graph to explain why y is not a function of x.

Input (x)	−2	1	0	−1	2	0
Output (y)	0	2	1	0	4	3

Set 2 Linear and Nonlinear Functions

➤ **Tell whether each function is *linear* or *nonlinear*.**

1 $y = 2x + 4$ _____

2 $y = \frac{x}{2} - 3$ _____

3 $y = x^2 + 2$ _____

4 $y = 2$ _____

5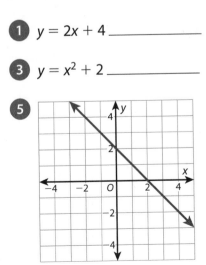

6

_____

_____

Set 3 Use Functions to Model Linear Relationships

➤ **Solve the problems. Show your work.**

1 The total cost of an order of custom jackets is a function of the number of jackets. The table shows the cost of ordering different numbers of jackets. Write an equation for the linear function that models this situation.

Jackets	Cost
10	$350
40	$1,100
50	$1,350

2 Rafael is biking home from work. The graph shows Rafael's distance from home as a function of time.

Find the initial value and rate of change for the function and describe what each quantity means in this situation.

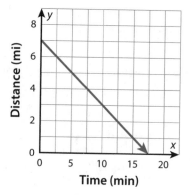

3 Diana observes a snail moving away from herself. The snail moves 2 inches in 4 seconds. The snail is 9 inches away from Diana after 3 seconds. Write an equation for the snail's distance from Diana, y, as a function of time, x.

4 The graph of a linear function passes through the point $(2, -3)$. The value of the function decreases by 4 when the input decreases by 3. Write the equation that models the function.

Set 4 Compare Functions

➤ **Solve the problem. Show your work.**

1 The graph shows the distance a dog runs over time. The equation $d = 13t$ gives the distance a cat runs in meters as a function of time in seconds. Which animal is faster, and by how much?

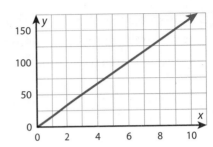

Set 5 Analyze Graphs of Functional Relationships

➤ **Use the graph at the right for problems 1–3. For each section, tell whether the graph is *increasing, decreasing,* or *neither,* and whether it is *linear* or *nonlinear*.**

1 Section A _____

2 Section B _____

3 Section C _____

➤ **Use the graph at the right for problems 4–6. Identify the entire interval for which each statement is true.**

4 For _____ $< x <$ _____ , the function increases at a constant rate.

5 For _____ $< x <$ _____ , the function increases slowly at first and then starts to speed up.

6 For _____ $< x <$ _____ , the function increases quickly at first and then starts to slow down.

Set 6 Graph Proportional Relationships and Calculate Slope

➤ **Solve the problems. Show your work.**

1 A train travels at a constant speed for 15 minutes and covers 20 miles in that time. Complete the graph to show the change in the train's distance over time. What is the slope of the line?

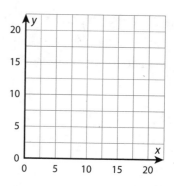

2 What is the slope of the line in the graph below?

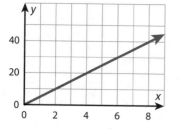

Set 7 Solve Systems of Linear Equations

➤ **Solve the systems of linear equations. Show your work**

1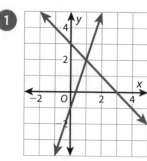

2 $y = 2x$

$y + 4x = 9$

3 $3x + 2y = 0$

$x + y = 1$

Set 1 Apply Exponent Properties for Positive Integer Exponents

➤ **Rewrite each expression as a single power for problems 1–6. Show your work.**

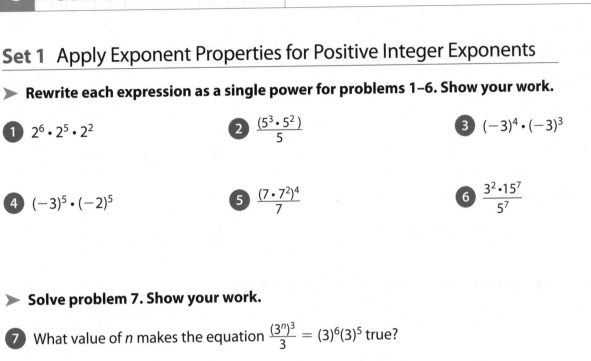

1 $2^6 \cdot 2^5 \cdot 2^2$

2 $\dfrac{(5^3 \cdot 5^2)}{5}$

3 $(-3)^4 \cdot (-3)^3$

4 $(-3)^5 \cdot (-2)^5$

5 $\dfrac{(7 \cdot 7^2)^4}{7}$

6 $\dfrac{3^2 \cdot 15^7}{5^7}$

➤ **Solve problem 7. Show your work.**

7 What value of n makes the equation $\dfrac{(3^n)^3}{3} = (3)^6(3)^5$ true?

Set 2 Apply Exponent Properties for All Integer Exponents

➤ **Evaluate the expressions for problems 1–6. Show your work.**

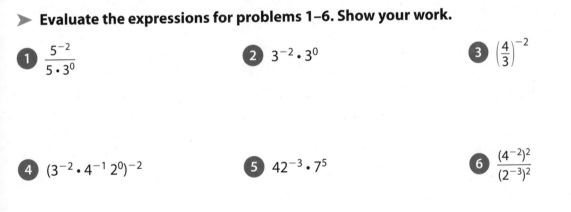

1 $\dfrac{5^{-2}}{5 \cdot 3^0}$

2 $3^{-2} \cdot 3^0$

3 $\left(\dfrac{4}{3}\right)^{-2}$

4 $(3^{-2} \cdot 4^{-1} 2^0)^{-2}$

5 $42^{-3} \cdot 7^5$

6 $\dfrac{(4^{-2})^2}{(2^{-3})^2}$

➤ **Solve problem 7. Show your work.**

7 What value of n makes the equation $8^{-n} = \dfrac{1}{2^3}$ true?

Set 3 Express Numbers Using Integer Powers of 10

➤ Write an estimate for each number as a single digit times an integer power of 10 for problems 1–3.

1 7.549 _____

2 0.00061 _____

3 9486 _____

➤ Write each number in standard form for problems 4–6.

4 $4 \times 10^6 =$ _____

5 $7 \times 10^1 =$ _____

6 $3 \times 10^{-5} =$ _____

➤ Fill in the blanks to compare the numbers for problems 7 and 8.

7 6×10^6 is _____ times as great as 3×10^5.

8 2×10^2 is _____ times as great as 5×10^{-2}.

Set 4 Scientific Notation

➤ Solve the problems. Write your answers in scientific notation. Show your work.

1 $(7.25 \times 10^6) - (6.47 \times 10^5)$

2 $6.2 \times 10^{-4} + 0.0025$

3 $(900,000) \times (2.2 \times 10^{-3})$

4 $(6.5 \times 10^9) + (1.2 \times 10^{10}) \times (3.4 \times 10^8)$

5 $(3.6 \times 10^4) \div (6 \times 10^3)$

6 $(3.1 \times 10^{-3}) \times (0.0025)$

Set 5 Functions

➤ **Tell whether each function is *linear* or *nonlinear*.**

1 $y = 2x$

2 $y = \dfrac{3}{x}$

3 $2y - 1 = 4x + 2$

_____   _____   _____

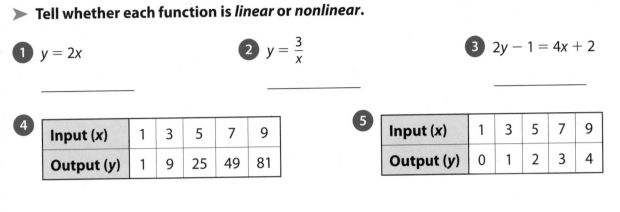

4

Input (x)	1	3	5	7	9
Output (y)	1	9	25	49	81

5

Input (x)	1	3	5	7	9
Output (y)	0	1	2	3	4

_____   _____

Set 6 Compare Functions

➤ **Solve the problems. Show your work.**

1 A used bookstore sells hardcover and paperback books. The equation $C = 4b$ gives the cost in dollars for buying paperback books. The cost is a function of the number of books. The table shows the cost for buying hardcover books.

What is the difference in cost of the two types of books?

Books	2	4	6	8	10
Cost ($)	12	24	36	48	60

2 Jada and Tom are racing to a finish line. The equation $d = 400 - 4.4t$ gives Jada's distance in meters from the finish line after t seconds. The graph shows Tom's distance from the finish line over time. Who is closer to the finish line at $t = 0$? Who is running faster?

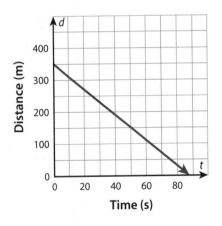

Set 7 Solutions to One-Variable Equations

➤ **Solve each equation for x and tell how many solutions it has. Show your work.**

1 $15 - 3x = 12 + 3x$

2 $4x + 6 = 4x + 9$

3 $3x + 8 = 2(x + 4) - x - 5$

4 $3(3x - 2) = 2(5x + 3) - x$

5 $3(x + 4) = 2(2x + 3)$

6 $4x - 1 = 3(2x + 1) - 2x - 4$

Set 8 Transformations Involving Dilations

➤ **Perform each sequence of transformations. Draw the image.**

1 Rotate $\triangle ABC$ 180° clockwise around the origin. Then dilate the image by a scale factor of 2 with a center of dilation at the origin.

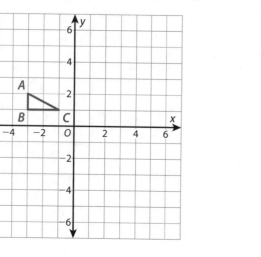

2 Dilate $\triangle ABC$ by a scale factor of $\frac{1}{3}$ with a center of dilation at the origin. Then reflect the image across the y-axis.

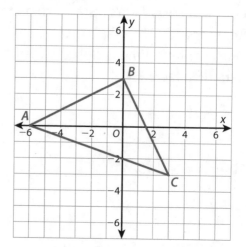

Set 1 Square Roots and Cube Roots

➤ **Solve the equations. Show your work.**

1 $s^3 = \frac{27}{64}$

2 $x^2 - 29 = 4$

3 $x^3 = 729$

4 $y^2 + 16 = 25$

5 $m^3 + 4 = 12$

6 $x^2 - 5 = -4$

Set 2 Use Functions to Model Linear Relationships

➤ **Solve the problems. Show your work.**

1 A plane flies toward an airport at a constant speed. After 40 minutes, it is 1,300 miles from the airport. After 1 hour, it is 1,100 miles from the airport. Write an equation for the plane's distance from the airport, y, as a function of flying time in hours, x.

2 Water is drained from a pool at a constant rate. The table shows the amount of water remaining in the pool as a function of time draining. How much water was in the pool when it started to drain? What is the rate of change?

Time (min)	Water (gal)
30	11,750
60	11,000
120	9,500

Set 3 The Pythagorean Theorem and Its Converse

➤ **Fill in the blank to describe the converse of the Pythagorean Theorem for problem 1.**

1 In a triangle, if the square of the length of one side of the triangle is equal to the sum of the squares of the lengths of the other two sides, then the triangle is

a _____ .

➤ **Solve problems 2 and 3.**

2 A right triangle has sides of length e, f, and g where $f^2 - g^2 = e^2$. Which side is the hypotenuse?

3 What is the length of the hypotenuse of the right triangle? Show your work.

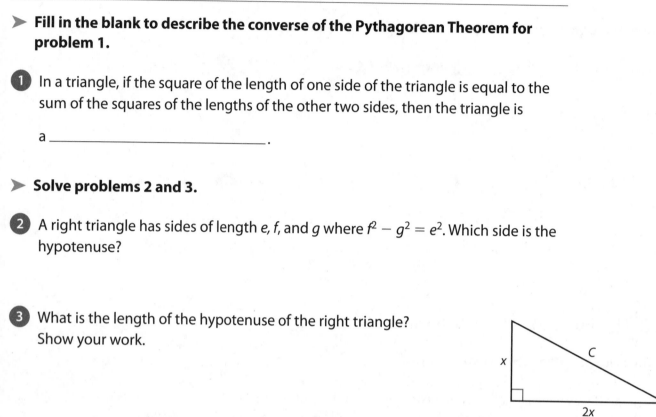

Set 4 Apply the Pythagorean Theorem in a Geometric Figure

➤ **Solve the problems. Show your work.**

1 The figure is a right rectangular prism. To the nearest tenth of a foot, what is the length of the diagonal from D to E?

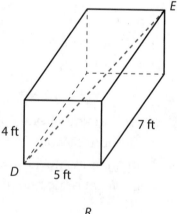

2 What is the height of $\triangle RST$?

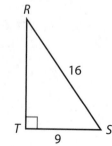

Set 5   Apply the Pythagorean Theorem in the Coordinate Plane

➤ **Use the figure at the right to solve problems 1 and 2. Show your work.**

1 What is the distance between points *R* and *S*?

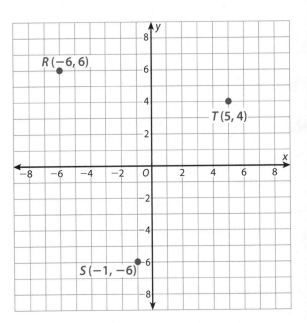

2 What is the distance between points *R* and *T*?

➤ **Solve problem 3. Show your work.**

3 What is the perimeter of trapezoid *ABCD*?

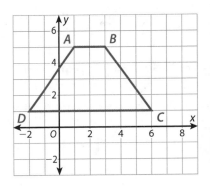

Set 6 Analyze Graphs of Functional Relationships

➤ **Use the figure at the right for problems 1–6. Identify the section(s) for which each statement is true.**

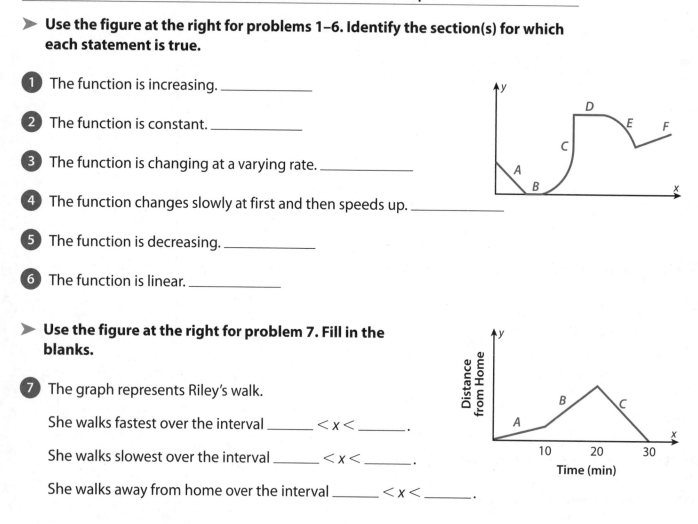

1 The function is increasing. _____

2 The function is constant. _____

3 The function is changing at a varying rate. _____

4 The function changes slowly at first and then speeds up. _____

5 The function is decreasing. _____

6 The function is linear. _____

➤ **Use the figure at the right for problem 7. Fill in the blanks.**

7 The graph represents Riley's walk.

She walks fastest over the interval _____ $< x <$ _____.

She walks slowest over the interval _____ $< x <$ _____.

She walks away from home over the interval _____ $< x <$ _____.

Set 7 Solve Linear Equations in One Variable

➤ **Solve the equations. Show your work.**

1 $5t - \frac{2}{3} = 4\left(\frac{1}{2}t - \frac{1}{4}\right)$

2 $5(m + 1) - \frac{5}{3} = 4\left(m - \frac{2}{3}\right)$

3 $0.5(2.5 - 5x) = 3.5 - 4x$

Interactive Glossary/Glosario interactivo

English/Español	Example/Ejemplo	Notes/Notas

Aa

absolute value a number's distance from 0 on the number line. Absolute value is never negative.

$|-3| = 3$
$|3| = 3$

valor absoluto distancia de un número desde 0 en la recta numérica. El valor absoluto nunca es negativo.

---

acute angle an angle that measures more than 0° but less than 90°.

ángulo agudo ángulo que mide más de 0° pero menos de 90°.

---

acute triangle a triangle that has three acute angles.

triángulo acutángulo triángulo que tiene tres ángulos agudos.

---

additive inverses two numbers whose sum is zero. The additive inverse of a number is the opposite of that number, i.e., the additive inverse of a is $-a$.

-2 and 2
$\frac{1}{2}$ and $-\frac{1}{2}$

inverso aditivo dos números cuya suma es cero. El inverso aditivo de un número es el opuesto de ese número; por ejemplo, el inverso aditivo de a es $-a$.

---

adjacent angles two non-overlapping angles that share a vertex and a side.

ángulos adyacentes dos ángulos que no se superponen y que comparten un vértice y un lado.

$\angle ADB$ and $\angle BDC$ are adjacent angles.

---

algorithm a set of routine steps used to solve problems.

$$\begin{array}{r} 17\ \text{R}\ 19 \\ 31\overline{)546} \\ -31\downarrow \\ \hline 236 \\ -217 \\ \hline 19 \end{array}$$

algoritmo conjunto de pasos rutinarios que se siguen para resolver problemas.

English/Español	Example/Ejemplo	Notes/Notas
alternate exterior angles when two lines are cut by a transversal, a pair of angles on opposite sides of the transversal and outside the two lines. When the two lines are parallel, alternate exterior angles are congruent. **ángulos alternos externos** cuando a dos rectas se cortan con una transversal, par de ángulos en lados opuestos de la transversal y fuera de las dos rectas. Cuando las dos rectas son paralelas, los ángulos alternos externos son congruentes.	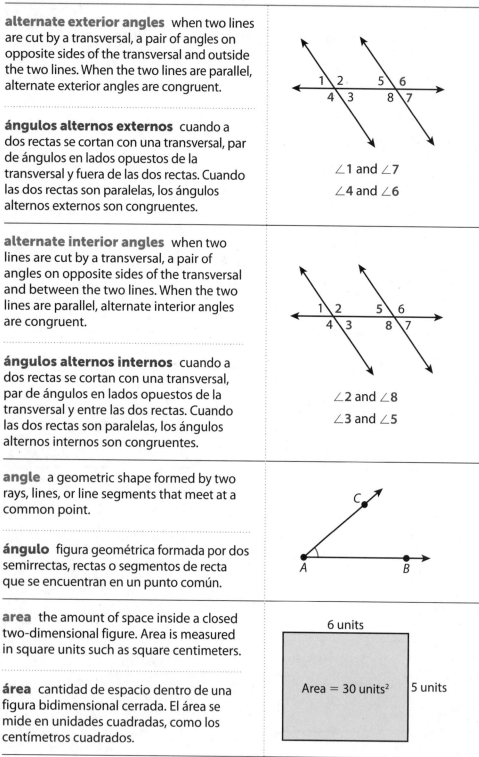 $\angle 1$ and $\angle 7$ $\angle 4$ and $\angle 6$	
alternate interior angles when two lines are cut by a transversal, a pair of angles on opposite sides of the transversal and between the two lines. When the two lines are parallel, alternate interior angles are congruent. **ángulos alternos internos** cuando a dos rectas se cortan con una transversal, par de ángulos en lados opuestos de la transversal y entre las dos rectas. Cuando las dos rectas son paralelas, los ángulos alternos internos son congruentes.	$\angle 2$ and $\angle 8$ $\angle 3$ and $\angle 5$	
angle a geometric shape formed by two rays, lines, or line segments that meet at a common point. **ángulo** figura geométrica formada por dos semirrectas, rectas o segmentos de recta que se encuentran en un punto común.		
area the amount of space inside a closed two-dimensional figure. Area is measured in square units such as square centimeters. **área** cantidad de espacio dentro de una figura bidimensional cerrada. El área se mide en unidades cuadradas, como los centímetros cuadrados.	6 units Area = 30 units² 5 units	

English/Español	Example/Ejemplo	Notes/Notas

association (between two variables)
a relationship between two variables. Two variables can be described as having a *linear association*, a *nonlinear association*, or *no association*. Linear associations can be described as *positive* or *negative*.

There is a positive association between x and y.

asociación (entre dos variables)
relación que existe entre dos variables. Dos variables se pueden describir como que tienen una *asociación lineal, no lineal,* o *ninguna asociación*. Las asociaciones lineales se pueden describir como *positivas* o *negativas*.

associative property of addition
regrouping the terms does not change the value of the expression.

$(a + b) + c = a + (b + c)$

$(2 + 3) + 4 = 2 + (3 + 4)$

propiedad asociativa de la suma
reagrupar los términos no cambia el valor de la expresión.

associative property of multiplication
regrouping the terms does not change the value of the expression.

$(a \cdot b) \cdot c = a \cdot (b \cdot c)$

$(2 \cdot 3) \cdot 4 = 2 \cdot (3 \cdot 4)$

propiedad asociativa de la multiplicación reagrupar los términos no cambia el valor de la expresión.

axis a horizontal or vertical number line that determines a coordinate plane. The plural form is *axes*.

eje recta numérica horizontal o vertical que determina un plano de coordenadas.

©Curriculum Associates, LLC   Copying is not permitted.

Interactive Glossary/Glosario interactivo   **GL3**

Bb

balance point the point that represents the center of a data set. In a two-variable data set, the coordinates of the balance point are the mean of each variable.

punto de equilibrio punto que representa el centro de un conjunto de datos. En un conjunto de datos de dos variables, las coordenadas del punto de equilibrio son la media de cada variable.

Data set: (1, 1), (3, 4), (5, 6), (7, 8)

$$\frac{1 + 3 + 5 + 7}{4} = 4$$

$$\frac{1 + 4 + 6 + 8}{4} = 4.75$$

Balance point: (4, 4.75)

base (of a parallelogram) a side of a parallelogram from which the height is measured.

base (de un paralelogramo) lado de un paralelogramo desde el que se mide la altura.

base (of a power) in a power, the number that is used as a repeated factor.

base (de una potencia) en una potencia, el número que se usa como factor que se repite.

8^2

base

base (of a three-dimensional figure) a face of a three-dimensional figure from which the height is measured.

base (de una figura tridimensional) cara de una figura tridimensional desde la que se mide la altura.

base (of a triangle) a side of a triangle from which the height is measured.

base (de un triángulo) lado de un triángulo desde el que se mide la altura.

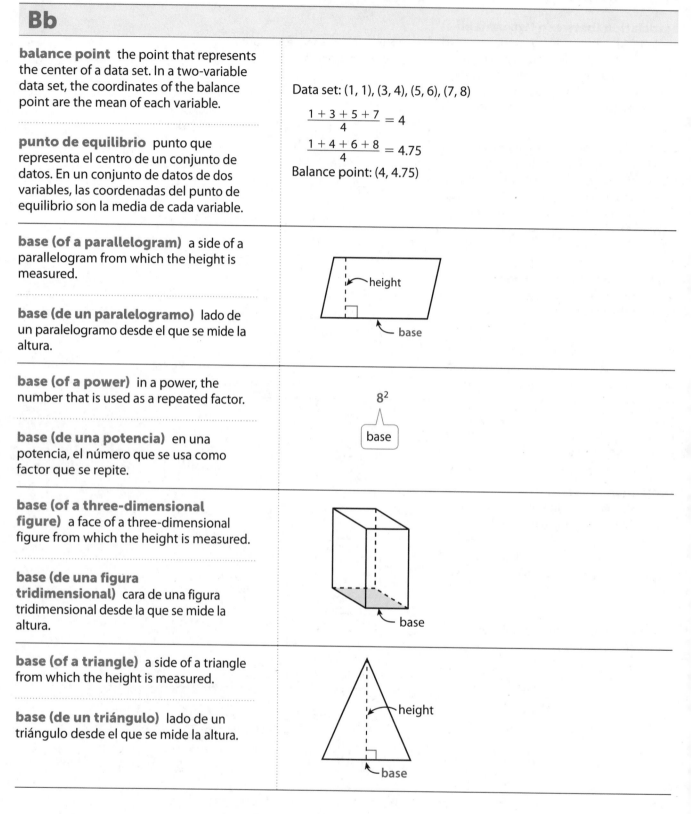

English/Español	Example/Ejemplo	Notes/Notas

bivariate involving two variables.

bivariante que tiene dos variables.

Car Data	
Years Old	**Color**
3	Red
4	Blue

box plot a visual display of a data set on a number line that shows the minimum, the lower quartile, the median, the upper quartile, and the maximum. The sides of the box show the lower and upper quartiles and the line inside the box shows the median. Lines connect the box to the minimum and maximum values.

diagrama de caja representación visual de un conjunto de datos en una recta numérica que muestra el mínimo, el cuartil inferior, la mediana, el cuartil superior y el máximo. Los lados de la caja muestran los cuartiles inferior y superior y la recta del centro muestra la mediana. Las rectas conectan la caja con los valores mínimo y máximo.

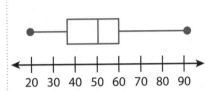

Cc

categorical data data that are divided into categories, such as characteristics of the population.

datos por categorías datos que se dividen en categorías, como las características de la población.

Car color: red, blue, white, black

---

center (of a circle) the point inside a circle that is the same distance from every point on the circle.

centro (de un círculo) punto dentro de un círculo que está a la misma distancia de todos los puntos del círculo.

---

center of dilation a fixed point from which a figure is dilated.

centro de dilatación punto fijo desde el que se dilata una figura.

---

center of rotation a fixed point around which a figure is rotated.

centro de rotación punto fijo alrededor del que se rota una figura.

---

circle a two-dimensional shape in which every point is the same distance from the center.

círculo figura bidimensional en que todos los puntos están a la misma distancia del centro.

---

circumference the distance around the outside of a circle. It can be thought of as the perimeter of the circle.

circunferencia distancia alrededor del exterior de un círculo. Se puede considerar como el perímetro del círculo.

English/Español	Example/Ejemplo	Notes/Notas
closed figure a two-dimensional figure that begins and ends at the same point.	Closed figure Open figure	
figura cerrada figura bidimensional que comienza y termina en el mismo punto.		
cluster a group of data points that are close to each other.	cluster 0 1 2 3 4	
agrupación conjunto de datos que están cerca unos de otros.		
coefficient a number that is multiplied by a variable.	$5x + 3$ coefficient	
coeficiente número que se multiplica por una variable.		
commission a fee paid for services, often a percent of the total cost. A salesperson who earns a commission often gets a percent of the total sale.	A 5% commission on $4,000 is 0.05($4,000), or $200.	
comisión tarifa que se paga por servicios, que suele ser un porcentaje del costo total. Un vendedor que gana una comisión por lo general recibe un porcentaje de la venta total.		
common denominator a number that is a common multiple of the denominators of two or more fractions.	A common denominator for $\frac{1}{2}$ and $\frac{3}{5}$ is 10 because $2 \cdot 5 = 10$.	
denominador común número que es múltiplo común de los denominadores de dos o más fracciones.		
commutative property of addition changing the order of the addends does not change the sum.	$a + b = b + a$ $4.1 + 7.5 = 7.5 + 4.1$	
propiedad conmutativa de la suma cambiar el orden de los sumandos no cambia el total.		

English/Español	Example/Ejemplo	Notes/Notas
commutative property of multiplication changing the order of the factors does not change the product. **propiedad conmutativa de la multiplicación** cambiar el orden de los factores no cambia el producto.	$ab = ba$ $4(7.5) = 7.5(4)$	
compare to describe the relationship between the value or size of two numbers or quantities. **comparar** describir la relación que hay entre el valor o el tamaño de dos números o cantidades.	$-4 < 8.5$	
complementary angles two angles whose measures sum to 90°. **ángulos complementarios** dos ángulos cuyas medidas suman 90°.	 $\angle AEB$ and $\angle BEC$	
complex fraction a fraction in which the numerator is a fraction, the denominator is a fraction, or both the numerator and the denominator are fractions. **fracción compleja** fracción en la que el numerador es una fracción, el denominador es una fracción, o tanto el numerador como el denominador son fracciones.	$\dfrac{\frac{1}{2}}{\frac{3}{4}}$	
compose to make by combining parts. You can put together numbers to make a greater number or put together shapes to make a new shape. **componer** formar al combinar partes. Se pueden unir números para hacer un número mayor o unir figuras para formar una figura nueva.		
composite number a number that has more than one pair of whole number factors. **número compuesto** número que tiene más de un par de números enteros como factores.	16 is a composite number because 1 · 16, 2 · 8, and 4 · 4 all equal 16.	

English/Español	Example/Ejemplo	Notes/Notas
compound event an event that consists of two or more simple events. **evento compuesto** evento que consiste en dos o más eventos simples.	Rolling a number cube twice	
cone a three-dimensional figure with one circular base and one vertex, connected by a curved surface. **cono** figura tridimensional que tiene una base circular y un vértice, conectados por una superficie curva.		
congruent (≅) same size and shape. Two figures are congruent if there is a sequence of rigid transformations that maps one figure onto the second. **congruente** (≅) del mismo tamaño y forma. Dos figuras son congruentes si hay una secuencia de transformaciones rígidas que hace coincidir una figura con la segunda.	Figure C' is congruent to Figure C.	
constant of proportionality the unit rate in a proportional relationship. **constante de proporcionalidad** tasa unitaria en una relación proporcional.	Unit rate: $10 per hour Constant of proportionality for dollars per hours: 10.	
converse of the Pythagorean Theorem in a triangle, if the square of the length of the longest side is equal to the sum of the squares of the lengths of the other two sides, then the triangle is a right triangle. **recíproco del teorema de Pitágoras** en un triángulo, si el cuadrado de la longitud del lado más largo es igual a la suma de los cuadrados de las longitudes de los otros dos lados, entonces el triángulo es un triángulo rectángulo.	If $c^2 = a^2 + b^2$, the triangle is a right triangle.	
convert to write an equivalent measurement using a different unit. **convertir** escribir una medida equivalente usando una unidad diferente.	60 in. is the same as 5 ft.	

English/Español	Example/Ejemplo	Notes/Notas

coordinate plane a two-dimensional space formed by two perpendicular number lines called *axes*.

plano de coordenadas espacio bidimensional formado por dos rectas numéricas perpendiculares llamadas ejes.

---

corresponding angles
(1) angles in the same relative position in figures. When figures are similar or congruent, corresponding angles are congruent.
(2) angles in the same relative position when two lines are cut by a transversal. When the two lines are parallel, corresponding angles are congruent.

ángulos correspondientes
(1) ángulos que están en la misma posición relativa en las figuras. Cuando las figuras son semejantes o congruentes, los ángulos correspondientes son congruentes.
(2) ángulos que están en la misma posición relativa cuando se cortan dos rectas con una transversal. Cuando las dos rectas son paralelas, los ángulos correspondientes son congruentes.

∠A and ∠S

∠2 and ∠6
∠4 and ∠8

---

corresponding sides sides in the same relative position in figures. When figures are congruent, corresponding sides are the same length.

lados correspondientes lados que están en la misma posición relativa en las figuras. Cuando las figuras son congruentes, los lados correspondientes tienen la misma longitud.

$\overline{AD}$ and $\overline{ST}$

---

corresponding terms terms that have the same position in two related patterns. For example, the second term in one pattern and the second term in a related pattern are corresponding terms.

términos correspondientes términos que tienen la misma posición en dos patrones relacionados. Por ejemplo, el segundo término en un patrón y el segundo término en un patrón relacionado son términos correspondientes.

Pattern A: 12, 18, 24, 30
Pattern B: 6, 9, 12, 15

---

cross-section a two-dimensional shape that is exposed by making a straight cut through a three-dimensional figure.

sección transversal figura bidimensional que se forma al hacer un corte recto a través de una figura tridimensional.

cube a rectangular prism in which each face of the prism is a square.

cubo prisma rectangular en el que cada cara del prisma es un cuadrado.

1 unit
1 unit
1 unit

cube root of *x* the number that when cubed is equal to *x*.

raíz cúbica de *x* número que cuando se eleva al cubo es igual a *x*.

$$\sqrt[3]{8} = \sqrt[3]{2 \cdot 2 \cdot 2}$$
$$= 2$$

2 is the cube root of 8.

cylinder a three-dimensional figure with two parallel curved bases that are the same size. The bases are connected by a curved surface.

cilindro figura tridimensional que tiene dos bases curvas paralelas que tienen el mismo tamaño. Las bases están conectadas por una superficie curva.

Dd

data a set of collected information. Often numerical information such as a list of measurements.

datos conjunto de información reunida. Con frecuencia, información numérica como una lista de medidas.

Commute length (mi):

15, 22, 10.5, 21, 9.5

---

decimal a number containing a decimal point that separates a whole from fractional place values (tenths, hundredths, thousandths, and so on).

decimal número que tiene un punto decimal que separa un entero de los valores posicionales fraccionarios (décimas, centésimas, milésimas, etc.).

1.293

---

decompose to break into parts. You can break apart numbers and shapes.

descomponer separar en partes. Se puede separar en partes números y figuras.

---

degree (°) a unit used to measure angles.

grado (°) unidad que se usa para medir ángulos.

There are 360° in a circle.

---

denominator the number below the line in a fraction that tells the number of equal parts in the whole.

denominador número debajo de la línea en una fracción que indica el número de partes iguales que hay en el entero.

$\dfrac{3}{4}$

---

dependent variable a variable whose value depends on the value of a related independent variable.

variable dependiente variable cuyo valor depende del valor de una variable independiente relacionada.

$y = 5x$

The value of y depends on the value of x.

| **English/Español** | **Example**/Ejemplo | **Notes**/Notas |

English/Español	Example/Ejemplo	Notes/Notas

English/Español	Example/Ejemplo	Notes/Notas

diameter a line segment that goes through the center of a circle and has endpoints on the circle. Also, the distance across a circle through the center.

diámetro segmento de recta que pasa por el centro de un círculo y tiene extremos en el círculo. También, la distancia de un lado al otro del círculo a través del centro.

diameter

---

difference the result of subtraction.

diferencia resultado de la resta.

$$\begin{array}{r} 16.75 \\ -\ 15.70 \\ \hline 1.05 \end{array}$$

---

digit a symbol used to write numbers.

dígito símbolo que se usa para escribir números.

The digits are 0, 1, 2, 3, 4, 5, 6, 7, 8, and 9.

---

dilation a transformation that makes a scale copy of a figure. A dilation is a proportional shrinking or enlargement of a figure.

dilatación transformación que produce una copia a escala de una figura. Una dilatación es una reducción o ampliación proporcional de una figura.

Figure *B* is a dilation of Figure *A*.

---

dimension length in one direction. A figure may have one, two, or three dimensions.

dimensión longitud en una dirección. Una figura puede tener una, dos o tres dimensiones.

5 in.
2 in.
3 in.

---

distribution a representation that shows how often values in a data set occur.

distribución representación que muestra la frecuencia con la que ocurren los valores en un conjunto de datos.

Pet	Frequency
Bird	7
Cat	12
Dog	8
Snake	3

English/Español	Example/Ejemplo	Notes/Notas
distributive property multiplying each term in a sum or difference by a common factor does not change the value of the expression. **propiedad distributiva** multiplicar cada término de una suma o diferencia por un factor común no cambia el valor de la expresión.	$a(b + c) = ab + ac$ $5(4 + 2) = 5(4) + 5(2)$	
dividend the number that is divided by another number. **dividendo** número que se divide por otro número.	$22.5 \div 3 = 7.5$	
divisor the number by which another number is divided. **divisor** número por el que se divide otro número.	$22.5 \div 3 = 7.5$	
dot plot a data display that shows data as dots above a number line. A dot plot may also be called a *line plot*. **diagrama de puntos** representación de datos que muestra datos como puntos sobre una *recta numérica*.		

Ee

edge a line segment where two faces meet in a three-dimensional shape.

arista segmento de recta en el que dos caras se unen en una figura tridimensional.

edge

---

equal having the same value, same size, or same amount.

igual que tiene el mismo valor, el mismo tamaño o la misma cantidad.

$50 - 20 = 30$

$50 - 20$ is equal to 30.

---

equation a mathematical statement that uses an equal sign ($=$) to show that two expressions have the same value.

ecuación enunciado matemático que tiene un signo de igual ($=$) para mostrar que dos expresiones tienen el mismo valor.

$x + 4 = 15$

---

equilateral triangle a triangle that has all three sides the same length.

triángulo equilátero triángulo que tiene los tres lados de la misma longitud.

---

equivalent having the same value.

equivalente que tiene el mismo valor.

4 is equivalent to $\frac{8}{2}$.

---

equivalent expressions two or more expressions in different forms that always name the same value.

expresiones equivalentes dos o más expresiones en diferentes formas que siempre nombran el mismo valor.

$2(x + 4)$ is equivalent to $2x + 2(4)$ and $2x + 8$.

English/Español	Example/Ejemplo	Notes/Notas
equivalent fractions two or more different fractions that name the same part of a whole or the same point on the number line. **fracciones equivalentes** dos o más fracciones diferentes que nombran la misma parte de un entero o el mismo punto en la recta numérica.	$-\dfrac{5}{10}$ $\dfrac{4}{8}$ $-\dfrac{1}{2}$ $\dfrac{1}{2}$ ← -1 0 1 →	
equivalent ratios two ratios that express the same comparison. Multiplying both numbers in the ratio $a : b$ by a nonzero number n results in the equivalent ratio $na : nb$. **razones equivalentes** dos razones que expresan la misma comparación. Multiplicar ambos números en la razón $a : b$ por un número distinto de cero n da como resultado la razón equivalente $na : nb$.	$6 : 8$ is equivalent to $3 : 4$	
estimate (noun) a close guess made using mathematical thinking. **estimación** suposición aproximada que se hace por medio del razonamiento matemático.	$28 + 21 = ?$ $30 + 20 = 50$ 50 is an estimate of $28 + 21$.	
estimate (verb) to give an approximate number or answer based on mathematical thinking. **estimar** dar un número o respuesta aproximada basados en el razonamiento matemático.	$28 + 21$ is about 50.	
evaluate to find the value of an expression. **evaluar** hallar el valor de una expresión.	The expression $4.5 \div (1 + 8)$ has a value of 0.5.	

English/Español	Example/Ejemplo	Notes/Notas
event a set of one or more outcomes of an experiment. **evento** conjunto de uno o más resultados de un experimento.	Experiment: rolling a number cube once Possible events: rolling an even number, rolling a 1	
experiment a repeatable procedure involving chance that results in one or more possible outcomes. **experimento** procedimiento repetible en el que se hacen pruebas y da uno o más resultados posibles.	Experiment: rolling a number cube once	
experimental probability the probability of an event occurring based on the results from an experiment. **probabilidad experimental** probabilidad de que un evento ocurra con base en los resultados de un experimento.	A coin is flipped 30 times and lands heads up 17 times. The experimental probability of the coin landing heads up is $\frac{17}{30}$.	
exponent in a power, the number that shows how many times the base is used as a factor. **exponente** en una potencia, el número que muestra cuántas veces se usa la base como factor.	8^2 exponent	
exponential expression an expression that includes an exponent. **expresión exponencial** expresión que tiene un exponente.	$3x^3$	

English/Español	Example/Ejemplo	Notes/Notas

expression a group of numbers, variables, and/or operation symbols that represents a mathematical relationship. An expression without variables, such as $3 + 4$, is called a *numerical expression*. An expression with variables, such as $5b^2$, is called an *algebraic expression*.

expresión grupo de números, variables y/o símbolos de operaciones que representa una relación matemática. Una expresión sin variables, como $3 + 4$, se llama *expresión numérica*. Una expresión con variables, como $5b^2$, se llama *expresión algebraica*.

$$\frac{32 - 4}{7}$$

$$3x + y - 9$$

exterior angle when you extend one side of a polygon, the angle between the extended side and the adjacent side. This angle forms a linear pair with the adjacent interior angle of the polygon.

ángulo externo cuando se amplía un lado de un polígono, se forma un ángulo entre el lado ampliado y el lado adyacente. Este ángulo forma un par lineal con el ángulo interno adyacente del polígono.

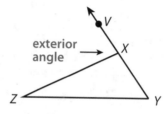

exterior angle →

Ff

face a flat surface of a solid shape.

cara superficie plana de una figura sólida.

face

factor (noun) a number, or expression with parentheses, that is multiplied.

factor número, o expresión entre paréntesis, que se multiplica.

$4 \times 5 = 20$

factors

factor (verb) to rewrite an expression as a product of factors.

descomponer volver a escribir una expresión como producto de factores.

$12x + 42 = 6(2x + 7)$

factor pair two numbers that are multiplied together to give a product.

par de factores dos números que se multiplican para dar un producto.

$4 \times 5 = 20$

factor pair

factors of a number whole numbers that multiply together to get the given number.

factores de un número números enteros que se multiplican para obtener el número dado.

$4 \times 5 = 20$

4 and 5 are factors of 20.

formula a mathematical relationship that is expressed in the form of an equation.

fórmula relación matemática que se expresa en forma de ecuación.

$A = \ell w$

Interactive Glossary/Glosario interactivo

English/Español	Example/Ejemplo	Notes/Notas

fraction a number that names equal parts of a whole. A fraction names a point on the number line and can also represent the division of two numbers.

fracción número que nombra partes iguales de un entero. Una fracción nombra un punto en la recta numérica y también puede representar la división de dos números.

$$-\frac{1}{2} \qquad \frac{4}{8}$$

frequency a numerical count of how many times a data value occurs in a data set.

frecuencia conteo numérico de cuántas veces ocurre un valor en un conjunto de datos.

Data set: 12, 13, 12, 15, 12, 13, 15, 14, 12, 12

Data Value	Frequency
12	5
13	2
14	1
15	2

function a rule in which each input results in exactly one output.

función regla en la que cada entrada resulta en exactamente una salida.

Rule: $y = \frac{3}{2}x$

Gg

gap an interval of the number line for which a distribution has no data values.

espacio intervalo de la recta numérica para el que una distribución no tiene valores.

gratuity an amount added on to the cost of a service, often a percent of the total cost. Gratuity is often referred to as a *tip*.

propina cantidad que se suma al costo de un servicio; suele ser un porcentaje del costo total.

A gratuity of 18% on a $20 bill is 0.18($20), or $3.60.

greatest common factor (GCF) the greatest factor two or more numbers have in common.

máximo común divisor (M.C.D.) el mayor factor que dos o más números tienen en común.

GCF of 20 and 30: $2 \cdot 5$, or 10

$20 = 2 \cdot 2 \cdot 5$

$30 = 2 \cdot 3 \cdot 5$

grouping symbol a symbol, such as braces {}, brackets [], or parentheses (), used to group parts of an expression that should be evaluated before others.

símbolo de agrupación símbolo, como las llaves {}, los corchetes [] o los paréntesis (), que se usa para agrupar partes de una expresión que deben evaluarse antes que otras.

$3 \div (7 - 2) = 3 \div 5$

$\dfrac{3}{7 - 2} = \dfrac{3}{5}$

Hh

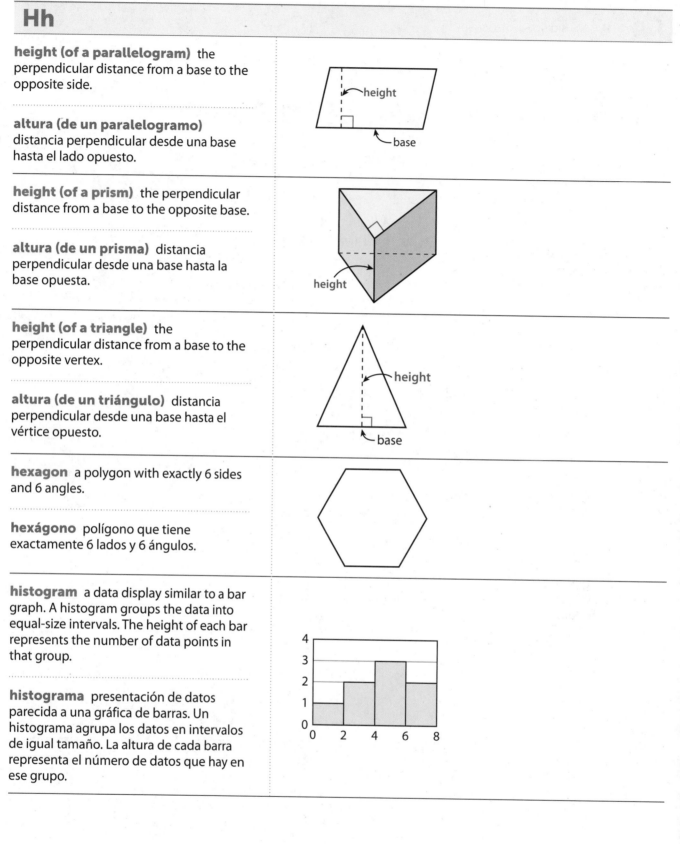

height (of a parallelogram) the perpendicular distance from a base to the opposite side.

altura (de un paralelogramo) distancia perpendicular desde una base hasta el lado opuesto.

height (of a prism) the perpendicular distance from a base to the opposite base.

altura (de un prisma) distancia perpendicular desde una base hasta la base opuesta.

height (of a triangle) the perpendicular distance from a base to the opposite vertex.

altura (de un triángulo) distancia perpendicular desde una base hasta el vértice opuesto.

hexagon a polygon with exactly 6 sides and 6 angles.

hexágono polígono que tiene exactamente 6 lados y 6 ángulos.

histogram a data display similar to a bar graph. A histogram groups the data into equal-size intervals. The height of each bar represents the number of data points in that group.

histograma presentación de datos parecida a una gráfica de barras. Un histograma agrupa los datos en intervalos de igual tamaño. La altura de cada barra representa el número de datos que hay en ese grupo.

English/Español	Example/Ejemplo	Notes/Notas
hypotenuse the side of a right triangle opposite the right angle. **hipotenusa** lado de un triángulo rectángulo opuesto al ángulo recto.	hypotenuse	

Ii

identity property of multiplication any number multiplied by 1 is itself. **propiedad de identidad de la multiplicación** cualquier número multiplicado por 1 es el mismo número.	$3 \cdot 1 = 3$	
image a figure that results from a transformation or sequence of transformations. **imagen** figura que resulta de una transformación o secuencia de transformaciones.	Figure C' is the image of Figure C after a reflection.	

English/Español	Example/Ejemplo	Notes/Notas
independent variable a variable whose value is used to find the value of another variable. An independent variable determines the value of a dependent variable.	$y = 5x$ The value of x is used to find the value of y.	
variable independiente variable cuyo valor se usa para hallar el valor de otra variable. Una variable independiente determina el valor de una variable dependiente.		
inequality a mathematical statement that uses an inequality symbol ($<, >, \leq, \geq$) to show the relationship between values of expressions.	$4{,}384 > 3{,}448$ $x \geq -2$	
desigualdad enunciado matemático que muestra con un símbolo de desigualdad ($<, >, \leq, \geq$) la relación que existe entre los valores de las expresiones.		
initial value in a linear function, the value of the output when the input is 0.	$y = \frac{1}{2}x + 25$ initial value	
valor inicial en una función lineal, el valor de la salida cuando la entrada es 0.		
input (of a function) the independent variable of a function.	$y = 2x + 1$	
entrada (de una función) variable independiente de una función.		Input (x): 0, 2, 3 — Output (y): 1, 5, 7
integers the set of whole numbers and their opposites.	$-3, -1, 0, 2, 3$	
enteros (positivos y negativos) conjunto de números enteros y sus opuestos.		
interquartile range (IQR) the difference between the upper quartile and lower quartile.	interquartile range IQR: $60 - 35 = 25$	
rango entre cuartiles (REC) diferencia entre el cuartil superior y el cuartil inferior.		

For the input/output example:

$y = 2x + 1$

Input (x)	0	2	3
Output (y)	1	5	7

inverse operations operations that undo each other. For example, addition and subtraction are inverse operations, and multiplication and division are inverse operations.

$300 \div 10 = 30$

$30 \times 10 = 300$

operaciones inversas operaciones que se cancelan entre sí. Por ejemplo, la suma y la resta son operaciones inversas, y la multiplicación y la división son operaciones inversas.

irrational number a number that cannot be expressed as a quotient of two integers. The decimal expansion of an irrational number never repeats or terminates.

$1.12112111211112\ldots$

$\sqrt{2}$

número irracional número que no se puede expresar como el cociente de dos enteros. La expansión decimal de un número irracional nunca se repite o termina.

isosceles triangle a triangle that has at least two sides the same length.

8 in.   8 in.

6 in.

triángulo isósceles triángulo que tiene al menos dos lados de la misma longitud.

Ll

least common multiple (LCM) the least multiple shared by two or more numbers.

mínimo común múltiplo (m.c.m.) el menor múltiplo que comparten dos o más números.

LCM of 20 and 30: $2 \cdot 2 \cdot 3 \cdot 5$, or 60

$20 = 2 \cdot 2 \cdot 5$

$30 = 2 \cdot 3 \cdot 5$

---

legs (of a right triangle) the two sides of a right triangle that form the right angle.

catetos (de un triángulo rectángulo) los dos lados de un triángulo rectángulo que forman el ángulo recto.

leg

leg

---

like terms two or more terms that have the same variable factors.

términos semejantes dos o más términos que tienen los mismos factores variables.

$2x^2$ and $4x^2$

1.2 and 5.1

$6xy$ and xy

---

line a straight row of points that goes on forever in both directions.

recta línea recta de puntos que continúa infinitamente en ambas direcciones.

---

line of fit a line drawn on a scatter plot to approximately model the relationship between the two sets of data.

recta de aproximación línea que se dibuja en un diagrama de dispersión para representar de manera aproximada la relación que existe entre los dos conjuntos de datos.

---

line of reflection a line across which a figure is reflected.

eje de reflexión línea a través de la que se refleja una figura.

A   B

line of reflection

English/Español	Example/Ejemplo	Notes/Notas
line of symmetry a line that divides a shape into two mirror images.		
eje de simetría línea que divide a una figura en dos imágenes reflejadas.		
line segment a straight row of points between two endpoints.		
segmento de recta fila recta de puntos entre dos extremos.	A • ————— • B	
linear association an association in which the relationship between the two variables can be generally approximated using a line.		
asociación lineal asociación en la que la relación que existe entre las dos variables se puede aproximar de manera general usando una recta.		
linear equation an equation whose graph is a straight line.	Equation: $y = \frac{3}{2}x$	
ecuación lineal ecuación cuya gráfica es una línea recta.		
linear function a function that can be represented by a linear equation. The graph of a linear function is a nonvertical straight line.		
función lineal función que se puede representar con una ecuación lineal. La gráfica de una función lineal es una recta no vertical.		

Interactive Glossary/Glosario interactivo

English/Español	Example/Ejemplo	Notes/Notas
linear pair two angles that are adjacent and supplementary.		
par lineal dos ángulos que son adyacentes y suplementarios.	$\angle BCA$ and $\angle ACD$ form a linear pair.	
lower quartile the middle number between the minimum and the median in an ordered set of numbers. The lower quartile is also called the 1st quartile or Q1.	lower quartile 20 30 40 50 60 70 80 90	
cuartil inferior el número del medio entre el mínimo y la mediana en un conjunto ordenado de números. El cuartil inferior también se llama primer cuartil, o Q1.		

Mm

English/Español	Example/Ejemplo	Notes/Notas
markdown an amount subtracted from the cost of an item to determine the final price. The amount subtracted is often a percent of the cost. **reducción de precio** cantidad que se resta al costo de un artículo para determinar el precio final. La cantidad que se resta suele ser un porcentaje del costo.	A discount of $20 is the same as a markdown of $20.	
markup an amount added to the cost of an item to determine the final price. The amount added is often a percent of the cost. **margen de ganancia** cantidad que se suma al costo de un artículo para determinar el precio final. La cantidad que se suma suele ser un porcentaje del costo.	A price increase of $25 is the same as a markup of $25.	
maximum (of a data set) the greatest value in a data set. **máximo (de un conjunto de datos)** mayor valor en un conjunto de datos.	Data set: 9, 10, 8, 9, 7	
mean the sum of a set of values divided by the number of values. This is often called the *average*. **media** suma de un conjunto de valores dividida por el número de valores. Suele llamarse *promedio*.	Data set: 9, 10, 8, 9, 7 Mean: $\dfrac{9 + 10 + 8 + 9 + 7}{5} = 8.6$	
mean absolute deviation (MAD) the sum of the distances of each data point from the mean of the data set divided by the number of data points. It is always positive. **desviación media absoluta (DMA)** suma de las distancias de cada dato desde la media del conjunto de datos dividido por el número de datos. Siempre es positiva.	Data set: 9, 10, 8, 9, 7 Mean: 8.6 MAD: $\dfrac{0.4 + 1.4 + 0.6 + 0.4 + 1.7}{5} = 0.9$	

English/Español	Example/Ejemplo	Notes/Notas
measure of center a single number that summarizes what is typical for all the values in a data set. Mean and median are measures of center.	Data set: 9, 10, 8, 9, 7 Mean: 8.6 Median: 9	
medida de tendencia central único número que resume qué es típico para todos los valores en un conjunto de datos. La media y la mediana son medidas de tendecia central.		
measure of variability a single number that summarizes how much the values in a data set vary. Mean absolute deviation and interquartile range are measures of variability.	Data set: 9, 10, 8, 9, 7 MAD: 0.9 IQR: 1	
medida de variabilidad único número que resume cuánto varían los valores en un conjunto de datos. La desviación media absoluta y el rango entre cuartiles son medidas de variabilidad.		
median the middle number, or the halfway point between the two middle numbers, in an ordered set of values.	Data set: 9, 10, 8, 9, 7 7, 8, **9**, 9, 10	
mediana el número del medio, o punto intermedio entre los dos números del medio, de un conjunto ordenado de valores.		
minimum (of a data set) the least value in a data set.	Data set: 9, 10, 8, 9, **7**	
mínimo (de un conjunto de datos) valor mínimo en un conjunto de datos.		
multiple the product of a given number and any other whole number.	4, 8, 12, 16 are multiples of 4.	
múltiplo producto de un número dado y cualquier otro número entero.		

English/Español	Example/Ejemplo	Notes/Notas
multiplicative comparison a comparison that tells how many times as many.	$\frac{1}{2} \times 6 = 3$ tells that 3 is $\frac{1}{2}$ times as many as 6 and that 3 is 6 times as many as $\frac{1}{2}$.	
comparación multiplicativa comparación que indica cuántas veces más.		
multiplicative inverse a number is the multiplicative inverse of another number if the product of the two numbers is 1.	3 and $\frac{1}{3}$	
inverso multiplicativo un número es el inverso multiplicativo de otro número si el producto de los dos números es 1.		

Nn

English/Español	Example/Ejemplo	Notes/Notas
negative association a linear association in which as the value of one variable increases, generally the other variable decreases.	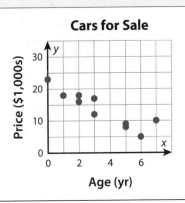	
asociación negativa asociación lineal en la que el valor de una variable por lo incrementa, generalmente cuando el valor de la otra variable disminuye.		

Cars for Sale

English/Español	Example/Ejemplo	Notes/Notas
negative numbers numbers that are less than 0. They are located to the left of 0 on a horizontal number line and below 0 on a vertical number line. **números negativos** números que son menores que 0. Se ubican a la izquierda del 0 en una recta numérica horizontal y debajo del 0 en una recta numérica vertical.	−3 −2 −1 0 1 2 3	
net a flat, "unfolded" representation of a three-dimensional shape. **modelo plano** representación plana "desplegada" de una figura tridimensional.		
no association when two variables have no relationship or association. **sin asociación** cuando dos variables no tienen relación o asociación.		
nonlinear association an association in which no line can reasonably describe the relationship between two variables. **asociación no lineal** asociación en la que ninguna recta puede describir razonablemente la relación que existe entre dos variables.		
nonlinear function a function with a graph that is not a straight line. **función no lineal** función que tiene una gráfica que no es una línea recta.		

English/Español	Example/Ejemplo	Notes/Notas
numerator the number above the line in a fraction that tells the number of equal parts that are being described.	$\dfrac{3}{4}$	
numerador número que está sobre la línea en una fracción y que indica el número de partes iguales que se describen.		

Oo

obtuse angle an angle that measures more than 90° but less than 180°.		
ángulo obtuso ángulo que mide más de 90° pero menos de 180°.		
obtuse triangle a triangle that has one obtuse angle.		
triángulo obtusángulo triángulo que tiene un ángulo obtuso.		

English/Español	Example/Ejemplo	Notes/Notas
opposite numbers numbers that are the same distance from 0 on the number line but in opposite directions. Opposite numbers have the same numeral, but opposite signs. The opposite of a number is also called the *additive inverse* of that number.	-3 and 3 $-\frac{8}{15}$ and $\frac{8}{15}$	
números opuestos números que están a la misma distancia del 0 en la recta numérica pero en direcciones opuestas. Los números opuestos son el mismo número, pero con el signo opuesto. El opuesto de un número también se llama *inverso de suma* de ese número.		
Order of Operations a set of rules that state the order in which operations should be performed to evaluate an expression.	Working from left to right: 1. Grouping symbols 2. Exponents 3. Multiplication/Division 4. Addition/Subtraction	
orden de las operaciones conjunto de reglas que establecen el orden en el que deben hacerse las operaciones para evaluar una expresión.		
ordered pair a pair of numbers, (x, y), that describes the location of a point in the coordinate plane. The x-coordinate gives the point's horizontal distance from the y-axis, and the y-coordinate gives the point's vertical distance from the x-axis.	(x, y) x-coordinate y-coordinate	
par ordenado par de números, (x, y), que describen la ubicación de un punto en el plano de coordenadas. La coordenada x da la distancia horizontal del punto desde el eje y, y la coordenada y da la distancia vertical del punto desde el eje x.		
origin the point $(0, 0)$ in the coordinate plane where the x-axis and y-axis intersect.		
origen el punto $(0, 0)$ en el plano de coordenadas donde el eje x y el eje y se intersecan.		

English/Español	Example/Ejemplo	Notes/Notas
outcome one of the possible results of a chance experiment.	Experiment: Rolling a number cube once	
resultado uno de los efectos posibles de un experimento aleatorio.	All possible outcomes: 1, 2, 3, 4, 5, 6	
outlier a data value that is much greater or much less than most of the other values in the data set. An outlier seems to not quite fit with the rest of the data points.		
valor atípico dato que es mucho mayor o mucho menor que la mayoría de los otros valores del conjunto de datos. Un valor atípico parece no ajustarse al resto de los datos.		
output (of a function) the dependent variable of a function.	$y = 2x + 1$	
salida (de una función) variable dependiente de una función.	Input (x): 0, 2, 3 — Output (y): 1, 5, 7	

For the output example table:

Input (x)	0	2	3
Output (y)	1	5	7

Pp

parallel (∥) always the same distance apart and never meeting.

paralelos (∥) que están siempre a la misma distancia y nunca se encuentran.

A ▢──────────▢ B

D ▢──────────▢ C

$\overline{AB} \parallel \overline{CD}$ and $\overline{AD} \parallel \overline{BC}$

---

parallel lines lines that are always the same distance apart and never intersect.

rectas paralelas rectas que siempre están a la misma distancia y nunca se intersecan.

---

parallelogram a quadrilateral with opposite sides parallel and equal in length.

paralelogramo cuadrilátero que tiene lados opuestos paralelos y de la misma longitud.

---

partial products the products you get in each step of the partial-products strategy. You use place value to find partial products.

productos parciales productos que se obtienen en cada paso de la estrategia de productos parciales. Se usa el valor posicional para hallar productos parciales.

218×6
Partial products:
6×200, or 1,200,
6×10, or 60, and
6×8, or 48

---

partial quotients the quotients you get in each step of the partial-quotient strategy. You use place value to find partial quotients.

cocientes parciales cocientes que se obtienen en cada paso de la estrategia de cocientes parciales. Se usa el valor posicional para hallar cocientes parciales.

$2,124 \div 4$
Partial quotients:
$2,000 \div 4$, or 500,
$100 \div 4$, or 25, and
$24 \div 4$, or 6

---

partial sums the sums you get in each step of the partial-sums strategy. You use place value to find partial sums.

sumas parciales totales que se obtienen en cada paso de la estrategia de sumas parciales. Se usa el valor posicional para hallar sumas parciales.

$124 + 234$
Partial sums:
$100 + 200$, or 300,
$20 + 30$, or 50, and
$4 + 4$, or 8

English/Español	Example/Ejemplo	Notes/Notas
partial-products strategy a strategy used to multiply multi-digit numbers. **estrategia de productos parciales** estrategia que se usa para multiplicar números de varios dígitos.	$\begin{array}{r} 218 \\ \times\ \ \ 6 \\ \hline 48 \\ 60 \\ +\ 1{,}200 \\ \hline 1{,}308 \end{array}$ (6 × 8 ones) (6 × 1 ten) (6 × 2 hundreds)	
partial-quotients strategy a strategy used to divide multi-digit numbers. **estrategia de cocientes parciales** estrategia que se usa para dividir números de varios dígitos.	$\begin{array}{r} 6 \\ 25 \\ 500 \\ \hline 4)\overline{2{,}125} \\ -\ 2{,}000 \\ \hline 125 \\ -\ 100 \\ \hline 25 \\ -\ 24 \\ \hline 1 \end{array}$ The quotient 531 is the sum of partial quotients (6, 25, and 500) and the remainder (1).	
partial-sums strategy a strategy used to add multi-digit numbers. **estrategia de sumas parciales** estrategia que se usa para sumar números de varios dígitos.	$\begin{array}{r} 312 \\ +\ 235 \\ \hline 500 \\ 40 \\ +\ \ \ 7 \\ \hline 547 \end{array}$ Add the hundreds. Add the tens. Add the ones.	
peak in a distribution, the shape formed when many data points are at one value or group of values. **pico** en una distribución, la figura que se forma cuando los puntos de muchos datos están en un valor o grupo de valores.	peak 0 1 2 3 4	
pentagon a polygon with exactly 5 sides and 5 angles. **pentágono** polígono que tiene exactamente 5 lados y 5 ángulos.		
per for each or for every. The word per can be used to express a rate, such as $2 per pound. **por** por cada. La palabra por se puede usar para expresar una tasa, como $2 por libra.	A price of $2 per pound means for every pound, you pay $2.	

English/Español	Example/Ejemplo	Notes/Notas
percent per 100. A percent is a rate per 100. A percent can be written using the percent symbol (%) and represented as a fraction or decimal.		
porcentaje por cada 100. Un porcentaje es una tasa por cada 100. Un porcentaje se puede escribir usando el símbolo de porcentaje (%) y se representa como fracción o decimal.	15% can be represented as $\frac{15}{100}$ or 0.15.	
percent change the amount of change compared to the original (or starting) amount, expressed as a percent. Percent change = $\frac{\text{amount of change}}{\text{original amount}} \times 100$	Saturday: 250 people Sunday: 300 people Change from Saturday to Sunday: $300 - 250 = 50$	
cambio porcentual cantidad de cambio en comparación con la cantidad original (o inicial) que se expresa como porcentaje. Cambio porcentual = $\frac{\text{cantidad de cambio}}{\text{cantidad original}} \times 100$	Percent change: $\frac{50}{250} \times 100 = 20\%$	
percent decrease the percent change when a quantity decreases from its original amount. Percent decrease = $\frac{\text{amount of decrease}}{\text{original amount}} \times 100$	Saturday: 250 people Sunday: 200 people Change from Saturday to Sunday: $250 - 200 = 50$	
disminución porcentual cambio porcentual cuando una cantidad disminuye desde su cantidad original. Disminución porcentual = $\frac{\text{cantidad de disminución}}{\text{cantidad original}} \times 100$	Percent change: $\frac{50}{250} \times 100 = 20\%$ There is a 20% decrease from Saturday to Sunday.	
percent error the difference between the correct value and the incorrect value compared to the correct value, expressed as a percent. Percent error = $\frac{\text{amount of error}}{\text{correct value}} \times 100$	A bag of flour weighs 4.5 lb. It should weigh 5 lb.	
error porcentual diferencia que hay entre el valor correcto y el valor incorrecto en comparación con el valor correcto, expresada como porcentaje. Error porcentual = $\frac{\text{cantidad de error}}{\text{valor correcto}} \times 100$	Percent error: $\frac{5 - 4.5}{5} \times 100 = 10\%$	

percent increase the percent change when a quantity increases from its original amount.

Percent increase =

$\dfrac{\text{amount of increase}}{\text{original amount}} \times 100$

incremento porcentual cambio porcentual cuando una cantidad se incrementa desde su cantidad original.

Aumento porcentual =

$\dfrac{\text{cantidad de incremento}}{\text{cantidad original}} \times 100$

Saturday: 250 people

Sunday: 300 people

Change from Saturday to Sunday: $300 - 250 = 50$

Percent change:

$\dfrac{50}{250} \times 100 = 20\%$

There is a 20% increase from Saturday to Sunday.

---

perfect cube the product when an integer is used as a factor three times.

cubo perfecto producto cuando se usa un entero como factor tres veces.

$27 = 3^3$

---

perfect square the product of an integer and itself.

cuadrado perfecto producto de un entero por sí mismo.

$9 = 3^2$

---

perimeter the distance around a two-dimensional shape. The perimeter is equal to the sum of the lengths of the sides.

perímetro distancia alrededor de una figura bidimensional. El perímetro es igual a la suma de las longitudes de los lados.

60 yd

40 yd   40 yd

60 yd

Perimeter: 200 yd
(60 yd + 40 yd + 60 yd + 40 yd)

---

perpendicular (⊥) meeting to form right angles.

perpendicular (⊥) unión donde se forman ángulos rectos.

A   B

D   C

$\overline{AD} \perp \overline{CD}$

---

perpendicular lines two lines that meet to form a right angle, or a 90° angle.

rectas perpendiculares dos rectas que se encuentran y forman un ángulo recto, o ángulo de 90°.

English/Español	Example/Ejemplo	Notes/Notas
pi (π) in a circle, the quotient $\frac{circumference}{diameter}$. Common approximations are 3.14 and $\frac{22}{7}$.	$\pi \approx 3.14$ or $\frac{22}{7}$	
pi (π) en un círculo, el cociente de $\frac{circumferencia}{diámetro}$. Las aproximaciones communes son 3.14 y $\frac{22}{7}$.		
place value the value of a digit based on its position in a number.	The 2 in 3.52 is in the hundredths place and has a value of **2 hundredths** or **0.02**.	
valor posicional valor de un dígito que se basa en su posición en un número. Por ejemplo, el 2 en 3.52 está en la posición de las centésimas y tiene un valor de 2 centésimas, o 0.02.		
plane figure a two-dimensional figure, such as a circle, triangle, or rectangle.		
figura plana figura bidimensional, como un círculo, un triángulo o un rectángulo.		
plane section a two-dimensional shape that is exposed by making a straight cut through a three-dimensional figure.	plane section	
sección plana figura bidimensional que se expone al hacer un corte recto a través de una figura tridimensional.		
point a single location in space.	A	
punto ubicación única en el espacio.		
polygon a two-dimensional closed figure made with three or more straight line segments that meet only at their endpoints.		
polígono figura bidimensional cerrada formada por tres o más segmentos de recta que se encuentran solo en sus extremos.		

population the entire group of interest. Samples are drawn from populations.

población grupo entero de interés. Las muestras se obtienen de las poblaciones.

Sample: 10 students from each Grade 8 homeroom in a school

Population: All Grade 8 students in the school

---

positive association a linear association in which as the value of one variable increases, generally the value of the other variable increases.

asociación positiva asociación lineal en la que el valor de una variable aumenta, generalmente cuando el valor de la otra variable aumenta.

Baseball Pitch and Hit

---

positive numbers numbers that are greater than 0. They are located to the right of 0 on a horizontal number line and above 0 on a vertical number line.

números positivos números que son mayores que 0. Se ubican a la derecha del 0 en una recta numérica horizontal y sobre el 0 en una recta numérica vertical.

---

power an expression with a base and an exponent.

potencia expresión que tiene una base y un exponente.

8^2

---

power of 10 a number that can be written as a product of 10s.

potencia de 10 número que se puede escribir como el producto de 10.

100 and 1,000 are powers of 10 because $100 = 10 \times 10$ and $1,000 = 10 \times 10 \times 10$.

---

prime number a whole number greater than 1 whose only factors are 1 and itself.

número primo número entero mayor que 1 cuyos únicos factores son 1 y sí mismo.

2, 3, 5, 7, 11, 13

English/Español	Example/Ejemplo	Notes/Notas
prism a three-dimensional figure with two parallel bases that are the same size and shape. The other faces are parallelograms. A prism is named by the shape of the base.		
prisma figura tridimensional que tiene dos bases paralelas que tienen el mismo tamaño y la misma forma. Las otras caras son paralelogramos. La base determina el nombre del prisma.		
probability a number between 0 and 1 that expresses the likelihood of an event occurring.	unlikely likely 0 $\frac{1}{2}$ 1 impossible equally certain likely as not	
probabilidad número entre 0 y 1 que expresa la posibilidad de que ocurra un evento.		
product the result of multiplication.	$3 \cdot 5 = 15$	
producto resultado de la multiplicación.		
proportional relationship the relationship between two quantities where one quantity is a constant multiple of the other quantity. If the quantities x and y are in a proportional relationship, you can represent that relationship with the equation $y = kx$, where the value of k is constant (unchanging).	$y = 8x$	
relación proporcional relación que existe entre dos cantidades en la que una cantidad es un múltiplo constante de la otra. Si las cantidades x y y están en una relación proporcional, esa relación se puede representar con la ecuación $y = kx$, en la que el valor de k es constante (no cambia).		
pyramid a three-dimensional figure whose base is a polygon and whose other faces are triangles. A pyramid is named by the shape of its base.		
pirámide figura tridimensional cuya base es un polígono y cuyas otras caras son triángulos. La base determina el nombre de la pirámide.		

Pythagorean Theorem in any right triangle, the sum of the squares of the lengths of the legs, a and b, is equal to the square of the length of the hypotenuse, c. So, $a^2 + b^2 = c^2$.

Teorema de Pitágoras en un triángulo rectángulo cualquiera, la suma del cuadrado de las longitudes de los catetos, a y b, es igual al cuadrado de la longitud de la hipotenusa, c. Por lo tanto, $a^2 + b^2 = c^2$.

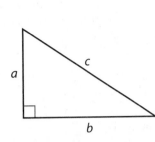

If the triangle is a right triangle, then $a^2 + b^2 = c^2$

Qq

quadrants the four regions of the coordinate plane that are formed when the x-axis and y-axis intersect at the origin.

cuadrantes las cuatro regiones del plano de coordenadas que se forman cuando los ejes x y y se intersecan en el origen.

Quadrant II y Quadrant I

Quadrant III   Quadrant IV

quadrilateral a polygon with exactly 4 sides and 4 angles.

cuadrilátero polígono que tiene exactamente 4 lados y 4 ángulos.

English/Español	Example/Ejemplo	Notes/Notas

qualitative description a description that focuses on the general relationship between quantities, often without using specific values.

descripción cualitativa descripción que se enfoca en la relación general que existe entre las cantidades, con frecuencia sin usar valores específicos.

Gas prices stay steady, then drop, then increase.

quotient the result of division.

cociente resultado de la división.

$$22.5 \div 3 = 7.5$$

Rr

radius (of a circle) a line segment from the center of a circle to any point on the circle. Also, the distance from the center to any point on a circle.

radio (de un círculo) segmento de recta desde el centro de un círculo hasta cualquier punto en el círculo. Además, la distancia desde el centro hasta cualquier punto en un círculo.

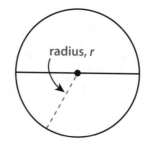

radius, r

random sample a sample in which every element in the population has an equal chance of being selected.

muestra aleatoria muestra en la que todos los elementos de la población tienen la misma probabilidad de ser elegidos.

The names of all of the students in the school are placed in a hat. Without looking, 30 names are selected. The 30 students are a random sample of the population.

English/Español	Example/Ejemplo	Notes/Notas
range the difference between the greatest value (maximum) and the least value (minimum) in a data set.	Data set: 9, 10, 8, 9, 7 Range: $10 - 7 = 3$	
rango diferencia entre el mayor valor (máximo) y el menor valor (mínimo) en un conjunto de datos.		
rate a ratio tells the number of units of one quantity for 1 unit of another quantity. Rates are often expressed using the word *per*.	5 miles per hour 2 cups for every 1 serving	
tasa razón que indica el número de unidades de una cantidad para 1 unidad de otra cantidad. Las razones suelen expresarse usando la palabra *por*.		
rate of change in a linear relationship between x and y, it tells how much y changes when x changes by 1.	$y = \frac{1}{2}x + 25$ rate of change	
tasa de cambio en una relación lineal entre x y y, indica cuánto cambia y cuando x cambia en 1.		
ratio a way to compare two quantities when there are a units of one quantity for every b units of the other quantity. You can write the ratio in symbols as $a : b$ and in words as a to b.	 4 circles : 2 triangles	
razón manera de comparar dos cantidades cuando hay a unidades de una cantidad por cada b unidades de la otra cantidad. Se puede escribir la razón en símbolos como $a : b$ y en palabras como a a b.		
rational number a number that can be expressed as the fraction $\frac{a}{b}$ where a and b are integers and $b \neq 0$. Rational numbers include integers, fractions, repeating decimals, and terminating decimals.	$\frac{3}{4}, -\frac{1}{8}, -3, 0, 1.2$	
número racional número que se puede expresar como la fracción $\frac{a}{b}$ en la que a y b son enteros y $b \neq 0$. Los números racionales incluyen los enteros, las fracciones, los decimales periódicos y los decimales finitos.		

English/Español	Example/Ejemplo	Notes/Notas

ray a part of a line that has one endpoint and goes on forever in one direction.

semirrecta parte de una recta que tiene un extremo y continúa infinitamente en una dirección.

A —————→ B

---

real numbers the set of rational and irrational numbers.

números reales conjunto de números racionales e irracionales.

Real Numbers

Rational Numbers	Irrational Numbers
27	$\sqrt{8}$
0.25	π
$\frac{1}{3}$	1.46829903...

---

reciprocal for any nonzero number a, the reciprocal is $\frac{1}{a}$. The reciprocal of any fraction $\frac{a}{b}$ is $\frac{b}{a}$. Zero does not have a reciprocal. The reciprocal of a number is also called the *multiplicative inverse* of that number.

recíproco para cualquier número a distinto de cero, el recíproco es $\frac{1}{a}$. El recíproco de cualquier fracción $\frac{a}{b}$ es $\frac{b}{a}$. El cero no tiene recíproco. El recíproco de un número también se llama *inverso multiplicativo* de ese número.

The reciprocal of $\frac{4}{5}$ is $\frac{5}{4}$.

The reciprocal of $\frac{1}{6}$ is 6.

The reciprocal of -8 is $-\frac{1}{8}$.

---

rectangle a quadrilateral with 4 right angles. Opposite sides of a rectangle are the same length.

rectángulo cuadrilátero que tiene 4 ángulos rectos. Los lados opuestos de un rectángulo tienen la misma longitud.

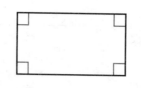

---

rectangular prism a prism where the bases are rectangles.

prisma rectangular prisma en el que las bases son rectángulos.

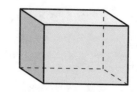

English/Español	Example/Ejemplo	Notes/Notas

reflection a transformation that flips (reflects) a figure across a line to form a mirror image. This line is called the *line of reflection*.

reflexión transformación que gira (refleja) una figura del otro lado de una línea para formar una imagen reflejada. Esta línea se llama *eje de reflexión*.

---

relative frequency the quotient that compares the number of times a data value occurs and the total number of data values. This can be expressed as a fraction, decimal, or percent.

frecuencia relativa cociente que compara el número de veces que ocurre un valor y el número total de valores. Esto se puede expresar como fracción, decimal o porcentaje.

Data set: red, green, red, red, blue, yellow, blue, white

Frequency of *blue*: 2

Total data values: 8

Relative frequency of *blue*: $\frac{2}{8}$, or $\frac{1}{4}$, or 0.25, or 25%

---

remainder the amount left over when one number does not divide another number a whole number of times.

residuo cantidad que queda cuando un número no divide a otro un número entero de veces.

$$7 \div 2 = 3 \text{ R } 1$$

remainder

---

repeating decimals decimals that repeat the same digit or sequence of digits forever. A repeating decimal can be written with a bar over the repeating digits.

decimal periódico decimales que repiten el mismo dígito o secuencia de dígitos infinitamente. Un decimal periódico se puede escribir con una barra sobre los dígitos que se repiten.

$0.\overline{3}$

$2.\overline{51}$

---

rhombus a quadrilateral with all sides the same length.

rombo cuadrilátero que tiene todos los lados de la misma longitud.

---

right angle an angle that measures 90°.

ángulo recto ángulo que mide 90°.

---

right prism a prism where each base is perpendicular to the other faces. In a right prism, the faces that are not bases are rectangles.

prisma recto prisma en el que cada base es perpendicular a las otras caras. En un prisma recto, las caras que no son bases son rectángulos.

---

right rectangular prism a right prism where the bases and other faces are all rectangles.

prisma rectangular recto prisma recto en el que las bases y las otras caras son rectángulos.

---

right triangle a triangle with one right angle.

triángulo rectángulo triángulo que tiene un ángulo recto.

---

right triangular prism a right prism where the bases are triangles and the other faces are rectangles.

prisma triangular recto prisma recto en el que las bases son triángulos y las otras caras son rectángulos.

English/Español	Example/Ejemplo	Notes/Notas
rigid transformation a transformation in which the size and the shape of the figure does not change. *Translations*, *reflections*, and *rotations* are examples of rigid transformations. **transformación rígida** transformación en la que el tamaño y la forma de la figura no cambian. Las *traslaciones*, las *reflexiones* y las *rotaciones* son ejemplos de transformaciones rígidas.	△A′B′C′ is a rigid transformation of △ABC.	
rotation a transformation that turns (rotates) a figure through a given angle and in a given direction around a fixed point. This point is called the center of rotation. **rotación** transformación que gira (rota) una figura a través de un ángulo dado y en una dirección dada alrededor de un punto fijo. Este punto se llama centro de rotación.	△P′Q′R′ is a rotation of △PQR.	
round to approximate the value of a number by finding the nearest ten, hundred, or other place value. **redondear** aproximar el valor de un número hallando la decena, la centena u otro valor posicional más cercano.	48 rounded to the nearest ten is 50.	

Interactive Glossary/Glosario interactivo

Ss

same-side exterior angles when two lines are cut by a transversal, a pair of angles on the same side of the transversal and outside the two lines. When the two lines are parallel, same-side exterior angles are supplementary.

ángulos externos del mismo lado cuando dos rectas se cortan con una transversal, par de ángulos del mismo lado de la transversal y fuera de las dos rectas. Cuando las dos rectas son paralelas, los ángulos externos del mismo lado son suplementarios.

$\angle 1$ and $\angle 6$

$\angle 4$ and $\angle 7$

same-side interior angles when two lines are cut by a transversal, a pair of angles on the same side of the transversal and between the two lines. When the two lines are parallel, same-side interior angles are supplementary.

ángulos internos del mismo lado cuando dos rectas se cortan con una transversal, par de ángulos del mismo lado de la transversal y entre de las dos rectas. Cuando las dos rectas son paralelas, los ángulos internos del mismo lado son suplementarios.

$\angle 2$ and $\angle 5$

$\angle 3$ and $\angle 8$

sample a part of a population.

muestra parte de una población.

Population: All students in the school

Sample: Three students in each homeroom

sample space the set of all possible unique outcomes for an experiment.

espacio muestral conjunto de todos los resultados posibles de un experimento.

Experiment: Rolling a number cube

Sample space: 1, 2, 3, 4, 5, 6

scale tells the relationship between a length in a drawing, map, or model to the actual length.

escala indica la relación que hay entre una longitud en un dibujo, un mapa o un modelo y la longitud real.

Scale from a map to actual distances in a town:

1 in. to 20 mi

English/Español	Example/Ejemplo	Notes/Notas
scale (on a graph) the value represented by the distance between one tick mark and the next on a number line. **escala (en una gráfica)** valor representado por la distancia que hay entre una marca y la siguiente en una recta numérica.	-10 -5 0 5 10 15 20 scale $= 5$	
scale drawing a drawing in which the measurements correspond to the measurements of the actual object by the same scale. **dibujo a escala** dibujo en el que las medidas se corresponden con las medidas del objeto real según la misma escala.	3 in. A 2 in. 6 in. B 4 in. $\triangle A : \triangle B$ is 1 : 2.	
scale factor the factor you multiply all the side lengths in a figure by to make a scale copy. **factor de escala** factor por el que se multiplican todas las longitudes laterales en una figura para hacer una copia a escala.	Scale from a map to the actual distance: 1 in. to 20 mi Scale factor from distances on the map to the actual distances: 20	
scalene triangle a triangle that has no sides the same length. **triángulo escaleno** triángulo que no tiene lados de la misma longitud.		
scatter plot a graph of two-variable data displayed as ordered pairs. **diagrama de dispersión** gráfica de datos de dos variables que se muestran como pares ordenados.	**Talking on the Phone**	

English/Español	Example/Ejemplo	Notes/Notas
scientific notation a way of expressing a number as a product in the form $n \times 10^a$, where a is an integer and n is a decimal number such that $1 \le n < 10$. **notación científica** manera de expresar un número como producto con la forma $n \times 10^a$, en la que a es un entero y n es un número decimal tal que $1 \le n < 10$.	$5{,}900{,}000 = 5.9 \times 10^6$	
sequence of transformations one or more transformations performed in a certain order. **secuencia de transformaciones** una o más transformaciones llevadas a cabo en un orden determinado.	A reflection followed by a rotation	
side a line segment that forms part of a two-dimensional shape. **lado** segmento de recta que forma parte de una figura bidimensional	side	
similar ($\approx$) having the same shape. Two figures are similar if there is a sequence of rigid transformations and/or dilations that maps one figure onto the second. **semejante** ($\approx$) que tienen la misma forma. Dos figuras son semejantes si hay una secuencia de transformaciones rígidas y/o dilataciones que hacen coincidir una figura con la segunda.	A B Figures A and B are similar.	
similar triangles triangles that are scale drawings of one another. Similar triangles have the same shape but may have a different size. **triángulos semejantes** triángulos que son dibujos a escala unos de otros. Los triángulos semejantes tienen la misma forma pero pueden tener diferente tamaño.	3 3 2.75 6 6 5.5	

English/Español	Example/Ejemplo	Notes/Notas
simple interest a percent of an amount that is borrowed or invested. **interés simple** porcentaje de una cantidad que se toma prestada o se invierte.	$I = Prt$ I = interest P = principal (amount borrowed or invested) r = interest rate t = time	
skewed left when most of the data points of a distribution are clustered near the greater values. **asimétrica a la izquierda** cuando la mayoría de los datos de una distribución se agrupan cerca de los valores más altos.	**Skewed Left**	
skewed right when most of the data points of a distribution are clustered near the lesser values. **asimétrica a la derecha** cuando la mayoría de los datos de una distribución se agrupan cerca de los valores más bajos.	**Skewed Right**	
slope for any two points on a line, the $\frac{\text{rise}}{\text{run}}$ or $\frac{\text{change in }y}{\text{change in }x}$. It is a measure of the steepness of a line. It is also called the *rate of change* of a linear function. **pendiente** para dos puntos cualesquiera en una recta, la $\frac{\text{distancia vertical}}{\text{distancia horizontal}}$ o $\frac{\text{cambio en }y}{\text{cambio en }x}$. Es una medida de la inclinación de una recta. También se llama *tasa de cambio* de una función lineal.	change in y (5, 2) (2.5, 1) change in x Slope: $\frac{1}{2.5} = 0.4$	
slope-intercept form a linear equation in the form $y = mx + b$, where m is the slope and b is the y-intercept. **forma pendiente-intercepto** ecuación lineal en la forma $y = mx + b$, en la que m es la pendiente y b es el intercepto en y.	equation: $y = 2x + 1$ slope: 2 y-intercept: (0, 1)	

Interactive Glossary/Glosario interactivo

English/Español	Example/Ejemplo	Notes/Notas
solution of an equation a value that can be substituted for a variable to make an equation true. **solución de una ecuación** valor que puede sustituir a una variable para hacer que una ecuación sea verdadera.	The value 5 is the solution of the equation $19 = 4x - 1$ because $19 = 4(5) - 1$.	
solution of an inequality a value that can be substituted for a variable to make an inequality true. **solución de una desigualdad** valor que puede sustituir a una variable para hacer que una desigualdad sea verdadera.	All values of x less than 5 ($x < 5$) are solutions of the inequality $5x < 25$.	
sphere a three-dimensional figure in which every point is the same distance from the center. **esfera** figura tridimensional en la que todos los puntos están a la misma distancia del centro.		
square a quadrilateral with 4 right angles and 4 sides of equal length. **cuadrado** cuadrilátero que tiene 4 ángulos rectos y 4 lados de la misma longitud.		
square root of x the number that when multiplied by itself is equal to x. **raíz cuadrada de x** número que cuando se multiplica por sí mismo es igual a x.	$$\sqrt{16} = \sqrt{4 \cdot 4}$$ $$= 4$$ 4 is the square root of 16.	
statistical question a question that can be answered by collecting data that are expected to vary. **pregunta estadística** pregunta que se puede responder reuniendo datos que se espera que varíen.	What is the typical amount of rain in April?	

English/Español	Example/Ejemplo	Notes/Notas

straight angle an angle that measures 180°. The sides of a straight angle form a straight line.

ángulo llano ángulo que mide 180°. Los lados de un ángulo llano forman una línea recta.

A B C

$\angle ABC$ is a straight angle.

---

sum the result of addition.

total resultado de la suma.

$$24 + 35 = 59$$

---

supplementary angles two angles whose measures sum to 180°.

ángulos suplementarios dos ángulos cuyas medidas suman 180°.

Z

W X Y

$\angle WXZ$ and $\angle ZXY$ are supplementary angles.

---

surface area the sum of the areas of all the faces of a three-dimensional figure.

área total suma de las áreas de todas las caras de una figura tridimensional.

5 units

4 units

5 units

Surface Area: $2(4)(5) + 2(4)(5) + 2(5)(5) = 130$ units^2

---

symmetric when a distribution has the same shape on both sides of a middle point.

simétrico cuando una distribución tiene la misma forma en ambos lados de un punto que está en el medio.

Symmetric

Interactive Glossary/Glosario interactivo

English/Español	Example/Ejemplo	Notes/Notas
system of linear equations a group of related linear equations in which a solution makes all the equations true at the same time. A system of equations can have zero, one, or infinitely many solutions.		
sistema de ecuaciones lineales grupo de ecuaciones lineales relacionadas en el que una solución hace que todas las ecuaciones sean verdaderas al mismo tiempo. Un sistema de ecuaciones puede tener cero, una o infinitas soluciones.	$y = 4x + 8$ $y = 3x + 8$	

Tt

English/Español	Example/Ejemplo	Notes/Notas
tax a percent of income or of the cost of goods or services paid to the government.		
impuesto porcentaje del ingreso o del costo de bienes o servicios que se paga al gobierno.	A 7% sales tax on a purchase of $40 is $2.80	
term a number, a variable, or a product of numbers, variables, and/or expressions. A term may include an exponent.	$4x + 9 + y^2$ ↑ ↑ ↗ term	
término número, variable o el producto de números, variables y/o expresiones. Un término puede tener un exponente.		

English/Español	Example/Ejemplo	Notes/Notas
terminating decimals decimals that end, or end in repeated zeros. **decimal finito** decimal en el que termina un número, o que termina en ceros repetidos.	0.25 5.6 −7.125	
theoretical probability the probability of an event occurring based on what is expected to happen. **probabilidad teórica** probabilidad de que ocurra un evento según lo que se espera que suceda.	There are two equally likely outcomes to flipping a coin: heads up or tails up. The theoretical probability of the outcome heads up is $\frac{1}{2}$, or 50%.	
three-dimensional solid, or having length, width, and height. For example, a cube is three-dimensional. **tridimensional** sólido, o que tiene longitud, ancho y altura. Por ejemplo, un cubo es tridimensional.	 height width length	
transformation a change in location, orientation, or size of a figure. **transformación** cambio de ubicación, orientación o tamaño de una figura.	 $\triangle A'B'C'$ is a transformation of $\triangle ABC$.	
translation a transformation that moves (slides) each point of a figure the same distance and in the same direction. **traslación** transformación que mueve (desplaza) cada punto de una figura la misma distancia y en la misma dirección.	 $\triangle A'B'C'$ is a translation of $\triangle ABC$ 5 units down.	

English/Español	Example/Ejemplo	Notes/Notas

transversal a line that cuts two or more lines. The lines cut by the transversal may or may not be parallel.

transversal línea que corta dos o más rectas. Las rectas cortadas por la transversal pueden ser o no ser paralelas.

Line *a* is a transversal that cuts lines *b* and *c*.

trapezoid (exclusive) a quadrilateral with exactly one pair of parallel sides.

trapecio (exclusivo) cuadrilátero que tiene exactamente un par de lados paralelos.

trapezoid (inclusive) a quadrilateral with at least one pair of parallel sides.

trapecio (inclusivo) cuadrilátero que tiene al menos un par de lados paralelos.

tree diagram a visual that shows all possible outcomes of an experiment.

diagrama de árbol representación visual que muestra todos los resultados posibles de un experimento.

There are 8 possible outcomes from flipping a coin 3 times.

trial a single performance of an experiment.

ensayo ejecución única de un experimento.

Rolling a number cube once

triangle a polygon with exactly 3 sides and 3 angles.

triángulo polígono que tiene exactamente 3 lados y 3 ángulos.

triangular prism a prism where the bases are triangles.

prisma triangular prisma en el que las bases son triángulos.

English/Español	Example/Ejemplo	Notes/Notas

two-dimensional flat, or having measurement in two directions, like length and width. For example, a rectangle is two-dimensional.

bidimensional plano, o que tiene medidas en dos direcciones, como longitud y ancho. Por ejemplo, un rectángulo es bidimensional.

width

length

two-way table a table that displays two-variable categorical data. One variable is shown along the top, the other down the side. Each entry in the table gives information about the frequency or relative frequency for the paired data.

tabla de doble entrada tabla que muestra datos categóricos de dos variables. Una variable se muestra arriba y la otra abajo al costado. Cada entrada en la tabla da información acerca de la frecuencia o frecuencia relativa para los pares de datos.

	Red Car	Black Car
New Car	16	22
Used Car	23	14

Uu

unit fraction a fraction with a numerator of 1. Other fractions are built from unit fractions.

fracción unitaria fracción que tiene un numerador de 1. Otras fracciones se construyen a partir de fracciones unitarias.

$\frac{1}{5}$

---

unit rate the numerical part of a rate. For the ratio $a : b$, the unit rate is the quotient $\frac{a}{b}$.

tasa por unidad parte numérica de una tasa. Para la razón $a : b$, la tasa por unidad es el cociente $\frac{a}{b}$.

Rate: 3 miles per hour

Unit rate: 3

---

unknown the value you need to find to solve a problem.

incógnita valor que hay que hallar para resolver un problema.

$20.5 + x = 30$

---

upper quartile the middle number between the median and the maximum in an ordered set of numbers. The upper quartile is also called the 3rd quartile or Q3.

cuartil superior número del medio entre la mediana y el máximo en un conjunto ordenado de números. El cuartil superior también se llama tercer cuartil, o Q3.

upper quartile

20 30 40 50 60 70 80 90

English/Español	Example/Ejemplo	Notes/Notas

Vv

variability how spread out or close together values in a data set are.

variabilidad la dispersión o cercanía de los valores en un conjunto de datos.

Gavin's Handstand Times

There is high variability in Gavin's handstand times.

---

variable a letter that represents an unknown number. In some cases, a variable may represent more than one number.

variable letra que representa un número desconocido. En algunos casos, una variable puede representar más de un número.

$$3x + 9 = 90$$

---

vertex the point where two rays, lines, or line segments meet to form an angle.

vértice punto en el que dos semirrectas, rectas o segmentos de recta se encuentran y forman un ángulo.

vertex

---

vertical angles opposite angles formed when two lines intersect. Vertical angles are congruent.

ángulos opuestos por el vértice ángulos opuestos que se forman cuando se intersecan dos rectas. Los ángulos opuestos por el vértice son congruentes.

$\angle 5$ and $\angle 7$

$\angle 2$ and $\angle 4$

---

volume the amount of space inside a solid figure. Volume is measured in cubic units such as cubic inches.

volumen cantidad de espacio dentro de una figura sólida. El volumen se mide en unidades cúbicas como las pulgadas cúbicas.

volume: 24 units^3

Ww

whole numbers the numbers 0, 1, 2, 3, 4, . . . Whole numbers are nonnegative and have no fractional part.

0, 8, 187

números enteros los números 0, 1, 2, 3, 4, . . . Los números enteros no son negativos y no tienen partes fraccionarias.

Xx

x-axis the horizontal number line in the coordinate plane.

eje x recta numérica horizontal en el plano de coordenadas.

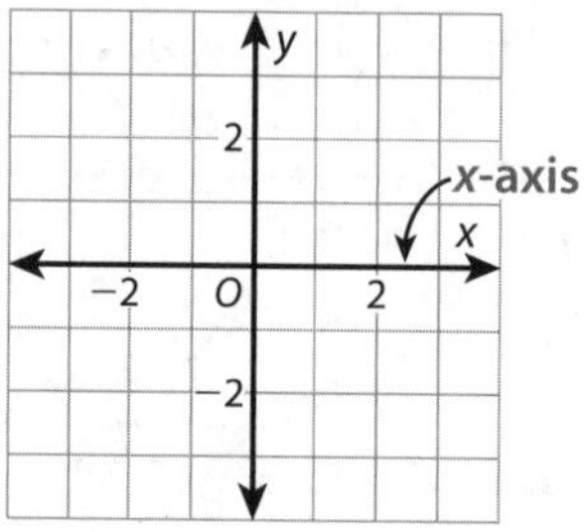

x-coordinate the first number in an ordered pair. It tells the point's horizontal distance from the y-axis.

(x, y)

x-coordinate

coordenada x primer número en un par ordenado. Indica la distancia horizontal del punto al eje y.

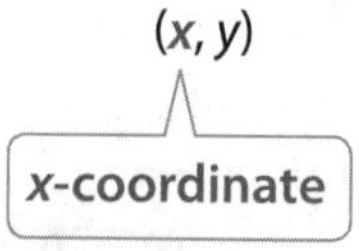

English/Español	Example/Ejemplo	Notes/Notas

x-intercept the *x*-coordinate of the point where a line, or graph of a function, intersects the *x*-axis.

intercepto en x coordenada *x* del punto en el que una recta, o gráfica de una función, interseca al eje *x*.

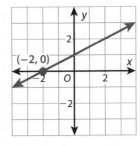

The *x*-intercept is −2.

Yy

y-axis the vertical number line in the coordinate plane.

eje y recta numérica vertical en el plano de coordenadas.

y-coordinate the second number in an ordered pair. It tells the point's vertical distance from the *x*-axis.

coordenada y el segundo número en un par ordenado. Indica la distancia vertical del punto al eje *x*.

(*x*, *y*)

y-coordinate

English/Español | Example/Ejemplo | Notes/Notas

y-intercept the *y*-coordinate of the point where a line, or graph of a function, intersects the *y*-axis.

intercepto en y coordenada *y* del punto en el que una recta, o gráfica de una función, interseca al eje *y*.

The *y*-intercept is 1.

Zz

zero pair two numbers whose sum is zero. Opposite numbers form a zero pair.

par cero dos números cuya suma es cero. Los números opuestos forman un par cero.

−3 and 3 form a zero pair.

1.2 and −1.2 form a zero pair.

Credits

Acknowledgment

Common Core State Standards © 2010. National Governors Association Center for Best Practices and Council of Chief State School Officers. All rights reserved.

Photography Credits

Cover: Taras Hipp/Shutterstock
Back Cover: 246, 448, 584 Eric Isselee/Shutterstock; 559 akiyoko/Shutterstock; 734 mipan/Shutterstock
Text: iii, 93 kuzmaphoto/Shutterstock, Artens/Shutterstock; iii, 79, 115 Makhh/Shutterstock; iv, 177 iStock.com/MR1805, solarseven/Shutterstock; iv, 214 Carlos Caetano/Shutterstock; iv, 294 Elena Noeva/Shutterstock, theendup/Shutterstock, IFH/Shutterstock; v, 349 JIANG DONGYAN/Shutterstock, Eddgars/Shutterstock; v, 435 CoolimagesCo/Shutterstock; vi, 459 StockImageFactory.com/Shutterstock; vi, 522 Sascha Burkard/Shutterstock, Vaclav Volrab/Shutterstock; vii, 642 Volodymyr Nikitenko/Shutterstock; viii, 747, 748 Photimageon/Alamy Stock Photo; viii, 774 Lopris/Shutterstock; 1, 3 kosolovskyy/Shutterstock; 4 Vadym Andrushchenko/Shutterstock, MarinaD/Shutterstock; 15 donsimon/Shutterstock.com; 16 Sarawut Aiemsinsuk/Shutterstock; 17 ne2pi/Shutterstock, Cube29/Shutterstock; 24 chanchai howharn/Shutterstock, eakasarn/Shutterstock; 31 NANTa SamRan/Shutterstock, MLWatts/Wikimedia Commons/CC0 1.0; 44 ma3d/Shutterstock, Alex Tuzhikov/Shutterstock; 45 Stock-Asso/Shutterstock, Amish Spirit; 48 Stanislav Samoylik/Shutterstock, MaxCab/Shutterstock; 65 GraphicsRF/Shutterstock; 73 FrameStockFootages/Shutterstock, Anna Komissarenko/Shutterstock; 81 Thomas Dutour/Shutterstock; 83 Michael Kraus/Shutterstock; 94 Daniel Doerfler/Shutterstock; 95 mTaira/Shutterstock, qonchajabrayilova/Shutterstock; 104 Aleksandar Grozdanovski/Shutterstock; 114 Piyawat Nandeenopparit/Shutterstock; 116 hrui/Shutterstock; 121, 122 Greg A Boiarsky/Shutterstock; 128 Photographee.eu/Shutterstock; 137 Anna Nahabed/Shutterstock; 138 Trompinex/Shutterstock; 139 ottoflick/Shutterstock; 142 Gearstd/Shutterstock; 143 Isaac Mok/Shutterstock.com; 159 iStock.com/Carol Hamilton; 164 Ambient Ideas/Shutterstock; 165 iStock.com/Talaj; 167 Yulia YasPe/Shutterstock; 173, 197 lovelyday12/Shutterstock; 175 denio109/Shutterstock; 180 Willyam Bradberry/Shutterstock; 181, 182 Julien Tromeur/Shutterstock; 185 LM Photos/Shutterstock; 186 CastecoDesign/Shutterstock; 187 Chandan Dubey/Moment/Getty Images; 188 Iakov Filimonov/Shutterstock.com; 190 sirtravelalot/Shutterstock; 191 Vaclav Sebek/Shutterstock; 195 foodonwhite/Shutterstock; 199 FocusDzign/Shutterstock.com; 202 Sergey Novikov/Shutterstock; 203 kurhan/Shutterstock; 204 MyImages - Micha/Shutterstock; 209 Denise Lett/Shutterstock, ppart/Shutterstock, Anne Kramer/Shutterstock; 210 Piotr Wytrazek/Shutterstock, Gina Stef/Shutterstock; 216 April Cat/Shutterstock; 218 Andrey_Kuzmin/Shutterstock, Vismar UK/Shutterstock; 220 Sergey Mironov/Shutterstock; 223 caimacanul/Shutterstock; 225 aradaphotography/Shutterstock; 227 Diane Garcia/Shutterstock; 230 Pratchaya.Lee/Shutterstock; 231 YAKOBCHUK VIACHESLAV/Shutterstock; 232 Naruedom Yaempongsa/Shutterstock, JIANG HONGYAN/Shutterstock; 234, 268, 348 Africa Studio/Shutterstock; 235 Ermolaev Alexander/Shutterstock; 237 Blake Alan/Shutterstock; 238 iStock.com/SarahPage; 240 pukkhoom_nokwila/Shutterstock.com; 242 David Porras/Shutterstock; 247 Manuel Ascanio/Shutterstock.com; 249 Anatoli Styf/Shutterstock; 253 ccarvalhophotography/Shutterstock; 254 Inspired by Maps/Shutterstock; 256 nullplus/Shutterstock, Anna Sastre Forrellad/Shutterstock; 259, 260 Thomas Soellner/Shutterstock; 260 Pop_Studio/Shutterstock; 268 Madlen/Shutterstock; 269 Parinya Feungchan/Shutterstock; 270 Cultura Creative (RF)/Alamy Stock Photo; 274 Bennyartist/Shutterstock, Tiger Images/Shutterstock, Nata-Lia/Shutterstock; 275 Dan Breckwoldt/Shutterstock; 278 WDG Photo/Shutterstock; 281 Nathapol Kongseang/Shutterstock; 282 home_sweet_home/Shutterstock; 286 Photo Melon/Shutterstock, Mego studio/Shutterstock; 288 Tim Jones/Alamy Stock Photo; 293 Marques/Shutterstock, Anton Kozyrev/Shutterstock, Felix Lipov/Shutterstock; 296 Dawid Galecki/Shutterstock; 302 Maria Kolpashchikova/Shutterstock; 309 Anton Gvozdikov/Shutterstock; 310 Lightspring/Shutterstock, Tyler Olson/Shutterstock; 314 Dmytro Zinkevych/Shutterstock; 315 Ev Thomas/Shutterstock; 316 Fascinadora/Shutterstock; 320 Mikayel Bartikyan/Shutterstock; 329 Kolpakova Daria/Shutterstock; 331 stephan kerkhofs/Shutterstock, Andre Seale/Alamy Stock Photo; 336 Konrawat/Shutterstock; 337 Seashell World/Shutterstock; 339 Volodymyr Goinyk/Shutterstock, Alex Stemmer/Shutterstock; 345, 387 ezphoto/Shutterstock.com; 347, 506, 668 New Africa/Shutterstock; 348 Archi_Viz/Shutterstock; 353 Dja65/Shutterstock, Picsfive/Shutterstock; 357 HEX LLC./Alamy Stock Photo; 359 Laura Crazy/Shutterstock; 360 theskaman306/Shutterstock; 361 adidas4747/Shutterstock; 364 dgbomb/Shutterstock; 365 Greg Epperson/Shutterstock; 366 worldinmyeyes.pl/Shutterstock; 368 bowoedane/Shutterstock, Infinity T29/Shutterstock; 370 spaxiax/Shutterstock, ben bryant/Shutterstock;

371, 372 Charlesy/Shutterstock, Kriengsuk Prasroetsung/Shutterstock; 372 fotorince/Shutterstock; 374 Mykola Mazuryk/Shutterstock, Iakov Filimonov/Shutterstock, elena09/Shutterstock; 377 Pixel-Shot/Shutterstock; 380 Chubarov Alexandr/Shutterstock; 381 leolintang/Shutterstock; 385, 498 Fotokostic/Shutterstock; 388, 393 adike/Shutterstock; 388 EVZ/Shutterstock; 389 iStock.com/ByronD; 392 Sugarless/Shutterstock; 393 RGB Ventures/SuperStock/Alamy Stock Photo, Linda Bucklin/Shutterstock, PHOTO JUNCTION/Shutterstock; 394 Willyam Bradberry/Shutterstock; 397 Brocreative/Shutterstock; 399 Marc Romanelli/Tetra Images/Getty Images; 400 Reid Dalland/Shutterstock; 403 Jim David/Shutterstock, iweta0077/Shutterstock; 407 Claudio Rampinini/Shutterstock, Olga Dubravina/Shutterstock; 409 jamesteohart/Shutterstock; 416 Gary Saxe/Shutterstock; 419 Ammit Jack/Shutterstock; 421 3DMAVR/Shutterstock; 422 Izf/Shutterstock; 436 Miceking/Shutterstock; 437 hobbit/Shutterstock; 439 TayebMEZAHDIA/Pixabay; 445, 447 Alina Lavrenova/Shutterstock; 453, 454 Rost9/Shutterstock; 460 Noah Seelam/AFP/Getty Images; 464 Marco Rubino/Shutterstock; 464 videoduck/Shutterstock; 468 aldarinho/Shutterstock; 469, 470 Fenton/Shutterstock; 474 Kateryna Kon/Shutterstock, Triff/Shutterstock; 475 Rvector/Shutterstock, KPG_Payless/Shutterstock; 476 Kia Nakriz/Shutterstock; 490 bluehand/Shutterstock; 491 View Apart/Shutterstock.com; 492 Maxx-Studio/Shutterstock; 493 r0ma4/Shutterstock; 496 imageBROKER/Alamy Stock Photo; 497 iStock.com/kyoshino; 500 Alex Mit/Shutterstock, BlueberryPie/Shutterstock, iStock.com/LueratSatichob; 502 Ermolaev Alexader/Shutterstock; 503 SoleilC/Shutterstock, kornn/Shutterstock; 504 Chatchai Somwat/Shutterstock; 506 Teacherx555/Shutterstock, iambasic_Studio/Shutterstock, Moolkum/Shutterstock; 511, 755 Tiger Images/Shutterstock; 511 soleilC/Shutterstock, Dancestrokes/Shutterstock, Ilya Andriyanov/Shutterstock, Khumthong/Shutterstock; 513 Neirfy/Shutterstock; 514 Oleksiy Mark/Shutterstock; 515 Aphelleon/Shutterstock; 518, 546 NASA; 519 Taiga/Shutterstock, mikeledray/Shutterstock, topseller/Shutterstock; 520 gg-foto/Shutterstock; 524 ixpert/Shutterstock; 525 Paul Crash/Shutterstock; 526 Chase Dekker/Shutterstock; 528 Lou Linwei/Alamy Stock Photo; 532 Poelzer Wolfgang/Alamy Stock Photo; 534 iStock.com/muendo; 534 iStock.com/Antagain; 539 Lidiya Oleandra/Shutterstock, iStock.com/Holcy, Goran Bogicevic/Shutterstock; 540 Checubus/Shutterstock; 541, 544 Christos Georghiou/Shutterstock; 541, 544, 548 Siberian Art/Shutterstock; 543 mijatmijatovic/Shutterstock; 546 nattha99/Shutterstock, John Rossie/AerospaceEd.org, 3D sculptor/Shutterstock; 547 Karl Yamashita/Shutterstock,

Barry Diomede/Alamy Stock Photo; 548 Golden Sikorka/Shutterstock; 549 gyn9037/Shutterstock; 555, 595 oxygen/Moment/Getty Images; 557 Natalya Erofeeva/Shutterstock; 558 ma3d/Shutterstock; 562 Kwangmoozaa/Shutterstock, Take Photo/Shutterstock; 564 Sean Pavone/Shutterstock; 566 faak/Shutterstock; 569 prapann/Shutterstock, Peter Olsson/Shutterstock, Michal Ninger/Shutterstock, Elnur/Shutterstock; 570 vvoe/Shutterstock, Sementer/Shutterstock, serg_bimbirekov/Shutterstock, Andrej Antic/Shutterstock; 572 Rashevskyi Viacheslav/Shutterstock; 574 David P. Lewis/Shutterstock, Vitalii Hulai/Shutterstock; 577 xpixel/Shutterstock; 578 RinArte/Shutterstock, Kanunnikov Vasyl/Shutterstock; 579 Yayayoyo/Shutterstock; 581 Evgeny Karandaev/Shutterstock, Amitofo/Shutterstock; 586 Lydia Vero/Shutterstock; 588 Mike Flippo/Shutterstock, Sergiy Kuzmin/Shutterstock, Nataliia K/Shutterstock; 590 Sebastian Janicki/Shutterstock; 593 John Le/Shutterstock; 594 arka38/Shutterstock; 596 Gts/Shutterstock; 597 G. Ronald Lopez/Alamy Stock Photo; 601 GraphicsRF/Shutterstock; 602 Irina Fischer/Shutterstock; 606 Jango/Stockimo/Alamy Stock Photo; 607 Yoshed/Shutterstock; 608 B Christopher/Alamy Stock Photo; 612 Runrun2/Shutterstock, Ivailo Nikolov/Shutterstock; 617 Stanislav Samoylik/Shutterstock; 618 Photoexpert/Shutterstock; 626 HelloRF Zcool/Shutterstock; 630 mihalec/Shutterstock, You Touch Pix of EuToch/Shutterstock; 636 iStock.com/oonal; 657 alicanozgur/Shutterstock; 664 iStock.com/Katiekk2; 668 MACVON/Shutterstock, Macrovector/Shutterstock; 670 naramit/Shutterstock; 672 art of line/Shutterstock; 674 Nyura/Shutterstock; 679, 682 Gines Valera Marin/Shutterstock; 679 tgavrano/Shutterstock, Travelerpix/Shutterstock; 685 J Davidson/Shutterstock; 687 Seksun Guntanid/Shutterstock, Baronb/Shutterstock; 693, 695 Denis Belitsky/Shutterstock; 700 Erik Lam/Shutterstock; 707 Matushchak Anton/Shutterstock, JoemanjiArts/Shutterstock; 710 Racheal Gazias/Shutterstock; 716 freesoulproduction/Shutterstock; 718 JeniFoto/Shutterstock; 723 Rawpixel.com/Shutterstock; 724 3000ad/Shutterstock; 725 PixieMe/Shutterstock; 728 Monkey Business Images/Shutterstock; 730 Samuel Borges Photography/Shutterstock; 735, 736 Yaran/Shutterstock; 738 Sergey Korkin/Shutterstock; 741 PetlinDmitry/Shutterstock; 745 Jenna Hidinger/Shutterstock; 755 Tiger Images/Shutterstock; 756 MilkyM/Shutterstock; 757 Khaled ElAdawy/Shutterstock; 762 Grigorita Ko/Shutterstock; 766 Ienjoyeverytime/Shutterstock; 767 Venus Angel/Shutterstock; 772 Josep Curto/Shutterstock; 777 Ana Prego/Shutterstock; 779 9george/Shutterstock; 784 Michael D Brown/Shutterstock;

Data Sets

541 https://nssdc.gsfc.nasa.gov/planetary/factsheet/; 700 https://www.akc.org/expert-advice/nutrition/breed-weight-chart/; 704 Rosenbaum, Mike. (2019, June 12). 100 Meter Men's Olympic Medalists. Retrieved from https://www.liveabout.com/100-meter-mens-olympic-medalists-3259179; 704 https://www.olympic.org/rio-2016/athletics/100m-men; 720 https://www.pewresearch.org/internet/fact-sheet/social-media/; 722 http://www.electproject.org/2016g; 743 https://data.worldbank.org/indicator/IT.NET.USER.ZS?end=2017&start=1960&view=chart; 743 https://en.wikipedia.org/wiki/Giant_pumpkin; 743 https://www.newsweek.com/world-record-pumpkin-mathias-willemijns-680566; 779 http://data.un.org/Default.aspx; 784 http://data.un.org/Default.aspx